Philosophy
of the Ancients

FRIEDO RICKEN

Translated by Eric Watkins

UNIVERSITY OF NOTRE DAME PRESS
NOTRE DAME   LONDON

Originally Published in 1988 as
Philosophie der Antike
Copyright © 1988 by W. Kohlhammer GmbH

Library of Congress Cataloging-in-Publication Data

Ricken, Friedo.
    [Philosophie der Antike. English]
    Philosophy of the ancients / Friedo Ricken ;
translated by Eric Watkins.
        p.   cm.
    Translation of: Philosophie der Antike.
    Includes index.
    ISBN 0-268-01587-2 (hard) —
ISBN 0-268-01588-0 (pbk.)
    1. Philosophy, Ancient.   I. Title.
B171.R5313   1991
180—dc20   90-70852
                                        CIP

Manufactured in the United States of America

Contents

Preface

This brief volume hopes to lead the reader to a personal involvement with the philosophical texts of the ancient period. Thus the most important methodological principle of this presentation is the referral to the sources. An introduction to ancient philosophy has many tasks: It ought to present historical philosophical connections, describe works, report doctrines, discuss questions critical for the sources, and, especially, interpret. In the limited space provided herein a compromise had to be struck among these various demands. For much a short note had to suffice, and only for a few central texts could an interpretation be attempted.

Concerning References: Commentated editions, commentaries, and translations with commentary are listed under Works. If a contemporary author referred to in the presentation is not found under Bibliography, please look to the relevant commentators. Books and papers are identified by their first year of publication insofar as this is provided in the references. If the page number refers to a new edition, a reproduction, or a translation, the corresponding year is added in parentheses.

Friedo Ricken

Abbreviations

DK   *Die Fragmente der Vorsokratiker,* griech./dt. hg. von H. Diels/W. Kranz, 6 Berlin Bd.1 1951, Bd. 2 m. 3 1952

       (*The Pre-Socratic Philosophers: A Companion to Diels, Fragmente der Vorsokratiker,* trans. by Mary Fitt, 2nd ed., Oxford 1949)

DL   Diogenes Laertius, *Lives of Eminent Philosophers,* trans. by R. D. Hicks, 2 vols., Cambridge, Mass. 1942

GK   *Grundkurs Philosophie,* Stuttgart 1988ff.

M   *Sextus Empiricus,* trans. by R. G. Bury, rev. ed., 4 vols., Cambridge, Mass. 1955–59

PH   Sextus Empiricus, *Grundriss der pyrrhonischen Skepsis* (Pyrrhoneae hypotyposes), übers. von M. Hossenfelder, Frankfurt 1968, 2 1985

RE   *Paulys Real-Encyclopädie der classischen Altertumswissenschaft.* Neue Bearbeitung, begonnen von G. Wissowa, Stuttgart 1984ff.

SVF   *Stoicorum veterum fragmenta,* ed. H. von Arnim, 4 Bde., Leipzig 1903–1924

A. Pre-Socratic Philosophy

I. Philosophy and Myth

1. THE QUESTION ABOUT THE TEMPORAL BEGINNING OF GREEK PHILOSOPHY

1. When and how does Greek philosophy arise? Where does the objective and temporal border between mythical and philosophical thought lie? In order to respond, the historian of philosophy is initially directed to a tradition that is markedly influenced by Aristotle and his school. The earliest extensive and continuous outline of the history of philosophy that we possess is found in chapters 3–10 in Aristotle's *Metaphysics*. However, Aristotle is not working here with the methodological tools of a modern historian. Rather, he is writing as a philosopher. His selection is determined by his own systematic approach; the teachings of the earlier philosophers are portrayed almost exclusively with the help of his own terminology.

One could of course attempt to free oneself from this tradition and advocate a different starting point for the beginning of philosophy by invoking a different concept of philosophy. After all, how we define a concept, one might say, is our business, and we are not forced to accept Aristotle's concept of philosophy. The question about the beginning of philosophy would then turn into a debate about how to determine the concept of philosophy. But here we can ascertain a minimal condition that an understanding of philosophy must satisfy in order for us to speak sensibly about

3

a beginning of philosophy: the conception must contain in its content a human mode of encountering reality that is distinct from other approaches, especially that of mythology.

2. For Aristotle (*Met.* 1, 1–2) philosophy is the highest form of knowledge. Knowledge is distinct from experience in virtue of its mark of strict universality. Ascertaining that a certain medicine has helped in various particular cases is not yet knowledge. Rather, knowledge is only given along with the awareness of the universal connection that a specific medicine always heals a specific illness, and that presumes in turn knowledge of the cause or the reason why the medicine heals. Thus, the concepts of cause (aitia) and principle (archē) are important for knowledge. As the highest form of knowledge, philosophy is concerned with first causes and principles. In the outline of the history of philosophy presented in the following chapters of his *Metaphysics* Aristotle examines the answers that his philosophical predecessors have given in response to the question about the first causes and principles.

3. If we view early Greek thought with this conception of philosophy, it becomes evident how difficult it is to draw a sharp line between philosophy and myth and to posit a temporal beginning of philosophy. Prototypes of a philosophical understanding of reality can be found in mythology. In order to illustrate this with an example, consider Hesiod's *Theogony* (ca. 700 B.C.). Next to Homer he had the greatest influence on the Greek's religious ideas.

2. HESIOD

4. The *Theogony* (genesis of the gods) portrays the genesis of the world, taking recourse to a host of Greek and oriental myths, and Zeus' path to rule over gods and human beings. In the present connection it is important to show how a transition from mythical to philosophical thought is intimated.

(1) In the proem Hesiod has the muses say: "We can say much false that resembles the real; but, if we desire, we can also proclaim truth" (V. 27f.). These verses express a critical attitude toward the mythical tradition. Not everything that the poets say on the authority of the muses is true. Hesiod searches for and claims to profess the truth.

(2) The muses give Hesiod the task of extolling "what will be and what previously was . . . and the species of the blessed, of the eternal beings" (V. 32f). The *Theogony* has a comprehensive thematic goal. It attempts to portray the entirety of what is. Thus, in these first verses we can see a first allusion to the basic question of Greek philosophy "What is being?" (*Met.* VII, 1 1028b4). Being is conceived with time: categories of time serve to determine the ontological order of being. Hesiod points out a dualism that is characteristic of the entire Greek understanding of reality. Eternal being is always opposed to becoming and passing away. Hesiod, influenced by the Greek's desire for immortality, gives clear priority to being.

(3) Hesiod inquires about the first or primary being. The first being for him is what has come to be earliest in time. Where it in turn comes from he does not ask. However, the first being is such that it enables coming to be and the being of all else. It is chaos (V. 116): the yawning emptiness, empty space into which all else comes to be and which encompasses all being.

(4) The *Theogony* orders mythology's gods into a genealogical scheme. After chaos the earth comes to be. Eros follows the earth. Chaos brings forth darkness and night. The descendents of night are, among others, death, sleep, age, and strife. The earth gives birth to the heavens, the mountains, the ocean, and the Titans. These genealogies represent an attempt to connect the powers and appearances of the world with one another and order them in a system. By providing the source of a god a genealogy reveals its essence; in the same vein, the essence of a mother, for example, of the night, is revealed in her offspring. The further up in the

genealogical order a creature stands, the greater is the ontological status developed in its offspring.

(5) Two classes of gods can be distinguished in the *Theogony*. First, there are the gods of whom stories are told as
in myths, who have effects and decide and act as humans
do. Besides these, Hesiod is acquainted with gods whose anthropomorphic features are removed and who function mainly as hypostases for natural powers. Hesiod's genealogical
system is determined in its structure, not by anthropomorphic divine persons, but rather by these hypostatized natural powers of life. "The divine persons live within the natural powers and not vice versa" (Diller, 1946 [1966], p. 706).
The importance of this observation lies in the fact that it
reveals traces of abstract thought in Hesiod. Mythology's
divine names develop into abstract concepts, anthropomorphic figures from myths into depersonified natural powers.

(6) The order of the world that is represented by genealogical connection derives from an ultimate principle, Zeus.
The allocation of areas of responsibility to the particular
gods, that is, the laws that govern the efficacy of the cosmic
forces, is his work (compare V. 73f.). Zeus' rule depends on
the superiority of his intelligence. His figure reveals a major
feature of monotheism in Hesiod's thought. Zeus symbolizes a supreme principle of reason that is the cause of the
world's order.

II. The Tradition of Pre-Socratic Philosophy

5. The works of the thinkers with whom Aristotle has the history of philosophy begin have not been entirely preserved. We possess *quotes* that can be found from Plato up to Byzantine authors. Age is no criterion for the exactness of a quote. It is often difficult to extract a literal quote from its context (which is sometimes paraphrase and sometimes protocol). The ancient authors quote not always according to original works but also according to handbooks and anthologies. For example, quotes of pre-Socratic philosophers have been preserved by the Skeptic Sextus Empiricus (second century A.D.), by the theologian author Hippolytus (third century A.D.) to whom we owe many fragments of Heraclitus, and by the Neoplatonic commentator of Aristotle, Simplicius (sixth century A.D.), who is an important source for Parmenides. Simplicius reports expressly that he is copying parts of Parmenides' poem because the exemplars have become rare (DK 28A21). Besides quotes we possess *reports* of the pre-Socratics' teachings. The first larger example of these so-called doxographical reports (doxa = teaching/opinion) is found in the first book of Aristotle's *Metaphysics*. Aristotle's portrayal is determined by the question to what extent his teaching of the four causes (material, efficient, formal, and final) can already be found in philosophers prior to him. The earlier thinkers are criticized according to the Aristotelian position. Such writing of the history of philosophy with systematic intent is continued to

a great extent by Theophrastus, a student and collaborator of Aristotle, in his work "physikōn doxai" (Teachings of the Natural Philosophers). Aristotle's approach is also characteristic for Theophrastus' selection of material and reports. He too presents the pre-Socratics' teachings extensively in Aristotelian concepts. This work by Theophrastus has not been preserved. The question has been debated recently whether an extensive fragment on sense perception is from this piece or another of his works. Our knowledge depends heavily on excerpts from ancient authors. To have reconstructed the tradition is to this very day the undisputed achievement of Hermann Diels (*Doxographi Graeci,* Berlin, 1879). The two most important sources are the "Epitome of Natural Philosophical Teachings," which comes to us under the name of Plutarch (second century A.D.), and the "Anthology" by Stobaeus (fifth century A.D.). Both depend upon Aetius' "Collection of Teachings" (ca. 100 A.D.), which has not been preserved. But even he used not Theophrastus directly but rather a lost compendium called the "Vetusta Placita" (prior to 50 B.C.) by Diels that contains excerpts from Theophrastus in addition to other material.

III. The Milesians

6. The doxographical reports have philosophy begin with Thales, Anaximander, and Anaximenes, who all lived in Miletos. The most important point of reference for dating them is the solar eclipse in 585 B.C. which Thales predicted. The role of interpretation is to ask in what sense something new begins with the Milesians. A well-known position, whose classical representative is J. Burnet, emphasizes the break with myth. The Ionians initiate European natural science as characterized by observation and experiment (1930, pp. 24–28). The Milesians are rationalists who break with the religious tradition. Thus it is mistaken to look for "the source of Ionian science in mythical ideas of any kind" (1930, p. 13). F. M. Cornford has reacted very strongly against this interpretation. In contrast to Greek medicine, Ionian natural philosophy is not acquainted with experimentation; its theses are speculative dogmas that cannot be verified by observation (1942). According to Cornford the Milesians are answering the same questions as the Genesis myths. On the whole they accept the same answers and are distinguished only by more abstract language (1952, pp. 187–201). W. Jaeger stands in between these two positions by not denying the Ionians' rationalist and empiricist attitude, while emphasizing that their theological interests should not be overlooked. One needs to distinguish between demythification and detheologification. Jaeger places the origin of Greek philosophical theology with the pre-Socratics.

1. THALES

7. Aristotle (*Met.* I, 3 = DK 11A12) reports that Thales viewed water as the principle (archē) of everything and for this reason claimed that the earth floats on water. The report utilizes Aristotelian concepts. Of the four causes (see par. 5) Thales was only acquainted with the material cause. He thought of water as a substrate or substance that neither comes to be nor perishes, but rather only changes its properties. Aristotle mentions circumstances that might have led Thales to his position: the wetness of food and seed and that warmth (for life) arises from wetness. The reservedness with which Aristotle states these reasons suggests that already he does not possess certain information about Thales anymore and that we can hardly assume that Thales is believed to have made these observations in order to provide support for these reasons. The report closes with the suggestion "that the ancients who inquired long before our time into divine things" had also viewed water as the origin of everything.

8. That Thales proceeds from mythical pictures of the world can hardly be disputed. For Homer (*Iliad* 18, 607f.) the earth is a plate that is surrounded by the Oceanis River. Oceanis, which also flows under the earth (*Iliad* 21, 195ff.), is designated as the origin (genesis) of everything (*Iliad* 14, 246; see 201). These statements are, however, isolated within Greek mythology. For this reason it is more probable that Thales is influenced by oriental myths (see Hölscher, 1968, pp. 40–48). A Babylonian myth, preserved in an Eridu poem, tells that in the beginning there was nothing other than the sea. Then Marduk build a reed raft. After that he created dust and poured it onto the raft. The earth lies on water that circumscribes the earth according to Egyptian ideas. "The Nile arises from this subterranean water and brings fertility to earth. On the edge of the earth . . . lies the heaven's vault. Water flows around the heaven as a second Nile from which the life-giving rain falls" (Hölscher, 1968, p. 42). That Thales is thought to have had connections with the orient speaks

in favor of the influence of these myths. He is supposed to have explained the Nile's flooding by the north wind blowing in the summer and to have developed a method of measuring the height of the pyramids with the help of their shadows (A21). The prediction of the solar eclipse (A5) would have been impossible for Thales without knowledge of Babylonian astronomy.

9. How Thales conceived of water becomes evident from the witnesses who attribute to him an animistic worldview. He viewed the soul as something that moves, for he claims that a magnetized stone has a soul because it moves iron. "And many claim that the soul is mixed in with the universe; perhaps for this reason Thales believed that everything is full of gods" (A22). Everything in the world, including stones, is alive. As with Hesiod the natural powers are gods. Thales' water ought not to be understood as matter in a modern sense. This archaic thought does not have at its command the distinctions between matter, life, movement, and soul. "Matter" lives and is the source of life. Here Thales can link up, for example, with the fact that the water of the Nile is the source of fertility. The Milesians are often called hylozoists (hylē = matter, zōē = life). This should not be understood such that matter is conceived of as living; rather this thought cannot yet make the distinction between matter and life.

10. Nonetheless, to what extent does something new begin with Thales as compared with mythology? Can the beginning of rational, scientific thought be dated to him? It is the tradition's unambiguous testimony that Thales attempted to find reasons for the ideas taken from myth. The mythical conception, according to which the earth is a plate that floats on water, becomes an hypothesis with the help of which he explains earthquakes. They are explained by recourse, not to the intervention of the god Poseidon anymore but rather to the movements of the water on which the earth floats like a piece of wood (A15; see A14). The swelling of the Nile is explained by the winds that blow against the current (A16).

For the view that everything is alive, the power of the magnet stone is given as a reason (A22). In all of this one should not overlook the fact that these are the first known attempts at rational explanation. It is questionable whether one may speak of observation. This becomes evident from, for example, the criticism that Herodotus (born 484 B.C.) raises against Thales' explanation of the swelling of the Nile: "In many years these winds are absent but the Nile still rises. Besides, if the winds were responsible, all other rivers that flowed against these winds would fare just as the Nile does. The effect would even have to be greater because these other rivers are smaller and their currents weaker. But there is a series of rivers in Syria and Libya in which flooding like the Nile's does not occur at all" (*The Histories,* II).

2. ANAXIMANDER

11. According to doxographic reports Anaximander designated the apeiron as the source (archē) of everything. The word probably stems from peran = on the other side, beyond; peraō = to cross (a sea or a room) and means "what cannot be crossed from one end to the other" (see Kahn, 1964, p. 231ff.). The following can be extracted from the reports for Anaximander's concept: 1. "Apeiron" initially has spatial import. It refers, in a manner similar to Hesiod's "chaos," to the space that "contains" everything else (DK 12A15, p. 85; A11, p. 84, line 2). This space is not, however, empty but rather is a body that consists of a material that is less dense than water and more dense than air (Aristotle, *De caelo* 303b10–13); Thus body and space have not yet been distinguished. 2. This space-body is the inexhaustible supply from which everything arises: "He also tells why it is unlimited: so that the present coming to be does not recede in any respect" (A14). 3. The source of everything must be different from the elements air, water, and fire, which is thus a criticism of Thales. For the elements are in conflict in order to

destroy one another. If one of them were unlimited, the others would have already been destroyed (A16, p. 86, lines 1–3).
4. The apeiron steers all processes of the cosmos. It is immortal and incorruptible. For this reason Anaximander taught that it is divine (A15, p. 85, lines 18–20).

12. The apeiron emits a seed from which the cosmos proceeds. Probably a moist element arises first, which then separates the earth inward and a fiery ball outward "like the bark around a tree". The fiery ball is ripped apart by the expansion of the moist element and is divided into circles of fire (A10). These circles are enclosed by empty wheel rims of air that have densified. The rims have openings through which flames of fire stick out as if out of the pipe of a pair of bellows: the stars. Solar eclipses and the phases of the moon are explained by these openings being blocked (A18; A21).

13. The earth according to Anaximander has the shape of a cylinder whose height is a third of its diameter (A10). Like Thales, Anaximander asks by what means the earth stays in its place in space. Thales only pushes the problem back a level, as Aristotle is quick to point out: if the earth rests on water, on what does water rest? Anaximander's solution is amazing. He relinquishes the idea that the earth rests on anything. Rather the earth remains at the same place due to a state of equilibrium, since it lies in the middle of the universe and has the same distance to the universe's limits in every direction (A26). This explanation relies on the thought that gravity depends on the attraction of masses. The earth cannot fall down because the attraction in one direction is offset by the attraction on the opposite direction. Up and down are to be determined according to the direction of movement, that is, with reference to the middle of the earth. Thus Anaximander assumed the existence of antipodes (A11, p. 84, line 8f.).

14. Living beings arose, and on this point Anaximander can look to Thales for help, from moisture. At first they are surrounded by thorny "barks," probably because they could not protect themselves and survive in any other manner. Fur-

ther along in their development they migrate to dry land, lose their "barks," and accommodate themselves to the new living conditions. We find in Anaximander the first traces of an evolution theory. Human beings stem from fish and are initially developed inside fish. Apparently Anaximander observed that man is born early, biologically speaking, and is incapable of sustaining life in the first years. Thus, the first human beings were held back inside of fish until puberty; only when they could nourish themselves did they see the light of the world (A30).

15. The oldest sentence of Greek philosophy preserved in its original form is by Anaximander: "the source of coming to be for existing things is that into which destruction also occurs; for they pay penalty and retribution to each other for injustice according to the assessment of time" (B1). The sentence does not, as it is often understood, express the things' debt to the apeiron that is to be retributed by their return into the apeiron. One cannot sensibly speak of an injustice that the things and the apeiron could do to *one another;* the apeiron commits no injustice by letting the things into existence. Rather it is exclusively the things which do injustice to each other and undergo punishment for one another. Anaximander has in mind phenomena such as the passage of night and day, summer and winter, and the circulation and interaction of the elements. They arise from one another and at the expense of one another. In this process each one comes into existence once. However, the possibilities of existence limit them. Time sets the just order for the duration of each one. The sentence extends beyond the regularity of natural occurrences and attempts to give an answer to human beings' mortality. It is "the first philosophical theodicy" (Jaeger, 1953, p. 48).

16. If we ask in Anaximander's case to what extent something new has occurred as opposed to mythology, a process of scientification can initially be observed. Natural processes are not derived from personified powers any more but rather are explained by models that have been taken from everyday experience. The antiquity of this thought is evident because

Anaximander works with a plurality of models that have not been unified: technical models (wheel of a wagon, bellows), biological models (the apeiron produces a seed; the bark that grows around a tree), and political models (the legislation of time). But Anaximander connects up with the mythical worldview as well. How did Thales and he ever come to ask about the source of the present world-order at all? Experience can hardly have given the impetus for this question, and it is enticing to look for an answer in mythology. Anaximander's worldview and teaching of the genesis of the world reveal similarities to the orient. The order of the series of astral spheres—farthest out is the sphere of the sun, then that of the moon, closest to the earth the fixed stars' sphere (A18)—corresponds to the Babylonian and Iranian worldview. In order to demonstrate Anaximander's proximity to ancient oriental ideas, Cornford (1952, p. 199f.) had compared Anaximander's cosmogony with the genesis account of *Gen.* 1, 1–2, 3: the creation in *Gen.* 1 proceeds from a primitive state in which the elements are mostly undifferentiated from each other; for Anaximander the elements are separated off from the apeiron with increasing differentiation. God divides light from dark; for Anaximander fire is divided from the other elements. Only after the division of light and dark does God create the stars; for Anaximander the stars are created from a fire ball that is initially placed around the moist-cold mixture. God creates the water animals prior to the land animals; for Anaximander the land animals are created out of the water animals. Anaximander's decisive accomplishment is to be seen in the fact that he attempted, albeit with several models, to view the process of creation as a unified developmental process in which every phase can be explained by the prior one.

3. ANAXIMENES

17. Thales and Anaximander want to answer the question about the cause or origin (archē) of everything. How-

ever, this concept remains unclear for them. They want to state from what everything else proceeds. Yet what does "from what" mean? To point out only two possibilities: 1. The origin produces the other by changing into the other, as, for example, in a burning process the material becomes energy. 2. The origin is the substrate that underlies everything else. All things that we find present in experience are nothing other than the various states of one and the same primitive material. We saw (par. 7) that Aristotle interpreted Thales in this manner. For Anaximenes (the acme of his work is estimated to be around 545 B.C.) the question has already been decided in favor of the second possibility. Like Anaximander, the origin is conceived of as infinite, whereby "infinite" is understood exclusively as spatial and temporal extension. The origin is a qualitatively determinate material: air. All other materials out of which things are constituted are merely air in one of its various densities. Anaximenes names two processes through which things come to be and perish: condensation and rarefaction. They are explained by the fact that air is in constant motion (A5).

18. When air becomes rarefied, it becomes fire. If it becomes more dense, it first becomes wind, then cloud, then water, then earth, and finally stone (A5). The differences in temperature are also explained by different densities. Anaximenes is thought to have found support in the following observation: If air is pressed through lips that are only opened a little, it becomes cold. If, on the contrary, it proceeds through a wide opening of the mouth, it becomes warm (B1). The earth has come to be through a "felting" of air. Because it is flat and wide, it "rides" (or floats) on air (A6). The stars proceeded from the earth's moist exhalations that have become more rarefied with increasing distance and have eventually turned into fire (A7, §5).

19. Anaximenes goes beyond Thales and Anaximander insofar as he does not make only one statement as to the origin, but with the help of a unified model he also describes the process through which the appearances have proceeded

from the origin. His theory is distinguished by its simplicity, large area of application, strong explanatory force, and a variety of observations upon which it can be based. Special note is to be given to the attempt at explaining all appearances with the *quantitative* concept of varying density. In this respect Anaximenes is a precursor of modern science. This does not exclude the possibility that we find animistic elements in his teachings. Air stands in a special relationship to life, as water does for Thales. The soul which holds the body of human beings together is (breath-) air (B2). Also the statement that air is in constant motion is to be understood such that air is alive and the principle of life.

IV. Xenophanes

20. Born around 570 B.C., Xenophanes leaves his home city Colophon in Ionia around the time of the Persian invasion (546/45) and leads from then on, presumably primarily in Sicily and Southern Italy, the life of a wandering rhapsodist (see DK 21B8). We possess fragments of his poems in various meters. Xenophanes concerns himself with the Milesians' cosmology. The corresponding fragments and reports can hardly be combined into a unified whole. Besides naive, popular views, astute theories and observations are found. To the question as to what the earth rests on, Xenophanes replies that it extends infinitely downward (B28). Everything is of earth—an idea that is already found in Homer (*Illiad* 7, 99)—or of earth and water (B29) and all becomes earth again (B27). Xenophanes' theory of the sun reminds one of Anaximenes: it is composed of fiery parts that are gathered together from moist exhalations (A40). Other testimony reveals a rationalistic tendency critical of religion. In this vein the rainbow, for Hesiod a goddess of the name Iris (*Theogony* 265ff.), is explained as a meteorological phenomenon: "And what they call Iris is only a cloud, purple and light red and yellow-green, to behold" (B32; see B39). Xenophanes taught, probably in connection with mythology, a periodical flooding of the earth (see, e.g., the flood *Gen.* 6f.; Deucalion and Pyrrha, Ovid, *Metamorphoses* 1,260ff.). The demonstrations that he adduces for it are amazing: "Shells are found both inland and in mountains, and in Syracuse,

18

he says, the imprint of a fish and seals was found in the stone quarries, while in Paros the impression of a bay leaf was deep in the stone and in Malta flat shapes [with imprints] of all possible marine animals were formed. He claims that it arose when long ago everything was covered with mud, and the impression was dried in the mud." (A33). B37 also displays that he is a shrewd observer: "And in certain caves water drips down." The stalactites serve as proof for him that water can petrify.

21. Xenophanes has a name in the history of philosophy especially as a critic of religion and as a theologian. His travels probably taught him that every people has its own ideas and pictures of the gods. "The Ethiopians claim that their gods are snub-nosed and black, the Thracians that theirs have blue eyes and red hair" (B16). From this he concludes that the gods of natural religion are anthropomorphic projections: "If, however, cows, horses, and lions had hands and could paint with their hands and create works as human beings do, then horses would paint pictures of the gods similar to horses and cows like cows, and they would create works with the very shape that they have" (B15). The anthropomorphism of the Homeric religion extends so far that he also ascribes human mistakes to the gods: "Homer and Hesiod attributed to the gods everything which is shameful and reprimandable: stealing and adultery and lying to one another" (B11). In contrast, Xenophanes claims: "A single god is the greatest among gods and humans, similar to humans neither in form nor in thought" (B23). Distinctive of his new concept of god is: 1. It is gained via a negative path; god is different from humans. 2. God can only be conceived with the help of superlatives. He is *the* greatest, *the* most perfect. From this it follows for Xenophanes that there can only be one god. The greatest cannot have a companion that is equally great. But how is it to be understood that for Xenophanes the one god is still one among other gods? Does B23 contain an admission to natural religion's polytheism? When Xenophanes allows for divine powers in addition to the one

god, they cannot be gods in the true sense of the word, and they cannot be conceived of in an anthropomorphic manner. The one god is pure perceiving and spiritual activity: "He sees as a whole, thinks as a whole, and hears as a whole." He acts in the world, but in contrast to human beings his action is free from the imperfections of motion and effort. He acts, as Aristotle would say, as an "unmoved mover." "He always stays in the same place without moving, for it is not appropriate for him to go here and there, but rather he brings everything into motion through the power of his thought" (B26; B25). It is reasonable to suppose that the Milesians paved the way for Xenophanes' concept of god. Anaximander is thought to have viewed the apeiron as divine because it has the attributes that are important for the Homeric concept of god: immortality and incorrigibility; like Xenophanes' god, the apeiron guides the universe (DK 12A15, p. 85, lines 18–20).

22. The doxographic tradition claims that Xenophanes is the founder of the Eleatic school and the teacher of Parmenides (A2; A31). It sees in Xenophanes' single unmoved god the point of departure for Parmenides' teaching of the unchangeable being (see par. 38). The common ground between the two thinkers is especially emphasized in the pseudo-Aristotelian work *De Melisso Xenophane Gorgia* (MXG; *Aristotelis opera,* ed. Bekker, pp. 978–980; DK 21A28), which characterizes Xenophanes' single god with Parmenidean predicates and proves its noncreation and singularity by means of Parmenidean proofs. K. Reinhardt (1916) and K. von Fritz (1967) attach great historical value to MXG, and, according to Reinhardt, Xenophanes relies on Parmenides. The arguments of the researchers who estimate the historical value as low (Zeller, 1919; Wiesner, 1974; Cassin, 1980) carry more weight. Xenophanes is largely a critic of Homeric religion; he does not, however, develop his own religion systematically, as MXG suggests. The reports according to which Xenophanes identifies the one god with the universe are hardly believable (A30; A31; A35). They

probably derive from Plato, who does not distinguish in the *Sophist* between Xenophanes and Parmenides and ascribes to both a teaching according to which the universe of things is a single being.

23. Xenophanes' sober, critical attitude becomes evident through his statements about human knowledge. B38 points out the relativity of certain perceptual judgments: "If god had not let honey exist, they would say that yellow figs are much sweeter." B34 is especially important: "No man has seen (iden) nor known (eidōs) the light with respect to the gods and everything of which I speak. For even if one were successful in saying the complete truth, one would still not know (oide) it, since for everything there is only presumption." The fragment observes a close connection between "knowing" (eidenai; oida; simple past) and "seeing" (idein; eidon; aorist). It alludes to the fact that two different forms of the same verb are at issue. Xenophanes denies that there could be knowledge that relies on seeing the states of affairs about which he is speaking. Human beings can only presume that such is the case. This ought not to be understood as a form of skepticism. Statements as to the degree of probability can be made based on the reasons in favor of a presumption (see B35). Xenophanes believes in progress in human knowledge (B18).

V. Pythagoras

24. Pythagoras was born on the island of Samos, not far from Miletos. During Polycrates' tyrannical rule he immigrated around 530 B.C., at approximately 40 years of age, to Kroton in lower Italy, probably due to political reasons. There he founded a community somewhat like a religious order that soon spread to other cities in lower Italy and gained political influence. Around 500 B.C. a resistance movement was formed in Kroton. For this reason Pythagoras resettles in Metapontion. However, the group regains its influence quite quickly. Around 450 B.C. actions against the Pythagoreans are taken in all of Italy; many flee to Greece and found new communities there. Various movements develop.

25. Pythagoras left no written works. His teaching was handed down orally within the order. It was forbidden to pass them on to outsiders. The literal formula "he himself has said it" testifies to the great authority that he had among his followers. Philolaus' fragments from Kroton (around 400 B.C.) (DK) and Aristotle's reports (*Met.* I, 5f.) count among the few reliable reports about the Pythagorean school. At most, however, they only allow inferences to Pythagoras himself. The remaining material is heavily influenced by Plato. Whether the mathematical and cosmological teachings of which Philolaus and Aristotle report actually derive from Pythagoras is controversial. For E. Frank (1923) and W. Burkert (1962), who deny this, Pythagoras is exclusively a religious prophet, whereas Ch. Kahn (1974) and J. Mansfeld (1983) place him in the cosmological-scientific tradition

of the Milesians. In favor of the latter position is the fact that Heraclitus testifies to Pythagoras' extensive empirical knowledge and for this reason mentions him along with Xenophanes and the geographer and historian Hecataeus (DK 22B40; B129).

26. With certainty Pythagoras maintains, and probably for the first time in Greece, the soul's immortality and the transmigration of souls. According to Herodotus III 123 (= DK 14A1) he is influenced by the Egyptians, who were the first to advance these theories. After death the soul is reborn in another human being or animal. That is attested to by Xenophanes (DK 21B7) in the sixth century and Ion of Chios (DK 36B4), Empedocles (DK 31B129), and Herodotus (II 123 and IV 95) in the fifth century. From this resulted the ban on butchering and eating animals. Empedocles reports that Pythagoras could remember everything from his previous ten or twenty lives.

27. From Philolaus and Aristotle the following cosmogony can be reconstructed: The world and everything in it consists of two principles: the unlimited (evens) and the limiters (odds) (DK 44B1f.). From both the One arises which is neither even nor odd (B5). The One breaths the empty in from the unlimited, like a newly born child breathes the air. In this manner the numbers and the world that consists of numbers arise from the One (DK 58B30; *Met.* 986a19–21). Thus the One can multiply itself. The Pythagoreans represent this plurality (the limiting) with points, whereas the space in between the points refers to the empty (unlimited). The perfect and complete number is ten (*Met.* 986a8). It is the sum of the four first numbers and is represented by an equilateral triangle, each of whose sides comprise four:

This figure is designated a "tetractys" (from tettara = four). Since the unlimited and the limiter are unequal to each other, another is required, according to Philolaus, in order to connect them: harmony. He understands by this arithmetic proportion and gives as an example the numerical relationships of musical intervals: the octave (1:2), the fifth (2:3), and the fourth (3:4) (DK 44B6). These three relationships which are fundamental for all of reality are contained in the tetractys. The number ten also defines the astronomical worldview. Philolaus relinquishes the Milesians' geocentric conception of the world. In the middle of the cosmos there is a central fire around which the heavenly bodies circle. In order to complete the set of ten, Philolaus postulates a heavenly body: the counterearth. It circles the closest around the central fire, followed by the earth, the moon, the sun, the five planets, and the sphere of fixed stars (DK 44A16; *Met.* 986a8–13). According to Aristotle the Pythagoreans claimed that the things themselves are numbers (*Met.* 987b28). This general claim apparently rests on the observation that numerical ratios underlie certain appearances, for example, the ratio of the lengths of the strings that produce a musical harmony underlies that harmony. However, it also has epistemological presuppositions. Philolaus assumes that only numerical ratios can be known. If reality is to be known, it can only be thought as mathematically structured (DK 44B3; B4).

28. To what extent does this cosmogony derive from Pythagoras? On this point only speculation is possible (see Kahn, 1974, pp. 180–185). The teaching of the unlimited and the limiters and of the harmony can be dated to the first half of the sixth century and can therefore be attributed to Pythagoras. The unlimited (ta apeira) reveals a certain similarity with Anaximander's apeiron and Anaximenes' unlimited air: the emptiness that the One breaths in from the unlimited is conceived as air. The concept of harmony plays an important role for Heraclitus, and it cannot be excluded that Pythagoras and Heraclitus have taken it over from Anaximander (see par. 15).

VI. Heraclitus

29. Heraclitus descends from an aristocratic family in Ephe-
sos. He was about forty years old around the year 500 B.C.
He criticizes Pythagoras and Xenophanes, who were presumably elder contemporaries (DK 22B40). He is thought to have
died in his sixtieth year. His fragments as well as Diogenes
Laertius' biography from the first half of the third century
A.D., which relies mostly on fragments, characterize him as
a lonely misanthrope, with a highly aristocratic haughtiness
and an antidemocratic attitude, who renounced any political activity. "One is ten thousand if he is the best" (B49).
"For what is their reason or understanding? They believe
folksingers and make the masses their teacher because they
do not know that the many are bad and the few good" (B104;
see B29; B121).

In addition to the doxographical remains we possess about
125 literal fragments. Most often they are pithy, extremely
dense and pregnant sayings; their style contributed to Heraclitus being dubbed "the obscure" by the ancients. Most of the
fragments have come down to us through the church author
Clement of Alexander and Hippolytus of Rome (both from
around 200 A.D.). With some certainty we can assume that
they had Heraclitus' original work in their possession. It is
as yet undecided whether these sayings were merely aphorisms
whose order is of no importance or rather were originally
composed by Heraclitus as a whole whose order cannot be
discerned due to the tradition. Diels maintains the former

position. On the converse side, Kahn 1979 advanced the thesis of an original composition. He compares Heraclitus' style with Pindar's and Aeschylus'. The work leaves an unfinished and inconsistent impression for Theophrastus (DL IX 6). Whether that speaks against a composition must remain unsettled. Perhaps Theophrastus prejudged the text with inappropriate Aristotelian premises.

30. In B67, 88 and 111, Heraclitus places the following pairs of opposites together: day/night, winter/summer, war/peace, sickness/health, hunger/satiety, effort/rest, life/death, wakefulness/sleep, youth/old age. In contrast to Anaximander's opposites these pertain to experience. Experience encompasses human beings and their world and combines them into a unity. The manner in which human beings experience themselves determines how they experience the world. The healthy man's attitude toward life and the world is different than that of a sick man. The feelings and attitudes of a hungry person toward fellow human beings are different than those of a well-nourished person. One's moods and feelings toward life depend on the rhythm of day and night and of summer and winter. The opposites that Heraclitus mentions in the three fragments encompass essential areas of human experience: nature, the human body and vitality, the social realm, one's relation to time, the past, and the future. Heraclitus refers to the pillars of the human condition: hunger, sickness, old age, death. The opposites pose a question to human beings: For what reason is there health *and* sickness, satiety *and* hunger, peace *and* war, life *and* death? The question as to the meaning of the opposites is the question as to the meaning of humanity itself: "I went searching for myself" (B101).

31. Consider next the method with which Heraclitus searches for a solution. He stands in the Ionian tradition insofar as he emphasizes the importance of empirical knowledge. "I prefer what one can see, hear, and experience" (B55). "Men who love wisdom must understand something of many things" (B35). Nonetheless, he shows unconcealed contempt

for *mere* empirical knowledge. "Knowing many things does not teach having understanding. For otherwise it would have taught Hesiod and Xenophanes and Hecataeus" (B40; see B129). "Eyes and ears are poor witnesses for human beings when they have barbaric souls" (B107). Barbarians are humans who do not understand *the* language, Greek. Whoever considers the senses exclusively is like one who hears a language but does not understand it. The fragment compares reality with a language. Human beings hear it without understanding it, even without wanting to understand it. They are not at one with the basic law of reality in which they live. "Since they hear without understanding, they are like the deaf. The saying testifies this about them: 'Present they are absent'" (B34; see B19). "That with which they are constantly interacting, the logos, with which they are not at one and upon which they come daily, appears foreign to them" (B72). For Heraclitus two levels of reality correspond to the two levels of knowledge: perception and understanding. The true essence, or basic law, of reality is hidden behind the phenomena (see B123). "The lord whose oracle is at Delphi does not speak out or conceal but rather gives a sign" (B93). The ambiguous prophecies of the oracle that Apollo sends to Delphi are signs of truth. The essence of things, the concealed *physis* (see B123), also does not speak out such that it must only be heard nor does it hide its message; it reveals it in signs.

32. The essence of reality according to Heraclitus is the unity of the opposites. "That which strives against each other concurs" (B8). What is opposed forms a unity with its opposite. Unity can only be conceived of as a unity of things resisting each other. Heraclitus illustrates this with the metaphor of a bow. "They do not comprehend how being brought apart corresponds with being brought together. There is a back-stretched connection as with a bow and the lyre" (B51). The unity of the bow's form and its functional capacity depend upon the bow's wood and the pull of the string in opposite directions. In this manner the string pulls the bow's

wood and the bow's wood the string. In order for the arrow
to fly, the archer's hands must pull the bow's wood and the
string in opposite directions. The unity that results from the
difference is revealed in the lyre in that only strings that are
strung at different tensions produce different tones and thus
a harmony. The fragment points out yet another unity: the
bow is a lethal battle weapon, whereas the lyre symbolizes
peace and agreement. "Connections: wholes and not-wholes,
things being brought together and things being brought apart,
being in tune and being out of tune, out of everything arises
unity and from unity everything" (B10). The various things
and the whole cosmos are a connection of opposites. The
opposites form a whole; they strive toward one another and
complement each other as a harmony. The whole, however,
can only exist if the opposites retain their opposing powers.
To this extent their connections are incomplete and disso-
nant. The whole only exists in the relation of its parts. Every
part is what it is only through its relation to all other parts
and its position in the order of the whole.

Heraclitus produces a number of examples of everyday
phenomena, of which we can only note a few, that exhibit
the basic law of reality. "It is not better for human beings
to get everything that they want. Sickness makes health pleas-
ant and valuable, like hunger satiety and effort rest" (B110f.).
Fire is "lack and satiety" (B65). Life's intensity is only possible in the experience of opposites. It is only with the background of the negative that the positive can be experienced.
Life is only possible in the tension of frustration and satisfaction. Human beings are constantly in danger of taking
the greatest goods for granted and not as a gift. Fire is a picture of life as the unity of satisfaction and dissatisfaction.
It only exists by satisfying itself through burning something
else. It is always dissatisfied and wants to reach out for more.

The ultimate opposition in experience is that of life and
death. "Since they are born they want to live and be deathless—or rather rest; and they leave behind children so that
deathless are born" (B20). Life wants to produce life; birth

is the realization of life. When life realizes itself in birth, it produces a living being that is determined to die. Life is lived in the tension between the will to live and the desire of death. It is experienced as effortful and as a burden. Death as rest is the secret desire of life. Only against the backdrop of uncertain death does life obtain its unique value. Only one who is aware of death lives intensely. The opposites battle one another; death wants to destroy life, and life defends itself against death. "One must know that war is common (universal), that right is strife, and that everything arises and is ordered by strife" (B80). "War is the father of everything; he proves some to be gods, others as human beings, some as slaves, and others as free" (B53). War is "common" in two senses: it omits no one and creates at the same time a deeper unity between the opposing forces. As the principle of polarity it is the cause of cosmic development and order. Order and right can only be realized through it. It gives to each what each deserves. B53 describes the resolution of war in the ancient period. The defeated are sold as slaves; the victors are free. To this extent the ancient social order is the result of war. All beings must prove themselves in war. It is only this extreme situation that brings out their essences.

33. Heraclitus designates the reality that is hidden behind the appearances with several names. "God is day and night, winter and summer, war and peace, satiety and hunger. He changes like fire which when it is mixed with spices is named according to each one's scent" (B67). The pairs of opposites that are attributed to god are exemplary for all pairs of opposites. God does not change. He appears in the opposites yet still transcends them. Heraclitus explains this with a comparison. When one places various spices in a fire, it produces a different scent in each case. Each one is named accordingly. Fire itself cannot be experienced directly by the sense of smell, but the spices can only develop their smell through the fire. God is immanent to the things as their living force. None the less he is different from them. Reality as we experience it is always only the scents and never the fire. B1 and

B2 signify this transcendental reality as logos. "Although logos always is, human beings never come to understand it, both before they have heard it and once they have heard it. For whereas everything occurs according to this logos, they are like inexperienced ones" (B1). "Although the logos is common (universal), the many live as if their thinking were peculiar to them" (B2). The logos is Heraclitus' teaching. At the same time it is said to be eternal. It is the relationship in which the opposites stand to one another as well as the law according to which they relieve each other, the dynamic, ordering dimension that determines all events. Every human being participates in the logos. The search for oneself leads to the logos: "You would not find the limits of the soul, even by walking every path. So deep is its logos" (B45). The central demand of Heraclitus' ethical theory is to follow the logos. The teaching of the moral law of nature that is later advanced by the Stoics is ultimately derived from Heraclitus. Only the logos as the universal can create unity among humans. Without laws no human society can subsist (see B44). However, all human laws "are sustained by the one divine" law that is valid without limit (see B114).

VII. The Eleatics

1. PARMENIDES

34. The history of ontology begins with Parmenides. He asks what we mean when we speak of "being" and notes characteristics that necessarily belong to a being by virtue of the fact that it is. Regardless of how much the Greek philosophy that follows objects to Parmenides' concept of being, ultimately it cannot avoid his influence. According to Parmenides being is uncreated, imperishable, immutable, and complete. Plato attributes these ontological predicates to the Forms. They are essential for Aristotle's and Neoplatonism's concept of God, the latter of which exercised an extensive influence on medieval Christian theology and philosophy. The ancient atomists ascribe these same predicates to the ultimate material components of reality. Through them a line reaches from Parmenides to modern natural science and materialism. Like Xenophanes and Heraclitus before him, Parmenides considers the possibility of human knowledge. With more force than Heraclitus he distinguishes between experience that the senses provide and knowledge through logos which alone reveals the truth.

35. There are two diverging methods of calculating the birth date of Parmenides, who lived in Elea in lower Italy. According to DL IX (DK 28A1) he was approximately forty years old in the years 504–501 B.C. This results in his birth date being circa 540 B.C. Plato (*Parm.* 127a–c; A5) reports

the meeting of an old Parmenides with a young Socrates. Accordingly, Parmenides would have been born between 515 and 510. He is to have been "converted" to philosophy by a Pythagorean (DL IX 21; A1). Whereas the Ionians wrote in prose, Parmenides composed a poem in hexameters.

36. The proem (B1) describes how Parmenides rides quickly through a gate on a wagon drawn by two steeds to a goddess and receives a revelation from her. The ride is not to be understood as the expression of a unique, personal, religious, or mystical experience. It is rather an allegory for the course of Parmenidean thought. "Every time the epic [namely, Parmenides' poem] is recited, such an ascent occurs, such a revelation issues forth" (Fränkel, 1960, p. 159). The position that Parmenides develops in the following passage in strict argumentative form contradicts everyday experience to such an extent that it is almost tantamount to a religious revelation. That it is placed in the mouth of the goddess underlines its claim to validity and truth. The detailed description of a gate stands in the middle of the proem (B1, 1–20). It symbolizes the border of the world (see Hesiod, *Theogony,* 748ff.) and of everyday experience which is to be presently transcended. The metaphor of light is emphasized: the wagon is steered toward light by the maiden of the sun; the gate separates the night's and the day's paths (lines 9–11). It makes clear that Parmenides conceives of being from the perspective of light and visibility and of knowledge from that of sight. The keys to the gate are in the possession of Dike (line 14; see line 28). For the Greeks Dike is the goddess of justice and right. For Parmenides she embodies the laws of thought and being, which are one and the same (see B812–15). Consistent thought leads him from the world of seeming to being.

37. The conclusion of the proem (lines 28–32) divides the following. Parmenides is to experience truth (Part I, B2–B8, 51) and human opinion (doxai) (Part II, after B8, 51) from the goddess. The first part especially influenced the ensuing development. According to H. Diels' assessment nine-

tenths of the poem has been recovered. How the second part
and its relation to the first part are to be understood is controversial. The concern with the second part asks how Parmenides judges the reality of experience. Two answers can
be mentioned here (see Jantzen, 1976, pp. 21–34): 1. Parts
I and II are distinguished due to their mode of knowledge.
The statements concerning being in Part I are self-evident,
whereas those concerning the perceivable world are only
probable hypotheses. Most often this epistemological distinction is combined with an ontological distinction: even the
perceivable world *is,* albeit in a limited sense. We shall see
that this interpretation can hardly be combined with Parmenides' concepts of knowledge and being. 2. Part II is concerned
with the false as such. It explains how people arrive at the
false opinions of the everyday worldview and thus guarantees the truth of the first part's portrayal.

38. The claim of Part I reads: being is, and is necessarily;
it cannot not be (B2). Statements about (the) being are derived from this claim in B8: 1. Being is uncreated and imperishable (5–21). 2. It is one and continuous (22–25). 3.
It is immutable (26–31). It is complete (32–49). These statements follow validly in the main from the claim. Their provocation lies in what they dispute. They exclude the possibility of attributing to things predicates that characterize our
world of experience: coming to be and perishing, change,
plurality, capacity for development, and difference. Parmenides' ontology disputes the reality of the world of experience.
Thought, to which alone Parmenides grants access to being,
contradicts experiential knowledge (B7).

39. How is this claim justified? B2 refers to the two paths
of enquiry which, according to Parmenides, are the only conceivable ones. The second is then excluded as impossible.
Thus, only the first path remains. The paths are formulated
as follows:

(1) that . . . is and that it is not possible not to be.
(2) that . . . is not and that it is necessary not to be.
The first notable feature about these formulations is that both

paths are portrayed not by complete sentences but rather by sentence functions. The subject term that is to be added proceeds from B6, 1, when the first path is repeated in the form "It is right to say and think that *being* is." The same results from B8, 2, when the sentence function is repeated, and then "being" is named as the subject. The second point deserving notice is the syntactical use of 'is'. Parmenides assumes a unary use of 'is' (i.e., 'is' as a single-place predicate) when he reflects on the concept of being. Third, it is to be remembered that the two paths are not the only possible ones. Hence the major premise of the proof does not present an exhaustive disjunction. Between necessary being and necessary not-being there is a third path, that of contingent being or not-being.

This formal inadequacy does not, however, influence the validity of the argument. For if it is inconceivable that being is not, then the conceivability of contingent being is also excluded. For contingent being is being that can be or not be. Thus it presumes the possibility that Parmenides excludes according to which being is not. This exclusion is proven in the following manner:

(3) Only what can be thought can be (B3).

(4) Not-being cannot be thought (B2, 7).

(5) Not-being cannot be.

The problem lies in (4). We can grant Parmenides that the question as to what can and what cannot be can only be decided by thought. However, how can he claim that not-being cannot be known? Apparent facts contradict this. We can know that something is not the case and that certain beings, for example, unicorns, do not exist. I suggest two interpretations here of which the second, taken historically, is more probable.

40. 1. If we understand 'is' as a term used to express a single-place predicate, the statement "Being is not" is a contradiction due to its form. It has the same form as, for example, the statement "Walking things do not walk." This contradiction does not arise when we use 'is' as a two-place

predicate, for example, "Being is not uncaused." Similarly, the first path would, according to this interpretation, be a tautology and thus necessary.

41. 2. Single-place predicate terms stand for properties. The most elementary and best-known properties are those which are transmitted to us through our senses, for example, colors or tactile qualities. Parmenides' concept of being rests on the fact that he does not sufficiently distinguish between thought and perception. "Being," according to his conception, stands for a property that is conceived as a kind of perceptual property. The act of perception depends upon its object. The color actuates the capacity to see. Whoever sees, sees colored. Parmenides understands the relationship between thought (noein) and being in a corresponding manner (see B8, 34–36). Thought relies on its object, being, in order for it to develop. It is an experience of being just as seeing is a perception of color. If thought cannot develop without being, then not-being cannot be thought. Whoever sees nothing, does not see, and whoever thinks not-being, does not think. That being is conceived according to perceivable content depends on two factors. First, there is the (inappropriate) single-place predicative use of 'is'. This deception is not suggested by its two-place (predicative) use. It becomes evident here that 'is' stands not for a property but rather serves to predicate a property of an object. Second, the grammatical construction of the Greek verb for thought (noein) is to be noted. It is constructed with an accusative (direct) object and not with a that-clause. When I think a being, this being cannot be the state of affairs that something is such and such or not such and such; that something exists or does not exist. When I think of states of affairs, I can also think of negative states of affairs and in this sense of not-being. Conversely, if the only construction possible is one with an accusative (direct) object, then thought can only have an unstructured content: I think of being as I see colors or feel warmth.

42. Three arguments from the text and doxographical

reports support this second interpretation. 1. According to B16 the faculty of knowledge in human beings (nous) relies upon the mixture of elements in the human body. We know only the element that predominates in us. The decisive point is emphasized by Theophrastus in his commentary on this fragment (A46): Parmenides equated thought and perception. That human beings know according to the mixture of elements in their bodies is also a theory of thought and perception. Theophrastus' interpretation is confirmed by Aristotle. For the ancients, as it is stated in *De anima* III, 3, 427a21f., thought and perception are identical. 2. B4 describes the mind (nous) as the capacity for sight. It views being as a unity for which the difference between presence and absence is abrogated. Being is an homogeneous whole. The mind will not disturb it, neither by analyzing it into distinct parts nor by letting it roll up into a ball at any place and thus destroy its homogeneity. 3. The same idea, that being is an homogeneous whole, is found in B8, 23–25, and B8, 42–49. The predicates that are attributed to and denied of being there ('divided', 'evenly spread', 'coherent', 'complete', 'continuous', 'larger', 'smaller', 'more intensive', 'less intensive') can only be meaningfully predicated of spatial constructs or of qualities that are ascribed to spatial constructs.

43. Part II sketches the opinions of the mortals about the cosmos and its genesis. The underlying mistake consists in the assumption suggested by sense experience that also not-being is (B6; B7). Plurality and change in the perceivable world are names that human beings have stipulated (B8, 38–41, 53; B19, 3). The cosmos is, according to human positing, built up out of two elements, light and night (B8, 53–61; B9). They reflect being insofar as each one of them is identical with itself, that is, is immutable. They participate in not-being insofar as they are distinct from one another (B8, 57f.). Parmenides explains the coming-to-be of individual things from these elements with a concept of mixture that will be so important for the natural philosophers who follow (B12, 4; A43; A43a). Both elements fill the en-

tire cosmos, so that it is a filled whole like the ball of being
(B9). The preserved details reveal that the opinion part is
to explain the entirety of appearances. Parmenides considers, among other things, age (A46a), sleep (A46b), the
difference between the sexes (A52), reproduction and em-
bryology (B17f.). Concerning his astronomical theories, it
is remarkable that, for example, the moon receives its light
from the sun (B14f.), the morning star is identical with the
evening star (A40a), and the earth is a sphere (B44).

2. ZENO

44. Zeno of Elea (born around 500 or 490 B.C.) proposes
to defend Parmenides' claim by showing that the assumption of plurality and motion leads to paradoxes. Two arguments against plurality (DK 29B1–3), four against motion
(A25–28), and one against the existence of space have been
preserved: Everything that is is in space. If space is something, it too must be in space, and so on ad infinitum (A24).
The first two proofs against motion read: 1. It is impossible
that a body traverse a certain stretch. For before it traverses
the whole stretch, it must have already traversed half of that
stretch, and prior to that half of that stretch, it must have
traversed half of that stretch, etc. Therefore, it must have
traversed infinitely many segments. However, that is not possible in a finite time. 2. The fast runner Achilles can never
pass the slow tortoise. Assume that Achilles runs ten times
faster than the tortoise, and the latter has a head start of
100 meters. When Achilles has traversed these 100 meters,
the tortoise still has a lead of 10 meters. When Achilles has
run these 10 meters, the tortoise will still have a lead of
1 meter. Although the lead always becomes progressively
smaller, Achilles will never succeed in passing the tortoise.
According to Aristotle (*Phys.* 239b5–29) both paradoxes
rest on the same mistake: in both cases the goal cannot be
reached due to the infinite division of a stretch of space or

time, respectively. Aristotle solves both paradoxes by distinguishing a twofold meaning of "infinite" (*Phys.* 233a21–31). Every kind of continuum can be designated as infinite with respect to either its extension or its divisibility. A stretch infinite according to its extension cannot be traversed in a finite time. On the contrary, however, a stretch finite in extension yet infinite in divisibility can be traversed in a finite time.

VIII. The Pre-Socratic Systems after Parmenides

1. EMPEDOCLES

45. Like Parmenides Empedocles, and with him Anaxagoras and the atomists, is of the opinion that being can neither arise from not-being nor perish into not-being (DK 31B11f.). What separates him from Parmenides and links him with the Ionians are his epistemological premises. Against Parmenides he presses expressly for the use and reliability of the senses (B3, 9–13). Empedocles, Anaxagoras, and the atomists want to exclude coming-to-be and passing-away without declaring the world of appearance to be an utter illusion.

46. The life, person, and death of Empedocles of Acragas (ca. 500–ca. 430 B.C.) are surrounded by legend (DL VIII 51–77 = A1). He is one of the most diversified personalities of the ancients: philosopher, natural scientist, politically active democrat, theologian, and poet. The preserved fragments stem from the poems *On Nature* and *Purifications*. The two works appear to contradict each other, especially with respect to their teachings on the soul. The *Purifications* speak of an original sin (B136–139) that must be expiated by continual reincarnations of the soul (B115; B117–121) until it is liberated from the cycle of rebirths (B146f.). On the contrary, the critical, materialistic tendency of *On Nature* appears to exclude the thought of immortality. Whether and how these

positions can be combined with one another is debated by scholars.

47. The ultimate components of the cosmos are the four "roots" earth, air, fire, and water (B6; B17, 18). Like Parmenides' being they are uncreated, imperishable, and qualitatively unchangeable. Only the ratio of their mixture changes (B17, 27–35; A28). They are contained in a never-ending cyclical process that is determined by the two efficacious powers of Love and Strife, and for which four stages can be distinguished (although this is controversial). A: When Love rules, the roots form an homogeneous ball, the Sphere, in which they permeate each other completely (B27–29; A41). B: Strife gains strength and dissolves the Sphere (B30f.). C: The roots are completely separated from each other (Plutarch, *De fac. lun.* 12 = prior to B27). D: Love reaches the middle of the chaos and gains more and more control over Strife (B35). Empedocles assumed (according to one interpretation) that in phases B and D mirroring worlds arise (B17, 3). We are living in phase B (Aristotle, *De gen. et corr.* 334a5 = A42). The whole cosmos and all living organisms consist of the four roots (B21). Empedocles compares them with the colors that a painter mixes in various ratios and from which he creates his forms.

48. The development of living organisms proceeds in different stages (A72). Initially the homogeneous things — blood, flesh, and bones — arise by a mixture of the roots according to certain proportions. Then the organs arise but are combined with one another by mere chance. Thus malfigurations occur: beings with two faces, humans with ox heads, and such (B59–61). Only the expedient organisms survive in the battle for existence (Aristotle, *Phys.* 198b29 = prior to B61) and reproduce. Perception depends upon the same elements being present in the perceptual organ and the perceived object. Like perceives like (B109). Effluences are constantly given off from everything, and if they fit, they will penetrate into the pores of a sense organ (B89; A86, 7). Empedocles did not distinguish between perception and thought

...ters into the pupil (68A135, par.
...qualities—temperature, color, and
...ing to opinion" (nomō) (68B125).
...above-mentioned properties of the
...ss consists of sharp-cornered, small
...ss, of smooth atoms (68A135, §63ff.).
...atomic theory is an important step toward
...nsofar as it supplies the thought that all
...minations are to be derived from quantita-
...ions (see Anaximenes, par. 19). In contrast
...mic theory Democritus' theory is one not of
...ce but rather ontological. Democritus was prob-
...opinion that atoms could not be observed but
...nferred by reason (68A37; A102; A124). His the-
...d to explain, not particular empirical facts, but rather
...ical states of affairs generally and especially the vari-
...rms of change. Nonetheless it prepares the way for
...ght in the vein of natural science. The difficulty with
...concept of the atom lies in the connection of extension
...d indivisibility. What is extended is also divisible. One of
...ristotle's reports (68A48) leads one to suspect that Democritus saw this difficulty and distinguished between mathematical and physical observation so that he could still admit
mathematically potential infinite divisibility while assuming
indivisible material body. Material bodies must be assumed,
because the limits of mathematical divisibility are unextended
points that cannot be the ultimate components of extended
bodies.

53. Almost all of Democritus' literal fragments stem from
his ethical works. Their authenticity is questionable. B35–
115 are passed down under the name of "Democritus." It
is also controversial how Democritus' atomism is consistent
with his ethics. The goal of life is inner harmony, temperance, being relaxed, joy, being free of fear, and other af-
fective excitements (68A1, par. 45; A167). The connection
between this ethical ideal and the atomic theory becomes
evident in 68B191: the concern is to avoid large movements

(Aristotle, *De anima* 427a21 = prior to B106). Human beings' capacity for thought is the blood around the heart
(B105), because all the elements are mixed most evenly in
this blood. The soul is thus no more than a certain propor-
tionate mixture (Aristotle, *De anima* 408a13 = A78); it is
destroyed when this proportion changes.

2. ANAXAGORAS

49. Anaxagoras (ca. 500–428 B.C.) originated from Cla-
zomenae in Asia Minor but spent a large portion of his life
in Athens. He was a friend of Pericles. Because he taught
that the sun is a glowing mass of stone, he was accused of
atheism. He died in Lampsacus (DL II 6–15 = DK 59A1).
"Of coming-to-be and perishing," Anaxagoras writes in agreement with Parmenides, "the Greeks have no correct opinion.
For nothing comes to be or perishes, but rather a composition or separation of things that are occurs. And accordingly
they would be correct to call coming-to-be composition and
perishing separation" (B17; see B5). How Anaxagoras conceived of the ultimate components of things can hardly be
reconstructed in a consistent manner. He proceeds from two
assumptions: 1. There can be no qualitative change: no "stuff"
or material can change its constitution. The infinite profu-
sion of all qualitatively diverse "stuffs"—for example, water,
fire, hair, bread, and meat (B8; B10)—must for this reason
be uncreated and imperishable. 2. Each "stuff" is quantita-
tively infinitely divisible. For every smallest part there is a
conceivably smaller part (B3). Every part of the infinitely
divisible stuff, regardless of how small, contains the entire
infinite wealth of qualitatively diverse stuffs (B4), which are
conceived of as infinitely small. However, since the infinitely
small cannot exist in reality, these qualitatively diverse parts
have no self-sufficient, separate existence (B6). Thus, they
cannot be experienced in their qualitative difference (B1; B4).
The diverse constitution of the objects in the world of ex-

perience is explained by the different allotments of the infinitely small, qualitatively diverse "parts" or "seeds." Every particular thing contains all seeds, but it shows the constitution of the seed of which it contains the most (B11; B12 end). How does this differentiation arise? In addition to the parts Anaxagoras assumes a second principle of mind (B12–14). It too is "stuff." In contrast to the other stuffs there is no other stuff in it, although it can mix itself with other stuffs such as in living beings. Hence, it is the finest and purest stuff and can thus determine itself and all others. Anaxagoras describes mind as a knowing, omniscient principle that orders the world. However, its ordering activity exhausts itself in being the origin of rotational motion, and Plato and Aristotle criticize him for maintaining this position (*Phaedo* 97b; *Met.* 985a18 = A47). In the beginning the stuff completely lacked qualities (B1). Via the rotational motion a process of separation arises that brings forth the cosmos in an ordered procession (first fire spews forth, then air, water, earth, stone) (A45, p. 18, line 13f.; see B15; B16).

50. It is evident that there are inconsistent strands in Anaxagoras' theory. The stuff conceived of as infinitely divisible contains, to use an Aristotelian formulation, potentially all qualities. If one interprets Anaxagoras in this manner, then he does not explain how the various qualities are realized. For the concepts "composition" and "separation" and the explanation of differentiation by rotational motion presume that parts of a real extension and of real diverse qualities are present and can be separated mechanically from one another by rotational motion.

3. THE ATOMISTS

51. The doxographic reports often mention Leucippus of Miletus (beginning of the fifth century B.C.) and Democritus of Abdera (ca. 460–ca. 370 B.C.) together. It is probable that Democritus worked out the particulars of the atomist

position who
ing to Ari
Eleatic ont
Parmenides h
be from not-be
ing. In contrast w
a principle. As emp
tion. Parmenides' one
finite mass of atoms foun
The atoms, also called "th
indivisible, because they do
(67A14). They differ only accor
in their size) (like the letters A a
Z from N), and their order (like AN
ferent weights arise from different sizes
have their own motions. How this is to b
clear from the reports. Through this motio
lide, and they either latch onto or repel one an
A15). The world arises out of a whirl that divide
according to their size. The larger ones gather in t
and form the earth. The smaller ones fly outward an
the stars (67A1). Since empty space and the mass of a
are infinite, Leucippus and Democritus assume an infin
number of worlds that come to be and perish in an inces
sant process (68A40). The various weights of the element
depend on the diverse empty spaces between the atoms. Hard
materials consist of atoms that latch together due to their
form; and soft materials, of those that can easily be pushed
against one another (68A135, §61ff.).

The materialistic explanation is also carried out consistently for the mental realm. Soul and mind consist of fire atoms. Because they are small and round, they are especially mobile (68A101). Perception depends on atoms being perpetually discharged from things (see Empedocles, par. 48). The theory of vision is worked out in more detail: The objects radiate small replicas (eidōla). They meet with emissions of the eye and imprint into the air between the eye and

among the soul's atoms, "for the souls that move in large intervals are neither in good balance nor in good spirits." Thus, Democritus teaches an ethics of measure and prudence (sōphrosunē). Human beings should not overestimate themselves (68B3) but rather direct themselves toward what is possible and be content with what is present (B191). Prudence leads to greater joy and holds one back from pleasure that ultimately leads to (greater) displeasure (B211; B70–74). Democritus emphasizes the ethical autonomy of human beings: "Whoever does shameless deeds must especially be ashamed of himself" (B84; see B244; B264). The polis can only achieve greatness with the unity of its citizens (B250). Disunity and strife injure both parties (B249). The rich ought to help the poor with their wealth. Democracy is to be preferred to other forms of government because it guarantees freedom (B251). The polis' duties have priority over all others (B252). Democritus urges respect for the law because it serves the well-being of humans (B47; B174; B245; B248).

B. The Sophists and Socrates

I. The Sophists

54. In the second half of the fifth century B.C. a thematic shift in Greek philosophy occurs in Athens. Whereas the focal point had been the cosmos, Socrates, according to Cicero, "is the first to have called philosophy down from the heavens, planted it in the cities, and even introduced it into houses, and forced them to ask about life, ethics, good, and evil" (*Tusculan* V 10). However, Socrates is to be seen in a larger context of a movement of enlightenment that is characterized as sophism. We owe our knowledge of sophism especially to Plato, one of its strongest historical opponents. Its value is thus controversial even today. According to one widespread judgment the Sophists are destroyers of morality, masters of rhetorical deception and an art of disputation with which everything can be proved and disproved, and "agents of apparent knowledge" (Aristotle). A more positive viewpoint is due especially to Hegel and E. Zeller: The Sophists validate the principle of subjectivity. Man loses his awe toward the tradition as such and avers not to accept what he has not proved himself. Without the Sophists Socrates and Plato would not have been possible. Socrates attempts to justify anew moral consciousness by a radicalization of the Sophist's enlightening activities and their critical questioning.

55. One important prerequisite of sophism is the development of Athenian democracy. Whoever wants to advance successfully his opinion in the public assembly or in court must master the art of rhetoric and argumentation. Language be-

comes an instrument of power. The Sophists are wandering teachers that proffer to sell such an education to the sons of leading families. They originated from various regions: Protagoras, the most important one, from Abdera in Thrace, Gorgias from Leontinoi in Sicily, Prodicus from the island of Keos in the Cyclades, Hippias from Elis on the Peleponnesos. The conservative circles were often suspicious of and disliked these foreigners who had no civil rights. Due to their jobs the Sophists are interested in philosophy of language. They discuss whether words have meaning naturally or by convention. They are concerned with the multiple meaning of words, synonymy, and etymology.

56. If rhetoric is viewed as a mere technical science, it can be used to convince audiences of any position whatsoever. From this perspective Protagoras' claim that two contradictory statements are possible for any state of affairs becomes understandable (DK 80A1, par. 51). Protagoras' epistemology also leads to relativism. It is summarized in the famous sentence "Man is the measure of all things, of existing things as they are and of nonexisting things as they are not" (80B1). Reality is constantly changing. Knowledge is exhausted in sense perception. It is a process that the subject undergoes passively. For this reason every perception is subject- and situation-relative. It does not reveal any reality in itself. However something appears to a person here and now in perception is how it is (see Plato, *Theaetetus* 166aff.). Protagoras is presumed to have disputed that the tangents only touch one point in a circle (80B7). This example illustrates the reduction of the real to the perceived. Moral norms are relative as well. However, Protagoras distinguishes here between the individual and the collective subject. Justice is what appears to be justice not to the individual but rather to the state. Nonetheless the laws that obtain in the various states are not equal, just as all perceptions are not. What appears sweet to the healthy person may appear sour to an ill person. Both perceptions are true, but that of the healthy person is more useful than that of the ill person. In the same

sense one can distinguish between useful and harmful laws and moral norms. Protagoras sees the task of the sophist at this point. As the doctor attempts to produce a change for the better in the physical condition of a person, the sophist attempts to influence the state such that the useful rather than the harmful will appear to be just (see Plato, ibid.).

57. The sophistical enlightenment questions the validity of the norms of human community life. The discussion is led by the phrases 'nomos' (custom, law, convention) and 'physis' (nature). For the traditional conception, which is found, for example, in Heraclitus, law is the expression of a divine order. It guarantees the interests of everyone. The unity of the polis and its power to protect its citizens' freedom rest on law (DK 22B114; B44). This understanding undergoes a crisis due to the increasing changes in law in the Athenian democracy. Similarly, the increased knowledge of the various ethics of other peoples leads to a relativization (Herodotus III 38). Sophism takes over the concept of physis from medicine. Physis is the normal state whose return is the goal of the medicinal art as well as the "equipment" given by birth that can only be changed at the price of the possibility of damage. The reference to it serves to criticize the nomos as unnatural and harmful. The Sophist Antiphon advises one to act in accord with the agreed-upon laws when one is being observed, but otherwise in accord with the necessities of nature. Man only suffers true damage if he acts against nature. Laws are the enemy of nature (DK 87B44A). This can certainly be understood positively as a criticism of the laws that only serve to advance a particular social caste and show disrespect for the needs of other human beings. In this manner Antiphon (DK 87B44B) and Hippias (Plato, *Protagoras* 337cd) stand for the equality of all human beings, regardless of racial and social differences, by referring to physis, that is, the same structure of needs. Apparently the rights of the stronger and a corresponding unlimited politics of might were justified by referring to the physis as well. This proceeds not only from Plato's admittedly very polemi-

cal portrayal (*Gorgias* 483bff.) but also, for example, from Thucydides' Melian dialogue (V 85ff.). In the discussion it becomes apparent that a human community is not possible when each one follows exclusively the physis. For this reason the state and laws are justified by a social contract (Plato, *Republic* 358eff.). Protagoras goes further and claims that human beings possess a natural social and moral capacity beyond their technological capacities (Plato, *Protagoras* 320cff.).

II. Socrates

58. The most important sources for Socrates' philosophy are: 1. Plato, especially the *Apology* and the dialogues *Crito, Euthyphro,* and the *Phaedo,* which are concerned with Socrates' trial and death; 2. Xenophon's (born ca. 426 B.C.) *Memorabilia* ("Remembrances of Socrates"); 3. the comedian playwright Aristophanes' *The Clouds* (debut 423 B.C.); 4. particular passages in Aristotle (*Met.* 987b1, 1078b27, *NE* 1144b14). These testimonies diverge immensely. According to Aristophanes, Socrates is a critical, atheistic philosopher of nature and a Sophist in the pejorative sense, as one who teaches young men how to turn wrong into right. Plato's Socrates is an opponent of the sophists on all levels. The Socrates of the early Platonic dialogues who questions, emphasizes his own ignorance, and reveals a deep irony presents a stark contrast to Xenophon's virtuous and upright citizen who represents a flat position of utility. Aristotle agrees with Plato and summarizes the method of Socratic dialog into a pithy phrase: Socrates discusses ethical questions, seeks the universal, and is the first to concern himself with definitions (*Met.* 987b1). Newer research emphasizes the source value of the early Platonic dialogues. J. Burnet's and A.E. Taylor's fundamental thesis (*Greek Philosophy,* London, 1932, and *Socrates,* 1932; rev. ed.: Boston, 1951, resp.) that all of Plato's essential philosophical thoughts, especially the theory of Forms, derive from Socrates, is hardly maintained anymore. *The Clouds* makes clear that the general opinion, confirmed

by Plato in the *Apology* (19bc; 23d), does not distinguish
Socrates and the sophists. Aristotle, who first came to Athens
30 years after Socrates' death, can be excluded as an independent source. Xenophon wrote his *Memorabilia* around
360. He combines in them personal memories with excerpts
from Socratics independent of Plato, whose works were not
preserved (see Gigon 1947).

59. Socrates (ca. 470–399 B.C.) was the son of the stone
mason Sophroniscus and the midwife Phaenarete and was
married to Xanthippe, who bore him three sons. He par-
ticipated in the battles at Potidaea (432–429), Delion (424),
and Amphipolis (422). In 406 he opposed as a committee
member the recommendation of the people's assembly that
sentenced the generals to death after the Athenian victory
at sea near the Arginousai Islands, because they could not
shelter the captives in stormy seas. He resisted the Thirty
Tyrants by refusing to help arrest Leon of Salamis, who was
believed to be executed (Plato, *Apology* 32a–d). In 399 he
was accused of corrupting the youth, not recognizing the
state's gods, and introducing new gods (ibid. 24b) and was
sentenced to death by hemlock.

60. According to the *Apology* and the early Platonic dialogs Socrates is initially concerned to attack apparent knowledge in discussion in order to bring humans to question
things. Whoever has only apparent knowledge knows less
than one who knows one's ignorance. For such a person has
no questions and cannot therefore be searching (*Apology*
21b–d). The Socratic method is the examination of life
(*Laches* 187e). An unexamined life is not worth living (*Apology* 38a). The question, posed repeatedly by Socrates, as to
the definitions of the virtues calls into question the ideas on
values that determine his discussion partner's life. Socratic
questioning is an expression of trust in the power of insight.
No man can voluntarily act against his own interests just
as no one can consciously will to err. Everyone necessarily
strives for the good. Only insight into the good can motivate one toward the good. In this sense virtue is knowledge.

Socratic method thus aspires to lead human beings from the apparent good to the really good, his true interest (see *Gorgias* 466de). Socrates explains what he means by knowledge of the good by a comparison with knowledge of the arts (technē). Like art, virtue (aretē) is understanding how to do something. To the extent that an artisan understands how to make his product, the work will succeed. The work that a virtuous person understands how to make is the good life. Every art finds its fulfillment in its exercise. Whoever exercises an art has more joy the better that person is at that activity. In the same sense the successful, happy life is only possible due to virtue. Virtue has a social importance: every art serves. Art as such does not seek advantage for itself but for another. The doctor as doctor strives toward the health of the sick. Art as such only seeks its exercise; in that lies its fulfillment. By being active it serves another (*Rep.* 352dff.; 341cff.; *Euthyd.* 279dff.).

These similarities should not obscure the essential difference between art and ethical knowledge. Every art is limited to bringing about a certain good. It is not, however, capable of judging this good in turn and answering questions about its correct use. The arts are knowledge of goods, but not of the Good. Doctors understand sickness and health. Yet they cannot decide whether it is better for a person to be sick or healthy (*Laches* 195c; *Euthyd.* 280bff.). What can be said about this knowledge of the Good? Socrates provides a primarily negative answer. He objects to an apparent knowledge that identifies *a* good with *the* Good, even if it be life itself. Whoever is afraid of death claims implicitly to know what he does not know. He claims to know that death is the greatest evil, although no one knows whether it might not be the greatest good (*Apology* 29a). Like the sophists, Socrates criticizes traditional religion. He is concerned with the unity of religion and morality. Traditional religion does not decide what is morally right, but rather the morally good is a criterion for the credibility of religion (see *Euthyphro* 10d). At the same time moral actions that are oriented toward insight have a theological dimension. At the conclusion of the *Apology* (41d) and the *Crito* (54e) Socrates expresses the conviction that whoever follows her insight into the good cannot ultimately suffer evil because god leads her, and her fate is important to the gods. One can interpret the reports as to the Daimon that advise Socrates whenever he is planning to do wrong (*Apology* 31cff.; 40aff.) in light of this conviction in providence.

C. Plato

Life and Works

61. The most important sources for Plato's biography are the seventh of the letters passed down under his name, which either he or one of his students composed, and Diogenes Laertius. Plato (427–347 B.C.) was born into an aristocratic Athenian family. His mother, Perictione, is believed to have blood lineage back to Solon and his father, Ariston, to the remarkable Athenian king Kodros. After their victory in the Peleponnesian War (404) the Spartans renounced the democracy in Athens and introduced an oligarchy, the rule of the "Thirty Tyrants." Critias and Charmides, a cousin and a brother of Plato's mother respectively, belonged to the Thirty. They encouraged Plato to take up a career in politics. Plato initially hoped that the new regime would create more just conditions but soon turned away from them disappointed. Plato again considered engaging in politics when democracy was restored in 403. However, the execution of his friend and teacher, Socrates, by the new occupants of power (399) lead him to be skeptical of political reform in Athens. He came to the opinion that justice can only be realized if the true philosophers become rulers or the rulers become true philosophers, that is, if political power and reason can be combined in one person (*Ep.* VII 326ab.).

His philosophy is to serve a just political order. Plato believed that he could only plausibly advance a political philosophy if he were to become involved in its practice within the limits of his possibilities (*EP.* VII 328c–329a). This conviction motivated his political activities in Syracuse, which turned out to be, however, a complete failure. Around 390 he undertook a research trip to Egypt, to Cyrene where he met the mathematician Theodorus, and to lower Italy where he met Archytas of Tarent and other Pythagoreans. Without any particular intentions he traveled on to Syracuse where he won over to his ethical and political ideals the young Dion, the brother-in-law of the ruling Dionysius I. His stay there is thought to have ended when Dionysius I had Plato sold as a slave.

After being bought back at the slave market at Aegina and returning to Athens, Plato founded the Academy on a plot of land outside Athens, named after the hero Academus. It had the legal standing of a religious club to honor the Muses and was a cohabitual community of teachers and students. The curriculum encompassed mathematics, natural science, and dialectic. Former students of the Academy were politically active in numerous cities. After Dionysius I's death (367) Dion convinced the former's son Dionysius II to invite Plato as a teacher and political advisor. Plato could not, however, succeed in overcoming the influences against him near the young ruler. Dion was found guilty of attempted high treason and was forced to leave Sicily. In 361 Plato followed a second, urgent invitation by Dionysius II. This trip too was a complete disaster. Dionysius and Plato disagreed vehemently about the exiled Dion. Plato was hindered from leaving Syracuse and only regained his freedom through Archytas' help.

62. Aristotle (*Met.* 1, 6) reports on Plato's philosophical teachers. Through Cratylus Plato is presumed to have learned the Heraclitean claim that there can be no knowledge of sensible perceivable reality, because it is in constant flux. Socrates' inquiry into the definition of moral predicates is thought to have alerted him to take note of the problem of universals. Aristotle especially emphasizes the Pythagoreans' metaphysics of numbers. According to DL III 6 Plato went to Euclid of Megara after Socrates' death. There he prob-

ably learned of Parmenides' ontology with which he was concerned in his later dialogs.

63. With the exception of 13 letters of which at most the sixth, seventh, and eighth are genuine, Plato's written works are composed of dialogs (even the *Apology* contains elements of dialog), all of which we possess. Thrasyllus' classification (first century A.D.) underlies the written works and many printed editions according to which the dialogs and letters are placed in nine groups with four works in each (tetralogies) (DL III 56–61). Already in ancient times several works passed down with Plato's name were considered spurious (ibid. 62). In addition to authenticity, modern criticism discusses the chronological ordering of the dialogs. The most important applied method is stylometrics, which observes the unintended and philosophically meaningless changes in style. Due to the results obtained with this method by W. Lutoslawski (1897), C. Ritter (1903; 1914), and H. von Arnim (1912) (see Leisegang [1950] 2375), there is widespread agreement today that Plato's dialog are to be ordered in three groups whereby the place of each particular dialog within its group is controversial, especially in the early and late dialogs. Early Dialogs: *Apology, Crito, Laches, Lysis, Charmides, Euthyphro, Hippias Minor, Hippias Major* (genuine ?), *Protagoras, Gorgias, Ion*. Middle Dialogs: *Meno, Phaedo, Republic, Symposium, Phaedrus, Euthydemus, Menexenus, Cratylus*. Late Dialogs: *Parmenides, Theaetetus, Sophist, Statesman, Timaeus, Critias, Philebus, Laws*.

64. Ethics is central to the early works. In the *Crito* Socrates argues against his friend of the same name who wants to help him escape from jail that even an unjustified death sentence does not permit him to violate the laws of his homeland. Concern with particular virtues is displayed in the dialogs *Laches* (courage), *Charmides* (temperance), *Euthyphro* (piety), and *Thrasymachus* (Book I of the *Republic*) (justice). The central theme of the *Lysis* is friendship, of the *Protagoras* the teachability and unity of virtue, and of the *Hippias Major* beauty. The majority of the early dialogs end

with no positive result. All of the definitions and attempts
at solutions given by Socrates' partner in discussion are refuted by Socrates. The interpreter must ask about the philosophical meaning of this lack of positive results. The *Gorgias,*
which introduces the second group of dialogs, is a discussion of rhetoric. As a technique of manipulating human beings it is an instrument of power. Plato shows that any power
without knowledge of the good is in truth powerless. The
Meno studies the epistemological presuppositions of Socrates' maieutic (the science of midwifery): How is it possible
that one can be led to knowledge exclusively through questions? How can one search for something with which one
is not acquainted? Plato answers with his theory of reminis-
cence, tied in with the traditional doctrine of the soul's immortality. The three classical dialogs of the mature period
reflect basic human dispositions: love (*Symposium;* it is, in
addition to rhetoric, the theme of the *Phaedrus*), social life
in the state (*Republic*), and death (*Phaedo*). The *Cratylus*
discusses from philosophy of language the problem whether
the names with which we refer to things are given naturally
or whether they are based on conventions.

65. The emphasis of the later dialogs is on ontology, dialectic, epistemology, and cosmology. The *Theaetetus* attempts
to clarify the concept of knowledge and in the process discusses Heraclitus' and Protagoras' relativism. In the *Parmenides* Plato raises objections to his own theory of Forms, which
will be picked up by Aristotle. The second part develops a
dialectic of the one and the many that influences Neoplatonic speculation. The *Sophist* concerns Parmenides' thesis
that not-being can be neither thought nor spoken. He solves
the problem by analyzing the predicative sentence. Like the
Phaedrus prior to it, the *Sophist* is important for Plato's
teaching of concept formation (dialectic). He mentions five
highest concepts (categories): Being, Rest, Motion, Identity, and Diversity. One of the most influential dialogs is the
Timaeus. Its themes are cosmology and anthropology as a
natural science. The demiurge creates the world according

to the pattern of the Forms. Since he wants to make the world as good as possible, he gives it a soul possessing mental capacities. Since Middle Platonism it has been debated whether the myth of creation presented in the *Timaeus* is to be understood as positing a temporal beginning of the world or, what is more probable, as a symbolic presentation of the atemporal order of the world. The importance of the *Timaeus* for modern natural science lies in the fact that Plato attempts to explain natural phenomena with the help of mathematical laws. He derives the four elements that he takes over from Empedocles from mathematical constructs. The fire atom is a tetrahedron, the earth atom a cube, the air atom an octahedron, the water atom an icosahedron. The *Philebus* asks again about the good. It defends a mixed life in which reason has priority, although pleasure too has its place. The latest work, the *Laws,* published by Philippus of Opus, is again concerned with the state. In contrast to the a priori procedure of the *Republic,* historical experience and respect for what is possible for man increase in importance. Rule by law replaces the *Republic*'s philosopher-king. Plato recommends a mixed constitution of monarchy and democracy. The importance of religion is emphasized. Book X asks about the causes of atheism and develops a theistic proof from the ordered motion of the heavenly bodies.

I. The Dialog Form

66. If we compare Plato's works with other great works from the history of philosophy—for example, Parmenides' poem, Aristotle's *Metaphysics,* or Kant's *Critique of Pure Reason*—their unique form is immediately apparent. Plato wrote no philosophical treatise that systematically developed a particular thesis. He uses no division of philosophy into particular disciplines. A glance at the *Gorgias,* the *Republic,* the *Phaedrus,* or the *Sophist* displays the wide gamut of themes that are broached in one dialog and can be combined into an organized whole. Plato portrays discussions; he alludes to situations in which they occur and describes the dialog's characters. Since the ancient period itself Plato's dialogs have been compared with dramas. Often the reader will be irritated by the impression of a lack of results. For what reason did Plato choose this literary form? How is it related to the philosophical content? Is it merely an outer costume from which a systematic teaching can be extracted? Or are the dialogs only protreptic works that are to stimulate and win over the reader without actually hitting on the real problems? Or are they (so-called exoteric) works directed toward a more popular and broad audience, whereas the (esoteric) systematic presentations of his philosophical teachings were reserved for lectures in the Academy?

67. Ever since Schleiermacher Plato researchers have repeatedly returned in discussing this question to the passage at *Phaedrus* 274c–278b where Plato compares evaluatively

the written word with oral discourse. Socrates tells the following myth: The Egyptian god Theuth discovers numbers, geometry, astronomy, and finally letters. He shows king Thamus his discovery, who inquires into their utility. Theuth answers that letters will make men wiser and ameliorate their memories. To the contrary, Thamus judges that written words will make men forgetful "because they will trust in the written word from without through foreign symbols instead of remembering from within through their own strength." The written word will only mediate apparent knowledge upon which men will imagine themselves to be wise. Only lively oral discourse that considers the person actually involved in the discussion, Socrates concludes from the myth, can teach true knowledge. Knowledge can be mediated through written discourse as little as mechanical aptitude can. The written word is as dead as a picture of an animal. It cannot answer questions. A smart and empathetic teacher knows what she can teach to whom. The written word is not capable of this differentiation. The written word is susceptible of misunderstandings; it requires interpretation. It cannot explain and defend itself. In oral discourse we can ascertain what the other person has understood. We can go into his difficulties and illustrate what is meant with other formulations. The written word is not in a position to accomplish this. The knowledge with which Plato is concerned here is knowledge of the morally good. This knowledge is distinct from its formulations. It is completely realized in none of them. For this reason it cannot be adequately tied down discursively. It only lives in the soul of the knower. It cannot be mediated from without. The student must be led to insight on her own. Thus, for whomever imparting this knowledge is important, he must implant it in the soul of the other through personal discussion and view writing merely as a fun game. A written work can only be a mnemonic device for one who already knows.

68. The devaluation of the written word as we have reported it from the *Phaedrus* renders comprehensible why

Plato chose the dialog form as his literary guise. A dialog forms a discussion and thus attempts to remedy the failings of the written word as much as possible. The situations, feelings, and emotions of life in which a discussion occurs and which influence it can be expressed. Plato can show how a philosophical question can arise from a particular life context with the means of the dialog form. He can point out phenomena that a thematizing and reflective discussion can never completely express. Many of Socrates' discussion partners are historical figures. The reader ought to understand their behavior with their background and character in mind. The people in the dialogs can explain and defend their claims. The process of knowledge can be retraced in its sometimes roundabout steps and fragmentary character. It becomes evident that a discussion of something is not that something itself and will always trail behind it. In contrast to philosophy as formulated knowledge, philosophy is emphasized as an activity and a path. The openness of the dialog is to make the ignorance of the reader evident to her and to engage her in the process of Socratic searching. Any interpretation that is to do justice to the unity of the literary form and the philosophical content would have to follow these points in the Platonic dialogs' events. Unfortunately that is not possible here due to external reasons. To this extent the following portrayal which picks out several thematic points is only an expedient.

II. The Form

1. THE FORM AS A PRESUPPOSITION
OF SOCRATIC DIALOGS

69. The central aspect of Plato's philosophy is the Form. According to the testimony of the early dialogs the question about the Form has Socratic dialog as its source. Because Socrates was convinced that one can only be just, courageous, and such when one knows what the Just, the Courageous, or other is, he attempts to clarify these concepts in a dialog. Socratic dialog presupposes that asking for a definition is intelligible. Plato thematizes this presupposition and thus arrives at an acceptance of the Forms. Whoever denies that Forms exist, Plato writes in the *Parmenides* (135bc) after he has raised apparently insoluble objections to the theory of the Forms, will have nothing toward which he can orient his understanding and will thus destroy the basis for the possibility of discussion. The relation between Socratic dialog and the acceptance of Forms becomes clear in, for example, the *Euthyphro*. The priest Euthyphro claims to know which actions are pious and which impious. He is preparing to take his father to court because he believes that he knows that this action is pious. Socrates tests this apparent knowledge and reveals the presuppositions behind the true knowledge of a predicative statement. He distinguishes between actions that are pious and piety itself. The various pious actions agree in that they are all pious. Plato formulates it as follows: In

all of them there is one and the same Form (eidos), the Pious. For this reason they all offer the same appearance (idea, idea) (6d9–e1). The statement "This action is pious" is true if the Form of the Pious is in fact in the action. True predication relies on the presence of the Form in the action. Despite the numerical diversity of the actions, the Form of piety, or the Pious, is one and the same in all actions. Regardless of how the various pious actions differ in various respects, the Pious in them is always identical with itself (5d1–5). Whoever, like Euthyphro, claims that an action is pious professes to know the appearance of the Pious, for only then can he decide whether the action in question shows this appearance. The appearance is thus the criterion for the truth of the statement. Whoever wants to judge the truth of the statement "This action is pious" must know the appearance of the Pious independently of this action and compare the action in question with the appearance (6e4–6).

How is the appearance known? Plato gives two answers whose consistency must at present remain undetermined. In the *Euthyphro* (6e4) and in many other dialogs he uses the metaphor of sight repeatedly. The words 'eidos' and 'idea' have the same root as a Greek word for sight (eido). In contrast there is the actual procedure of the dialogs: The viewing of the Form is the task of the Socratic *dialog:* The Form becomes known with the help of the art/science of leading a discussion well, that is, dialectic. The *Euthyphro* asks: What is the Pious? (5d7) The answer to this question tells what the Pious is, in short: its essence. Plato calls the essence the being-ness (ousia) of the Pious (11a7). In the tradition ousia in the sense of being-ness is translated as essence (essentia). Knowledge of the Form is knowledge of the essence, and this is only possible due to the art of discussion. Using the example of shame, the *Euthyphro* indicates what Form the correct essential definition of the Pious would have to have. Shame falls under the broader concept of fright. It is distinguished from other kinds of fright in that it has the mark of having something bad as its object (12bc). The example

illustrates that there must be relations between the Forms
that must be clarified if the question about an essence is to
be answered.

2. THE FUNCTIONS OF THE FORMS

70. Our look at the *Euthyphro* showed what Plato's concept of the Form is to explain. 1. The theory of Forms is
a *semantic* theory. It answers the question about the meaning of general terms (predicate words). 2. The semantic question leads to an *ontological* question. Plato advances claims
about the mode of being of this meaning and about the ontological presuppositions of predication. The Form is the
meaning of a general term, and it is intended to explain why
the same general term can be predicated of various singular
terms. 3. The Form is an *epistemological* concept. The Socrates of the early dialogs asks about the meaning of moral
predicate terms. We use them for statements, not about what
is in fact the case, but rather about what should be the case
or what is desirable. For this reason experience cannot teach
us the meaning of these terms; we must know them a priori,
prior to experience. How is such knowledge possible? Plato
refers us to dialectic as a method. These various functions
and interrelations of the Forms are to be spelled out more
fully in the following, especially in light of the middle dialogs. One should pay attention to decide whether these functions are consistent with one another or whether a concept
of Form that is to do justice to all of these points leads to
difficulties.

3. THE FORM AS MEANING

71. How does Plato analyze an elementary predicate sentence? Take as an example "Socrates is beautiful." The word
'Socrates' involves no difficulty. Plato understands it as a sing-

ular term that refers to the individual Socrates. The word 'beautiful' is an ambiguous word according to Plato (*Phaedo* 78e2; 102b2; 103b7; *Republic* 596a7). First, it can be used as a neuter plural with its definite article: "the [various] beautiful things" (ta kala). Second, Plato uses 'beautiful' as a neuter singular with its definite article, whereby he often amplifies the expression with the pronoun 'itself': 'the Beautiful itself'. There exists a dependency relation between the two that Plato calls eponymy. The use last described is primary; it designates the acutal bearer of the name: the Form of the Beautiful. The former use is secondary and derivative. It designates things that are not the Beautiful itself but rather only stand in a certain relation to it and for this reason bear the same name (*Phaedo* 78de; 102b1f.; *Republic* 596a). In the sentence to be analyzed 'Socrates is beautiful' 'beautiful' is used in the secondary sense. However, this use can be traced back to the primary use: A beautiful thing is something that participates in the Beautiful itself. Thus the complete analysis reads: "Socrates participates in the Beautiful itself." According to the presently most widely held view the sentence 'Socrates is beautiful' consists in a singular term and a one-place predicate. To the contrary, Plato analyzes it into two singular terms and a two-place predicate expression. Now we need to clarify what ontological claims Plato makes about objects that are designated by expressions of the type "the F itself," and how exactly he understands the relation represented by the two-place predicate expression.

4. THE FORM AS PARADIGM

72. Plato explains the concept of the Form with examples from the crafts in the *Cratylus* (389a–d) as well as in the *Republic* (596a–598d). The passage in the *Republic* connects up expressly with the semantic question: For every class of things for which we use the same name we posit exactly *one* Form (596a6f.). Plato uses tables and chairs as examples of

such classes. The various tables or chairs have the same name because they each originally depend on one common pattern. The Form of the chair is what the craftsperson looks to when she makes a chair. She can form a particular chair but not the Form of the chair, which is given to her previously by nature. The *Cratylus* uses the example of a weaver's shuttle. It is not arbitrary for the weaver how he forms his shuttle. He is bound to the original pattern as a norm. The original pattern is determined by the function in question, weaving. It is "what is naturally there for weaving" (389a8). A craftsperson who makes a tool or a commodity must find out what is naturally suited to fulfill a function (e.g., weaving or drilling) in order to then impart the corresponding Form to the (suitable) material (*Cratylus* 389c).

73. The examples display the ontological foundation of predication. The particular chair is a chair because its shape is a copy or imitation of the Chair itself. The particular chair and the Chair itself belong to different ontological orders. The Form of the chair is not a part of the perceivable reality but rather is prior to it. Chairs only exist because the craftsperson is given a goal, sitting, and knows what is best suited for it. Similarly, for the Forms of the virtues the relation to the Good is essential. Virtues make men good and enable them to perform good actions. Commodities serve to realize goals or goods: their Forms are conceived of as ideal objects that fulfill their functions *completely*. In the *Parmenides* (130a–e) Plato asks whether Forms correspond to all predicate expressions. Are there Forms for worthless things like mud and dirt, or does every Form imply the concept of the good? Parmenides' counterpart is a very young Socrates. It goes against his good sense to accept Forms for worthless things, but he admits that his refusal is inconsistent. This passage intimates that the later Plato carries his semantic approach through consistently and accepted Forms for all general terms independently of their value. In contrast to the various particular chairs, there can only be one Chair itself. If there were two, both would have the Form

of the chair, and this chair would in turn be a Chair itself
(*Republic* 597c). Only the Chair itself *is* in a full sense. The
carpenter, Plato argues, does not manufacture the Form of
the chair but rather only a chair. However, the Form of the
chair is "what a chair is." When the carpenter does not manufacture "what is," then she manufactures not being but rather
something that resembles being but *is* not (being). Only the
Form of the Chair is in the true sense of the word a being
(*Republic* 597a). It is the "truly (ontos) existing chair" (*Republic* 587d).

5. PLATO'S CONCEPT OF BEING

74. How does Plato arrive at this two-world theory? What
concept of being underlies it? Understanding the expression
"what a chair is," formulated more generally "what X is"
or "what X itself is" (*Republic* 597a2.c3; *Cratylus* 389b5;
Phaedo 78d3.5), is important. The symbol "X" is a variable
for predicate expressions. The expression is to be understood
as a Socratic question. Socrates asks, "What do you say virtue is?" (*Meno* 71d5), "What do you say Piety is?" (*Euthyphro* 5d7). Thus Socrates asks about the being of virtue, piety,
and such. "What X is" is the empty formula of the answer
to this question. "What is X?" "X is what it is." The word
'ousia' can take the place of the variable in the formula (*Meno*
72b1; *Phaedo* 78b5–d13); it is the substantive of the infinitive 'to be' in the Socratic question. The task of Socratic dialog is the clarification of this being or ousia (*Phaedo* 78d1).
Ousia is comprehended in the correct answer to the question "What is X?" We encounter the object of the "What is
X?"-question in various linguistic guises: as an abstract singular term, for example, "Temperance" (*Charmides* 159a10),
"Courage" (*Laches* 190d8); as a neuter (amplified by a re-
flexive pronoun) with the definite article, for example, "the
just" (*Republic* 332c1), "the Beautiful itself" (*Hippias Major* 286d8); as a concrete general term without an article,

for example, "Bee" (*Meno* 72b1). Despite these various formulations the "What is X?"-question always strives after one and the same goal: It searches for a definition of or at least a necessary condition for the object in question. It asks, expressed in the jargon of the philosophical tradition, about its essence. The expression "What X is" is an empty formula for a sentence that encompasses a definition of X and the essence X. The "being" of the Form is the "is" of a necessary statement. Its being is its essence (*Phaedo* 78d1). That the Form *is* means: one can make necessary statements about it that indicate what it is.

6. PARTICIPATION (METHEXIS)

75. In light of his concept of being it becomes evident why Plato can claim that the place of visible objects lies between being (ousia) and not-being (*Republic* 479c7). In the *Phaedo* Plato objects that the linguistic formulation of the sentence "Simmias is taller than Socrates" does not faithfully represent the true state of affairs. For in reality Simmias is not taller than Socrates by being Simmias "but rather by the size that he happens to have." In what do correct and incorrect understandings of the sentence consist? The linguistic formulation suggests, according to Plato, that Simmias insofar as he is Simmias is taller than Socrates, or, in other words, that being taller than Socrates follows necessarily from being Simmias. This misunderstanding is only possible because Plato assumes that 'is' ought always be understood as the 'is' of a necessary position. Such a relation does not, however, obtain for the state of affairs when Simmias is taller than Socrates. It is not necessary, but rather contingent. It does not have its cause in "being Simmias." Plato expresses this contingent relation with the words 'participates' (*Phaedo* 101c3, 102b2; *Republic* 476d2), 'partakes' (*Phaedo* 100c5; *Symposium* 211b3), and 'presence' (*Phaedo* 100d5). When a visible thing is beautiful, the reason for it

is the presence of the Beautiful, or the fact that it partakes of, or participates in, Beauty itself. Simmias is taller than Socrates due to the size which he happens to have contingently. In the literature on Plato this relation is often designated as methexis (participation) (*Parmenides* 132d3).

Thus visible things are only similar to being because their determinations can only be ascribed to them contingently. This statue *is* beautiful not in the same sense as the number three *is* odd. It is not of the essence of the statue to be beautiful. It is not beautiful per se or as such. The cause of its beauty is rather the contingent presence of Beauty itself. This piece of iron is only contingently a drill. It is a drill because the craftsperson gave it the Form *of* the drill (see *Cratylus* 389c–e). Because the determinations of visible things are ascribed to them contingently, there is change and genesis in the visible world. A piece of wood can take on the Form *of* the weaver's carriage. An object can lose a determination and take on the opposite one. What is beautiful can become ugly, and what is small can become large. In the realm of being, that is, of the Forms, change and genesis are excluded (*Phaedo* 78d). A visible object can lose being-large and take on being-small. Being-large itself is not altered by this process. What can be predicated of it is a necessary and immutable property of it. A variety of determinations can be attributed to visible objects. A beautiful statue is not just beautiful; it also has a shape, a size, a weight, a position, various colors, and so on. A Form, on the converse, is invariable (*Phaedo* 78d5). A Form cannot be the bearer of other determinations that would constitute a contingent relation with it. One can only predicate of it what it is per se. Redness (being red) is a color but is not itself colored, extended, and so on.

76. In the *Republic* (479ab) Plato supports his claim that visible objects lie between being and not-being with the following argument: "[I]s there any one of these many fair and honorable things that will not appear sometimes ugly and base? And of the just things, that will not seem unjust? [. . .]

do the many doubled things appear any the less halves than doubles? — No. — And likewise of the great and the small things, the light and the heavy things — will they admit these predicates any more than their opposites?" One should not misunderstand Plato to be denying the principle of noncontradiction and overlooking the difference between one- and two-place predicates. Plato knew very well that 'double' and 'half' are two-place predicates and that it is an abbreviated manner of speaking to say that something is both half and double. These phrases are to be completed by inserting their second term: "Six is the double of three and half of twelve." Apparently Plato was of the opinion (about which we do not wish to argue with him) that 'tall', 'short', and 'beauty' could be understood as two-place predicates. "Simmias is tall and short" (*Phaedo* 102b10) would then mean, for example: "Simmias is taller than Socrates and shorter than Phaedo." That something can be both beautiful and ugly can also be understood differently: because various contingent determinations can be attributed to a single visible object, it can appear beautiful under one aspect yet ugly under another (*Symposium* 211a2). A vase, for example, can be beautiful and ugly because it has an attractive shape but an unattractive coloring. The point of the quoted passage can only be understood with recourse to the comparison with the Form. The Form is what it is of itself. What is ascribed to it, is true of it as such (*Phaedo* 78d5; *Symposium* 211b1). When Plato, in support of his claim that visible objects lie between being and not-being, introduces two-place predicates and understands one-place predicates as two-placed predicates, he intends to point out that visible objects are not what they are of themselves. They are what they are through others: because they stand in various relations to others things or are due to a determination contingent to them. What we attribute to them depends on the point of view from which we observe them. Visible objects have their ontological place between being and not-being because they are not what they are of themselves nor as such.

7. THE *PARMENIDES'* OBJECTIONS

77. The first part of the *Parmenides* formulates three arguments against the theory of Forms. This text passage provides difficult riddles for Plato scholars. It begins with a short portrayal of the theory of Forms. Does it reproduce the position of the middle dialogs adequately? Do the objections stem from Plato himself, or were they raised against him by someone else? The young Aristotle of the Academy should be considered seriously as a candidate for this role. In his works (see Bonitz, *Index* 771a36) he repeatedly raises the second objection which he calls the "third man." Aristotle assumes that his readers are acquainted with the argument. It is apparently a standard objection then. Plato solved the *Parmenides'* objections nowhere in his public works. Did he think that they could not be solved? Did he relinquish the theory of Forms with the *Parmenides*? Or did he only wish to show how the theory was not to be understood? Here we shall only discuss the first two objections.

The short portrayal of the theory of Forms in *Parmenides* 130b upon which the objections rest emphasizes the separation (of which Plato was accused by Aristotle [Bonitz, *Index* 860a35]) of reality into the world of independent Forms and that of the things that participate in them. Both objections are directed against the concept of participation.

a) The Arguments

78. Argument (1) (131a–e): Every particular thing that participates in a Form must participate in either (a) the whole of the Form or (b) in part of the Form. There is no third possibility. Either one of these possibilities, however, compromises the unity of the Form. (a) If one Form is to be in independent and separate things as a whole, then it multiplies itself with every new thing. (b) In order to avoid this consequence Socrates suggests that one might think of the unity of the Form like the unity of the day which is present

at various places at one and the same time. In the same way
every Form could be one and the same in the multitude of
things named after it. Parmenides reifies this picture with
the comparison with a sail that covers many people. It is in
this sense that the Form is one among many. But then the
whole sail would not be over any particular person, but rather
only a part, that is, every individual would only participate
in a part of any Form. However, this sacrifices the unity of
the Form. Nonsensical consequences follow. We would have
to, for example, divide the Form of Large, and the various
individual things would be large due to something that is
smaller than Largeness.

79. Argument (2): The third man (132a–133a). This objection also shows that the concept of participation destroys
the unity of the Form. Plato develops it in two versions. (2a)
When we look at many large things, we see one and the same
determination, Largeness, in all of them. That is the reason
why we assume that Largeness is one, that is, why we assume a single Form of Largeness. When we observe Largeness
along with the various large things, the same process is repeated. We see one and the same determination that can be
attributed to both Largeness and the various large things,
for Largeness too is large. Thus we are forced to assume a
second Form of Largeness. This second Largeness is, in turn,
large like the various large things and the first Form of Largeness. Thus we must assume a third Form of Largeness and
so on ad infinitum. Therefore it follows from the concept
of participation that for every predicate expression we must
assume not one but an infinite number of Forms (132ab).
(2b) The Forms are patterns or models (paradeigmata), and
the numerous visible things are their copies. The relation
of participation is nothing more than this relation of similarity or copy-imitation. Similarity, however, is a symmetri-
cal relation. If the things are similar to the Form, then the
Form is similar to the things. However, a particular thing
and a Form can only be similar if the same attribute is true
of both of them, that is, if they both participate in the same

determination. If one conceives of the Form as an original pattern and participation as a relation of similarity, one is led into the same infinite regress as in (2a) (132d–133a).

80. What import did Plato himself attach to these arguments? They did not occasion him to abandon the theory of Forms. The dialogs *Theaetetus, Sophist,* and the *Philebus,* all of which most probably date after the *Parmenides,* attest to this. From the text of the *Parmenides* it becomes clear that Plato considered these objections to be difficult but not insoluble (133b; 135ab). If Socrates is not in a position to defend the theory of Forms against Parmenides, this is due to his youthfulness (127c). He has no idea of the difficulties which his theory brings with it (130e1; 133b1), and he is still lacking the necessary dialectical practice (135cd). But, and this is Plato's decisive reply to the objections, the young Socrates has correctly observed that the assumption of Forms is a necessary condition of any conversation (135c).

b) The Assumptions

81. Can the objections be resolved? Upon what mistakes do they rest? Arguments (1) and (2b) aim at a similar negative goal. They are directed at a misunderstanding of participation and the accompanying reification of the Form in order to illustrate how participation and the Form are *not* to be conceived. Argument (1) works with the words 'part' and 'whole'. They are ambiguous. Their application is not restricted to spatial objects. One can also speak of the parts of a concept (e.g., in the context of a definition). Argument (1), however, uses these words in the sense in which they can only be used for spatial objects and thus commits a category mistake. Participation is a relation between a spatial and an abstract object. Thus it belongs to a different category than the relation between spatial objects.

82. Argument (2b) understands participation as similarity. There are two reasons why that is not possible. *First,* the determinations due to which beings are similar to one

another must belong to the same category. (The following prescinds from similarities due to transcendental predicates that are not the topic of this discussion. Transcendental predicates "transcend" the limits of categories because they are predicated of all categories, for example, "being," "good"; see Aristotle *EN* I, 4). Two things can be similar with respect to color or shape, but we cannot compare the color of one thing with the shape of another thing. In this sense the relation of similarity is not restricted to spatial objects. It can also hold for abstract objects. Thus the color red is similar to the color orange, or the number three to the number 17 because both are prime numbers. On the contrary, the relation of participation is one between objects that do not belong to the same category but rather belong to different orders. For this reason it is improper to think of this relation as one of similarity. Whoever misunderstands it as similarity assumes that basic determinations from the same category can be applied to both the abstract and the concrete object. In this sense the relata of the relation are treated as objects from the same category. The tall Phaedo can only be similar to the Tall under the supposition that it is true that "The Tall is tall." This statement commits the mistake of self-predication (see par. 83).

Second, similarity admits of degrees whereas the relation of predication does not. *a* can be more similar to *b* than *c* to *b*. The various copies can be similar to the original pattern in various degrees. However, the "is" expressed by the copula does not admit of any degrees. Granted that a universal concept has no fuzzy boundaries, it is then true that either an object falls under it or it does not. Socrates either participates in being-human or Courage or he does not. As a counterexample, the sentence may be brought forth: "Socrates is more courageous than Meno." Does this not display sufficiently that participation admits of degrees? It obviously shows that Socrates partakes of courage in a higher degree than Meno. We can also form sentences with one-place predicates that illustrate the same point, for example,

"Socrates is extraordinarily courageous." The answer to this objection reads: We can speak of degrees of courage but not of degrees of participation in Courage. "Being extraordinarily courageous" and "being only a little courageous" are different predicates. Between them there is similarity. But either Socrates is extraordinarily courageous or he is not. Thus, participation does not admit of degrees. On the contrary, the original pattern/copy model that works with the relation of similarity understands 'Courage' as a univocal singular term for an abstract entity in which the concrete individuals participate in varying degrees.

Is Plato criticizing in argument (2b) a conception of participation that he maintained prior to the *Parmenides?* That will remain open here but is not to be excluded because Plato does repeatedly call the Form a paradigm (paradeigma) and likes to utilize picture metaphors. The discussion of argument (2b) revealed that this understanding is incompatible with the Form as a predicate.

c) Self-Predication and Pauline Predication

83. The regress in argument (2a) results from a mistake that Vlastos has designated with the expression "self-predication" in the literature on Plato (1954). Self-predication consists in a determination whose abstraction just is the Form being ascribed to that very Form. From a predicate expression we form the singular term of a Form of which we then predicate this predicate expression. Examples are "Beauty itself is beautiful" and "Largeness (the Large itself) is large." Through self-predication Largeness becomes a member of the class of large things since the predicate "is large" can be said of both. According to Plato's theory every predication depends upon participation in a Form. But self-predication leads to an infinite regress, for Largeness can only be large by participating in another Largeness. "Largeness is large" thus means: Largeness$_1$ participates in Largeness$_2$. If one omits self-predication, the regress does not arise.

84. Was the third man a real difficulty for Plato or did he know of a solution? The answer depends on whether Plato committed the mistake of self-predication or rather, after committing it, he recognized it in the *Parmenides*. There are passages in Plato that would appear to be self-predications (e.g., *Prot.* 330c; *Phaedo* 74c; *Symposium* 211a; *Parmenides* 129b; *Sophist* 252d). The question is, however, whether they can be interpreted in a different way. Vlastos suggested interpreting them as Pauline predications. He claims that an expression of the form "F-ness (The F itself) is G" is ambiguous. It could be a typical predication. Then the expression means: The F-ness is itself a member of the set of things that are G. But it could also be a Pauline predication (named by Vlastos after I *Cor.* 13:4). In this case the expression: "If something is a member of the set of things that are F, then it is necessarily also a member of the set of things that are G." Thus a Pauline predication says that one class necessarily includes another class. The sentence "Largeness is large" would then mean, if taken as a Pauline predication: "All large things are necessarily large." Thus the regress will not arise. Another possible way of avoiding the regress is to understand the sentence as an identity statement. Largeness is identical with itself. According to this interpretation it means: whereas perceivable objects participate in Largeness and are large due to it, Largeness participates in itself. But this participation relation is to be understood differently than that of concrete objects. It is not participation of predication but that of identity.

III. Knowledge

85. How can a Form be known? Until now (par. 69) there were two hints whose connection was not evident. Plato often uses the metaphor of sight and describes knowledge as a mental viewing. On the other hand he emphasizes the importance of discourse that alone can answer a "What is X?" question. The *Republic*'s simile of the divided line (509d–511e) provides a succinct overview of the various epistemic modes and their interconnections.

1. THE DISTINCTIONS IN THE SIMILE
OF THE DIVIDED LINE

86. We are to draw a line and divide it into two unequal parts and then divide each of these parts once more according to the same proportion as the initial line. From these directions we have the following proportions: AC:CB = AD:DC = CE:EB. With an intermediary step it follows that DC = CE. The sections of the line symbolize epistemic modes and the objects of knowledge that correspond to them. The increasing size of each section of the line represents the increasing degree of clarity. The division by point C distinguishes the epistemic modes of opinion and knowledge. The object of belief is the visible world which is at the same time the world of genesis and change. The lower section is divided again into the epistemic modes of assuming (AD) and

belief (DC). More easily comprehended than this distinction is the one on the side of the objects of knowledge. Assumption refers to a special kind of pictures: shadows and reflections that arise off the surface of smooth reflecting bodies. The objects that cause these pictures correspond to belief: animals, plants, artifacts. The higher section CB is divided into mathematical knowledge (knowledge of the understanding) (CE) and knowledge of the Forms (knowledge of reason) (EB).

2. THE PICTURE AS THE BASIC CATEGORY OF PLATONISM

87. Section AC has a twofold function: 1. It symbolizes two epistemic modes and two realms of objects. 2. It symbolizes the relation between the realm of objects of knowledge and that of opinion, that is, the relation between the world of being and the world of becoming. The correspondence CB:AC = DC:AD thus intends to say: the world of becoming is a copy of the world of being just as shadows and reflections are copies of the visible world. Plato sees a correspondence between the realms AD (copies) and CE (the mathematical). Just as the realm AD is merely a copy of the realm DC (visible objects), the realm of CE is a mere copy of the realm EB (the Forms). For this reason we can initially put these realms on hold in our present considerations. When we speak of the world of becoming being a copy of the world of being in the following, we intend this to refer to the relation DC:EB. Before we inquire about the conceptual statement of the individual sections, we shall first want to consider that the relation of the Forms to the world of visible objects corresponds to the object-copy relation in the visible world.

88. The comparison leads us to a central category of Plato's philosophy and Platonism: the concept of the picture, or the relation of a pattern to its copy. This relation can be

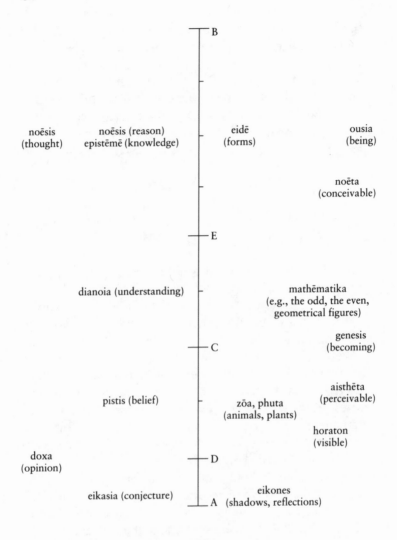

found in our visible world. We use it as a device to help to explain the relations that exist between the intelligible and the visible world. That we can do this is a fundamental hypothesis for Plato (see par. 95). Criteria with which the question as to its truth can be decided are its explanatory power and simplicity. This hypothesis is of great importance for

Plato's philosophical language. Because different kinds of pattern-copy relations can be found in reality, the language of philosophy is not limited to that of dialectic (par. 93–102). The use of pictures is a legitimate philosophical language game. Plato's dialogs are permeated with pictures, beginning with simple metaphors through similes on to various kinds of myths. The use of pictures in philosophical language is justified by an assumption about the structure of reality, but the pictures must prove themselves with their explanatory power. Their use is especially indispensable when conceptual language reaches its upper and lower borders. Beyond its upper border lies the Form of the Good, beyond its lower border the realm of variable reality. Plato understands his whole philosophy of nature that he presents in the *Timaeus* as a myth: "As being is to becoming, so is truth to belief. If then, Socrates, amidst the many opinions about the gods and the generation of the universe, we are not able to give notions which are altogether and in every respect exact and consistent with one another, do not be surprised. Enough if we adduce probabilities as likely as any others, for we must remember that I who am the speaker and you who are the judges are only mortal men, and we ought to accept the tale (mythos) which is probable and inquire no further" (*Timaeus* 29cd). The Greek word for 'probable' (eikōs) that occurs twice in this passage stems from the same root as eikōn: 'picture'.

89. Plato determines more precisely the concept of picture in AD. The subject at hand is shadows and reflections in water and on the surfaces of smooth bodies. Thus an ontological statement has been made initially. Copy and original stand in a relation of causal dependency. The shadow of a stick only exists as long as the stick that is responsible for it is present. Both have a different ontological status. The real thing is independent of the shadow, whereas the shadow is not independent of the real thing. The being of the shadow consists exclusively in its appearance or its form. The real object acts as a cause exclusively through its form. It brings

forth another being by communicating its form and only its form. A shadow only *is* by participating in the form of the real object. The relation thing-shadow can illustrate the relation *universal-particular*. The numerically single thing can be represented in numerically different copies. In this manner the various copies can depict the same original in different aspects. A picture can limit itself to showing a single aspect of the real thing. In the same sense one Form can show itself in a variety of things with the most varying reflections. The relation Form-thing is not to be understood as a relation of abstraction, so that the Form, as the universal, would be less rich in content compared with the individual. The Form is the abundance of content that is always only visible from one perspective for a particular thing.

From the ontological relation an *epistemological* relation follows. A building's shadow enables the calculation of its height. Without mirrors we would not know what our faces look like. The simile of the line emphasizes the varying degree of distinctness and truth in the various sections of the line. Every picture is only a makeshift for knowledge of what is pictured because in its being, that is, in the abundance of appearances in which it reveals itself, it falls short of the original pattern. Thus, pictures can, according to the medium in which they depict the original, display various degrees of clarity and thus various degrees of being as pictures. Whoever wants to recognize a picture must know what the picture depicts, and that is possible in a full sense only via knowledge of the original pattern. The metaphor of the picture thus alludes to ascending and descending movements of knowledge: from the picture to the pictured original and from the pictured original to the picture. The problematic of *appearance* is contained in the concept of the picture. It is the essence of a picture to represent something and to refer to something that it is not. The picture is a way in which another thing can appear. However, as an appearance it can also become a mere appearance, an apparition. This is the case when it is not recognized as a picture but is taken for the thing itself. The distinction between conjecture (AD) and belief (DC) is important for Plato's philosophy of art, his relation to myth, and his political philosophy. Plato is, on the one hand, a radical critic of poets and myths, but, on the other hand, he constantly works with pictures. The core of his criticism of myths and art is that they mislead people when their derivative character is not recognized. Politics uses appearances by deceiving the citizens with rhetoric. It is a mere appearance with respect to seeing the true interests that are hidden behind the camouflage.

3. OPINION

90. AC's epistemic mode is that of opinion. It is to be distinguished from knowledge and perception. It is different from perception in its predicative structure. In opinion something is perceived as something. For perception a predicate is attributed to a perceptual content. By placing opinion as the lowest epistemic mode Plato is denying that there are mere perceptions. He is claiming that all perceptions always have a predicative structure. The predicative structure of opinion joins the two halves of the divided line. Every opinion, whether true or false, implicitly assumes a knowledge of the meaning of the predicate, and Plato places this knowledge on the upper half of the line (CB).

91. On the distinction of opinion and knowledge: For Plato four conditions are necessary and, if taken together, sufficient for the truth of the sentence 'a knows that p': 1. a must assume that p is true; 2. p must be true; 3. a must be in a position to justify p; 4. p must be a necessary proposition; contingent states of affairs cannot be objects of knowledge. In the *Theaetetus* 201cd Plato provides the following definition: "Knowledge is true opinion with an account/justification." A true opinion is present when the first and second conditions obtain: a assumes that p is true, and p is true, but p is not in a position to justify p. The first through third

conditions are still true for the modern conception of knowledge, but not the fourth. The simile of the line illustrates clearly that knowledge can only be of immutable mathematical objects and Forms. There is only opinion of the perceivable world, which is subject to change and whose states of affairs are contingent. On the contrary, our concept of knowledge allows us to say of a contingent proposition that we know it, for example, that Caesar was murdered in March 44 B.C. The difference between the modern and the Platonic concept of knowledge lies in the concept of justification, which thus proves to be central for the concept of knowledge. Today we have no difficulty in admitting that there are methods, for example, in the historical sciences, that can justify contingent propositions. For Plato and Aristotle, however, the concept of justification is restricted to the realm of universal and necessary propositions.

4. MATHEMATICAL KNOWLEDGE

92. Plato designates the main cut in the line marked C as the "conversion from the world of generation to essence and truth" (*Republic* 525c). A change of perspective occurs at this point. How can it best be described? We must orient ourselves in our interpretation of Platonic epistemology toward the predicative sentence. We saw that opinion reveals a predicative structure. This structure can be viewed from different directions (see Wieland, 1982, p. 210): first in the direction from the predicate to the perceivable object. The predicate serves to know the object. This direction is characteristic for opinion. Our perception is always already determined by predicates. However, it is the perceivable objects that we know. Second, in the direction from the perceivable object to the predicate. The goal of knowledge is the predicate. The perceivable object serves to know the predicate. The change in perspective occurs in the mathematical sciences (arithmetic, geometry, astronomy and harmonics).

They have the task of turning the soul's eye from becoming to being. The cut C can be illustrated as follows for the example of geometry: Plato distinguishes between the circular object, the drawn circle, the imagined circle, all of which are to be assigned to the realm AC, and the circle about which the mathematician speaks. The mathematician does not converse about a visible construct to which we attribute "is a circle." Rather she speaks, as we would say in Platonic terminology, about the Circle itself, the ideal circle, the entity that is the meaning of the predicate expression "is a circle." She thus establishes a change in direction because she does not talk anymore about what is designated by the subject expression in the predicate expression "this is a circle" but rather about what is designated by the predicate expression. In contrast to the dialectician the conversion of directions for the mathematician is incomplete for two reasons. They characterize the section CE.

a) Reflection about the predicate remains tied down to intuition. The mathematician must use the objects of the section DC as pictures. The geometer issues statements about the ideal, not the drawn circle, but he can only discover the laws of the ideal circle with the help of the drawn circle. Geometry, for Plato, is not an exclusively axiomatic science that is solely concerned with consequences from specified axioms. Geometry's concepts and propositions can only be discovered with the help of intuition, and the definitions, axioms, and consequences must be able to be represented in intuition.

b) The mathematical sciences start with hypotheses. Their failure lies in the fact that they do not recognize their hypotheses as hypotheses. The mathematician thinks of her hypotheses as highest principles that neither require nor are capable of any further justification. What are these hypotheses? Plato mentions as examples the even and the odd, figures, and the three kinds of angles. In connection with Aristotle (see *Met.* VI, 1) the following interpretation is suggested: the mathematician presuposes propositions that tell what a

circle, an odd number, and so on is, that is, she presupposes
definitions. Second, she presupposes that the objects about
which she converses, for example, the circle, the obtuse angle,
and so on, exist. The hypothetical character of these propositions consists in the fact that they are not questioned further, do not lead back to an ultimate principle, and are not
then in turn justified in a descending process by such an ultimate principle. Plato considers such a final justification in
principle possible. The mathematician's definitions presuppose basic concepts that the mathematician can neither clarify nor relate to the basic concepts of other sciences, for example, that of number and of space. The mathematician
can explain just as little the concept of existence that is presupposed. In what sense do numbers or figures exist? How
is the existence of numbers related to the existence of perceivable objects? Because mathematicians are not in a position to clarify the concept of existence, they also cannot
prove that there are numbers. They must presuppose the existence of numbers.

5. DIALECTIC

93. The epistemic mode of the uppermost section of the
line (EB) to which the Forms are assigned bears the name
of dialectic. Like mathematics its goal is knowledge of the
predicate. Dialectic is initially the art of carrying on appropriate discourse, "asking and taking questions" (*Republic*
531e). The object of this discussion is the "What is X?"-
question (*Republic* 532a). Dialectic overcomes the limits of
mathematical knowledge. It is not tied down to intuition and
does not proceed from presuppositions that are unques-
tioned, but rather ascends to a presuppositionless beginning
or principle (archē) (*Republic* 511b). The simile of the line
and its explanation only provide short allusions to dialectic. These allusions can only be understood wilth the help
of other dialogs. However, Plato approaches the problem of

dialectic from a different perspective in the various dialogs. These perspectives complement each other. One can speak of an historical development in the sense of depth being accrued.

a) The Elenchus of the Early Dialogs

94. The early dialogs proceed from a suggested definition that Socrates' partner in discourse has given in answer to the "What is X?"-question, for example, "What is piety?" or "What is courage?" Socrates checks whether this suggestion is consistent with other statements and assumptions held by that person. The result is always negative; the early dialogs end in difficulties. Plato designates this procedure elenchus. Elenchus in a broad sense is the examination and analysis of a definition or statement with the help of the indicated procedure. In a narrower sense the word signifies examination with a negative result, refutation. The refutation does not necessarily depend on an objective difficulty. Initially it displays the discussion partner's inability to argue consistently. The difficulty, according to Plato's interpretation in the *Meno* (84ad) and *Sophist* (229e–230e), has the task of destroying alleged knowledge. It is a necessary presupposition of true knowledge. Only one who is convinced of not having a satisfactory answer can search for the correct answer. The desire to know how a state of affairs stands is only awakened when elenchus destroys the alleged knowledge. The *Sophist* (230a–e) observes in elenchus a process of catharsis of the soul. Whoever desires to learn must first eliminate the opinions that stand in the way of the acquisition of true knowledge. This occurs when elenchus reveals any contradiction among opinions. The experience of the difficulty serves to cleanse the character. It is to shock the confident dogmatist. Whoever sees that his own conceptions contradict each other becomes (in the ideal case which does not always correspond to the practice of the early dialogs) critical of himself and more tolerant toward others.

Elenchus should not be understood as an exclusively nega-

tive procedure with no results. The mere fact that two statements contradict each other does not provide any information
as to which of the two is true. The refutation of a definition
is only possible when there is unearthed a contradiction between the definition and component statements of the discussion all claiming to be true. The interpretation of an
early Platonic dialog must make explicit the assumptions
on which the refutation of the various suggested definitions
depends and are not themselves refuted in the course of
the discussion. They may be seen as the first hint toward
a solution.

b) *The Hypothetical Procedure of the* Phaedo

95. The positive function of the art of discussion only
alluded to in the early dialogs becomes clearer in both of
the methods of dialectic that the *Phaedo* describes. According to the first procedure (100a) we proceed from the proposition which we think the strongest (most likely to be true).
We use it as an assumption for every further argument. We
take to be true what follows from it and false what contradicts either it or what follows from it. In the second procedure (101de), too, we start with the strongest proposition.
In contrast to the first procedure Plato mentions here a
method of how we can examine and eventually justify this
proposition. We can take the proposition as an hypothesis
and ask what consequences follow from it. If these consequences contradict either each other or the initial hypothesis, we must give up the hypothesis. If such a contradiction
does not arise, we look for a higher hypothesis from which
the first hypothesis can be derived. This higher hypothesis
is in turn examined to ascertain whether its consequences
are free of contradiction. This procedure is repeated until
we reach a "sufficient" hypothesis, that is, one for which
none of the discussion partners desire a higher hypothesis
for justification. In the *Phaedo* this "sufficient" hypothesis
is that there are Forms. Whoever would want a dispute them

would be questioning the possibility of discourse itself (see
Phaedo 73a). The *Phaedo*'s dialectic does not lead beyond
hypothetical knowledge. An absolute certainty about ultimate
states of affairs is not possible for human beings. What humans can achieve is an hypothesis that is stronger than all
other hypotheses. Humans can and must live with this hypothetical knowledge even about matters that concern them
deeply like the mortality or immortality of the soul.

c) Collection and Division in the Phaedrus

96. The *Republic*'s dialectic is distinguished from that of
the *Phaedo* in two essential points: whereas in the *Phaedo*
the concern is the examination of propositions, the procedure in the *Republic* has knowledge of the meaning of predicate terms as its goal, and in contrast to the *Phaedo*'s hypothetical knowledge the *Republic*'s dialectic leads to the
abrogation of all hypotheses in a presuppositionless, absolute principle (*Republic* 510b), the Form of the Good. The
most important information about method in the *Republic*
is that dialectic presupposes the capacity for gathering and
unifying (*Republic* 537c). This information connects the
Republic's considerations with those of the early dialogs and
the *Symposium* (210a–211c), the *Phaedrus* (249bc; 265d–
266a), and the *Sophist* (253de). The early dialogs recognize
the inference from various examples to one universal proposition. In connection with Aristotle this inference is called
induction (epagōgē). Socrates argues in this manner in, for
example, the *Protagoras:* "Again, said I, do you recognize
the existence of the fair?—He did.—Has it any contrary except the foul?—No.—And the good too you recognize?—
Yes.—Has it any contrary except the bad?—No.—And also
high pitch in sound? And has it any other contrary but low?—
No.—In short, said I, to everything that admits of a contrary there is one contrary and no more.—He conceded the
point" (332c; see *Euthyphro* 10a–c; Robinson, 1953, pp. 33–
48). According to the *Phaedrus* we form a predicate by col-

lecting a plethora of sensual perceptions under the unity of
a universal concept. This collection is not to be understood
as an empirical generalization, however. It is only possible
due to a priori knowledge. For this reason Plato designates
it as recollection (anamnēsis). Knowledge of the universal
is latent a priori knowledge. It is actualized by perceptions,
but it is not abstracted from them. The particular perceptions and the universal concept belong to different orders
of knowledge. Collection is continued on the level of predicates. There it recognizes the universal predicate that sub-
sumes several specific predicates under it.

97. Corresponding to the procedure of collection on the
level of predicates (synagōgē) there is in the *Phaedrus* that
of division (diairesis) through which universal predicates are
ordered into more specific ones. The division is not simply
the reversal of collection, so that we return from the universal to the more specific predicates with which the collection
began. The specific predicates from which the collecting, ascending movement proceeds must be subsumed under a
higher concept. However, they need not stand in any systematic relation to each other. They can overlap, and there
can be vague concepts. The task of the dividing, descending
movement of dialectic is to divide the higher concept such
that the specific concepts are precisely determined and are
ordered in a system. The division may not be undertaken
arbitrarily. The dialectician must, like a good cook skilled
in the art of carving, find the joints and divide the concept
at these joints. He may not break up the proportions of the
members (*Phaedrus* 265e). Plato uses the process of division (dichotomy) for the analysis of concepts. The *Sophist*
attempts to gain practice in this art by inquiring into the
definition of the angler (218e). It divides activities into those
that require and those that do not require an art for their
exercise. Art is then divided into the acquisitive and the productive arts, and the acquisitive further into one that acquires
its object via exchange and a second that acquires it on its
own. This latter category is divided into hunting, battle, and

so on. The dichotomy is repeated until one reaches a concept that cannot be divided anymore (*Phaedrus* 277b; *Sophist* 229d).

98. Like the *Phaedrus'* dialectic the *Republic* also dictates an ascending and a descending movement. It too emphasizes the preliminary, "hypothetical" character of the concepts that were not developed in the descending movement from the uppermost concept (511b). Nonetheless, the *Republic's* procedure cannot be equated with that of the *Phaedrus*. The dialectic collection in the *Republic* cannot be understood such that we step up from specific predicates to ones that are always more universal. That results from the predicate whose knowledge is the goal of the ascent. "Good" is not, in contrast to, for example, "animal," a generic concept under which other, more specific concepts are subsumed. It shares this property with Beauty, which is the goal of the ascending dialectic in the *Symposium*. It is also common to the Good and Beauty that both are the ultimate reference point for all human activities. The *Symposium* sees a close connection between the Good and Beauty (204e–206a). Thus we shall take a look at collection in the *Symposium* in order to work out its difference from the *Republic*.

d) The Symposium's Ascent

99. In the *Symposium* (209e–212a) dialectic is described as intuitive knowledge. Plato utilizes the metaphor of sight. The starting point is the erotic-aesthetic experience when viewing a beautiful body. It is cleansed by a collection in the horizontal and vertical dimensions. The lover's perspective initially spreads out horizontally from the one beautiful body to all beautiful bodies. It discovers that the beauty of the one is related to that of all of the other bodies. This horizontal collection leads from the particular beautiful body to bodily beauty as such. A first vertical step leads from the corporeal to the spiritual level. Love is now directed at a human being because she is spiritually beautiful, that is, mor-

ally good or virtuous. (The Greek word 'kalos' means "beautiful" and "morally good.") The horizontal collection follows the ascent. The lover discovers the beauty of the moral as such in modes of behavior and laws. Plato emphasizes that it is a Form of beauty higher than that of the body. The next step is the ascent to the beauty of the sciences. Here, too, an horizontal collection follows.

The horizontal collection on the various levels leads to knowledge of the particular Form in common. This common Form is, however, a specific Form that is characterized by an essential relation to its realm of objects: the Form of *corporeal* beauty, or beauty *of* bodies, and so on. In the last step of the dialectic ascent the Form of beauty is released from these relations. The correctly led student apprehends the pure, relationless, independent Form of beauty, existing for itself. The prior steps can be practiced. The last step is withdrawn from human beings' control. It has the character of a gift. The absolute Form of beauty lights up "suddenly" (see *Ep.* VII 341cd).

The horizontal and vertical collections are not to be understood in the sense of abstraction such that the Form becomes increasingly poorer in content as the dialectic ascent proceeds. Although the absolute Form does not contain any explicit relations to the various specifications and concretizations, the latter are necessary, indispensable steps of the dialectic ascent. Only through them can humans know the abundance of the absolute Form. In this Form the content of the steps is abrogated like the various colors in unbroken light. The steps of beauty only obtain their quality through participation in absolute beauty that is reflected in them and is developed by them.

e) The Presuppositionless Beginning of the Republic

100. The *Symposium*'s dialectic ascent occurs within the realm of *one* Form. The starting point is sensual, perceivable beauty and the goal absolute Beauty. In contrast the

Republic's dialectic has as its object the entirety of Forms. The Form of the Good is the principle of all Forms. Plato presents this relation with the analogy of the sun (*Republic* 507b–509b). The sun actuates the sense of sight and colors with its light such that the sense of sight can see and the colors can be perceived. The sun is also the cause of the genesis and growth of visible substances. The Form of the Good fulfills the same functions in the intelligible world. It is the cause of knowledge and truth as well as the being and essence of the Forms. The Form of the Good belongs to another order higher than the other Forms. It is the cause of the essence of other Forms; yet it is itself not an essence but rather lies "beyond essence."

101. An interpretation of the analogy of the sun must assume that it is in a *practical* context within which the *Republic* searches for the Form of the Good. Knowledge of the Good is the goal of the ruler's education in an ideal state. The Good is the ultimate, albeit the most unclearly realized, goal of human actions. "The good which every soul pursues and for its sake does all that it does, with an intuition of its reality, but yet baffled and unable to apprehend its nature adequately, or to attain any stable belief about it as about other things" (*Republic* 505e). While many humans are content with appearances in other things, even in the ethical realm, with respect to the Good no one is satisfied with a mere appearance. Rather everyone seeks the truly Good (*Republic* 505d). The relation of the other Forms to the Form of the Good is to be interpreted in light of this practical context. In the tenth book of the *Republic* (601c–602a) Plato distinguishes three levels of reality: the picture, the thing, and the Form. Three kinds of art correspond to them: the mimetic (painter), the maker's (cobbler), and the user's (rider). Knowledge is assigned to the user's art, and opinion to the maker's. The passage understands the relation between the essence or Form of a thing and the Form of the Good as follows: one knows what a saddle is when one can work with a saddle, that is, when one knows for what a saddle is good.

The essence of a thing is its capacity for fulfilling its function, that is, realizing a good. Its essence consists in the relation to a good. The goods which the particular things, for example, a saddle, serve are in turn only relative goods. One can use them well or badly, and one can ask again for what they are good. The Form of the Good is the vanishing point of this hierarchy of goods. It makes the goods desirable in the first place without itself being one of these goods. Knowledge of the Form of the Good is the insight into an ultimate meaning, always already obscurely presupposed, upon which the affirmation of life and the entirely of reality depend and whose content cannot be further determined.

102. Plato emphasizes that knowledge of the moral is worthless as long as one does not recognize that it is good to live justly (*Republic* 506a). The Form of the Good is the principle of the Forms of the virtues in the sense that a virtue is only known when we have understood that it is good to live according to it. Only this knowledge can motivate one to corresponding behavior; it alone is *practical* knowledge. Knowledge of what just behavior is and the capacity to apply this knowledge in various situations is not yet knowledge of justice as long as we do not know that it is better to act justly than unjustly. Yet the value of moral behavior is not exhausted in the utility that is brought forth by it. Plato is of the opinion that justice deserves to be chosen for its own sake (*Republic* 358a). That it is good in itself to act justly is a synthetic statement. The quality of goodness must be supplemented to a descriptively conceivable mode of behavior. In this sense the Good for Plato is beyond essence. The description of what just behavior consists in is not an answer to the question why this behavior is good in itself.

IV. The Soul

103. If one is searching for a word that Plato uses to summarize his statements about human beings, there is none more fitting than the adjective "in between" (metaxu) with which the *Symposium* (202de) expresses the essence of Eros. Human beings live in an intermediary realm that is an area of tension between opposites: between animal and god; between death and immortality; between the visible, changing cosmos and the intelligible world of immutable being; between freedom and necessity; between isolation that drives them into egoism and the good fortune of a just society. Whereas we speak of human beings, Plato uses the word 'soul' (psychē). The soul is the Inbetween in which the opposites meet each other, and it has the capacity to choose between them and thus to determine itself. It is everything that human beings experience. Corresponding to their themes, each dialog concerning the soul does so under a specific respect.

1. THE *REPUBLIC*'S TEACHING
OF THE SOUL'S THREE FACULTIES

104. Plato's *Republic* discusses the age-old problem whether it is worthwhile to live justly. Is justice, as the sophist's thesis claims, only a convention to which we necessarily adapt ourselves in order to avoid greater evils, although it does violence to our true nature and stands in the way of

happiness, or is it a value in itself? Central to Plato's solution is the concept of unity. Happiness is the unity of human beings in the community of a state and the unity of each person with himself. Both influence each other. Only one who is at one with oneself is capable of living in a society with others, and only an ordered society can educate and raise one to be at one with oneself. This unity is not already present; it is to be achieved, and only justice has the capacity to accomplish this. For the relations among human beings it is obvious: human beings have varying talents and interests that they must coordinate for the common good. But is the individual human being also originally a plurality? Plato answers with the display of the soul's three faculties (435e–441c). He proceeds from the description of various mental phenomena. Human beings are, first of all, beings that are oriented toward acquiring knowledge. They ask about truth. They are, second, aggressive beings; this enables them to overcome difficulties and assert oneself against others. Third, they have the vital needs of nutrition and sexuality. From these three phenomena Plato infers a threefold division of the human soul.

His argument can be summarized in four steps. 1. The principle of noncontradiction: one thing cannot simultaneously do or suffer opposites under the same aspect and with respect to the same object. 2. Every mental activity is specific to a realm of objects peculiar to it through which it is defined. Thus, for example, thirst is desire for drink. Thirst as thirst is necessarily related to drink due to a definition-like connection. Thus, when a thirsty person does not want to drink in order to attain another good, for example, health, then it is not due to the thirst. 3. Human beings can do or suffer opposites with respect to the same object. The thirsty person, for example, who does not want to drink both wants a drink and does not want a drink. 4. We can only avoid a violation of the principle of noncontradiction by assuming that whatever (faculty) wants to drink is distinct from whatever (faculty) does not want to drink, that is, that two different faculties of the soul are involved. Plato calls them appetite (epithumia) and reason (logistikon). With the same method Plato works out the difference between the capacities for aggression and emotion with respect to appetite and reason. The contradiction between emotion and appetite is exposed when we desire something which we know to be wrong. We give in and are angry with ourselves. The difference between emotion and reason becomes evident in the fact that reason turns against emotion, can appeal to it on behalf of its better insight and attempt to appease it.

105. All three of the soul's faculties are related to goods. Appetite is concerned with nutrition and reproduction, hence with biological preservation. Emotion pursues the social goods of power, superiority, and recognition (581a). Appetite is reasonless desire or drive. Emotion participates in reason to the extent that it is triggered by a judgment. It is not, however, a judgment of reason. It is not knowledge but rather merely opinion that is expressed. Plato presents the relation of reason to both of the lower faculties of the soul with the political metaphor of rule. It results from the composition principle of the *Republic:* the state is a human being on a macro scale, and the human being is the state on a micro scale. The relations between the faculties of the soul correspond to those between the classes of the state. Rule in the ideal state is just when it is exercised in the interest of all and meets upon the consent of all. The same is true for the relation of the soul's faculties. Reason must rely upon the other two faculties; its dictates only become effective if they are followed by these faculties. It is in the interest of both emotion and appetite that they are steered by reason because otherwise they would be in danger of missing the goods toward which they are directed. Reason alone can *know* the good: it can deliberate, consider, and foresee. It takes up a higher standpoint which does justice to the interests of all faculties. The goal of its rule is the complete harmony of all human drives.

2. EROS

106. The threefold division of the soul in the fourth book of the *Republic* is, however, only a preliminary view for Plato. This is evident from the tenth book. Because the soul is immortal, as he argues there, it cannot be composed. The plurality connected with the threefold division of the soul must result rather from its connection with a body. The true essence of the soul is its transcendent relation. "And we must note the things of which it has apprehensions, and the associations for which it yearns, as being itself akin to the divine and the immortal and to eternal being" (611e). In the *Symposium* it becomes clear that the faculties of the fourth book of the *Republic* are only various manifestations of *one* mental power, of Eros. Eros is moved by a transcendent reality that shows up in an abundance of reflections that can be comprehended by erotic-aesthetic experience in the sensual realm and by conceptual thought in the intelligible realm. Transcendent reality itself can only be characterized by negations. Temporality, mutability, relativity, and inherence are all negated. It is the absolute Form of Beauty, dissolved of all concretizations, existing in itself, and the reference point of an experience that encompasses all perfections of every conceivable erotic-aesthetic experience and any intellectual activity. The absolute moves one's basic drive by being capable of being experienced in a variety of pictures: as corporeal beauty, in the beauty of a work of art, in every form of proportion, order, or harmony, whether it be that it reveals itself in a human community (the ethical is also an aesthetic phenomenon), in the cosmos, or in the laws of arithmetic and geometry. One's basic drive is differentiated such that it is directed at each of these reflections. Directed toward corporeal beauty it is experienced as erotic, toward the beauty of mathematics or the cosmos as the love of science, and so on.

107. The essence of Eros is presented with a fairy tale that characterizes it as a philosopher. Plato bestows upon

it Socrates' traits of one who knows that he knows nothing and is thus searching for wisdom. The erotic and intellectual search of philosophy are two interwoven developments of one basic power. The erotic experience is the initiative of dialectic through which alone it can find its perfection. Both are fulfilled in the grasp of the absolute in which the difference between knowledge and love is abrogated. That intellectual ascent has its origin in an erotic aesthetic experience is necessary due to the special nature of beauty. As a Form it belongs to the intelligible realm. But it is simultaneously the only Form that is also grasped by sensual knowledge because it appears in every visual beauty (*Phaedrus* 250cd). The Form of Beauty abrogates the division between the visible and the intelligible. Through it the elementary and the highest realm of reality are combined into a unity.

108. Appetite and emotion from the *Republic*'s threefold division are interpreted as striving for the divine in the *Symposium*. The basic drive of Eros is concretized as the drive for reproduction. Its goal is participation in the immortality of the divine. Mortal living beings realize immortality as it is possible for them: as an eternal subsistence in species. In the same way the emotive drive for recognition and validity is a mode of striving for the absolute, since honor and memory represent a higher mode of immortality than bodily offspring. Knowledge of the goods toward which the soul's faculties are directed, as pictures of the divine, is also motivation to act. Whoever knows the relation between the acts of life and the absolute also knows that an ultimate meaning lies in them and that they are worth being lived with complete intensity. In intensive, conscious experience of the various realms of human existence the absolute can be found.

3. IMMORTALITY

109. The fate of the soul after death counts as one of the central themes of Plato's philosophy and Platonism. The

Meno (81a–86b), the *Republic* (608c–611a), the *Phaedrus* (245c–246a), and especially the *Phaedo* consider the immortality of the human soul. These considerations are often considered to be proofs of the soul's immortality. This can lead to misunderstanding Plato as conceiving them to be conclusive arguments in the sense of a rationalistic metaphysics. The phenomenal basis, the intent of the statement, and the limits of these "proofs" only become clear from the context of the particular setting of each dialog. The *Phaedo*'s outer conversation shows that a lived attitude, Socrates' confidence with respect to his impending death, is the starting point of the discussion about immortality. This attitude relies upon Socrates' theological understanding of existence. He is convinced that his life is sheltered in the protection of the gods and that he can expect community with the gods after his death (60c–64a). Connected with this religious belief is the moral conviction or experience of conscience that death does not liberate human beings from the responsibility for their lives (107c). This conviction is especially developed in the *Republic* (608c–611a). The *Phaedo* conversation is Socrates' attempt to justify his attitude toward death. He is not successful in convincing all involved in the conversation. He himself points out that the "proofs" of immortality depend on assumptions that require further examination (107ab). The dialog emphasizes the practical consequences that result from the hypothesis of immortality: the only important goal is to be concerned with a moral existence (107c). The *Phaedo* closes, as do the *Gorgias* and the *Republic,* with a myth about the fate of the soul in the afterlife. It is the expression and illustration of consciousness of moral responsibility that reach past death. Belief in this myth is, like that in immortality, ultimately a risk. However, Plato emphasizes that it is a beautiful risk and that human beings need it in order to captivate themselves. It strengthens them in the conviction that whoever strives for a moral existence can look confidently toward death.

110. The four "proofs of immortality" from the *Phaedo*

are to be read against this background. The *first* proof (69e–72e) relies upon the doctrine from natural philosophy that everything proceeds from its opposite: the dead from the living and the living from the dead. As the human being survives the changes of sleep and wakefulness, so does the soul life and death. This view of the soul taken from the philosophy of nature is overcome in the *second* thought process (72e–77d). As in the *Meno*, Plato infers from the fact of a priori knowledge (which he explains by recollection of a prenatal grasp) to the preexistence and immortality of the soul. The *third* argument (78b–84b) proceeds from the dichotomy of being into simples which cannot be dissolved and composites, and shows that the soul along with the Forms belongs to the simples. An essential assumption of the *fourth* proof (102a–107b) is that there are relations between Forms. There are Forms that necessarily exclude each other and Forms that necessarily include each other. Life is necessarily attributed to the soul; the soul is the bearer of life. Death is opposed to life; they both exclude each other. The soul, essentially bound up with life, cannot take on death.

111. Except for the first, all proofs rely upon the hypothesis that there are Forms. It is the common undisputed foundation of the discussants; especially the third argument maintains an expressly dualistic view of man and knowledge. The body belongs to the realm of plurality, mutability, and the perishable, whereas the soul is related to the One, the immutable, and the imperishable. Sensual and rational knowledge are clearly separated from each other, and sensual knowledge is devalued as is the body. Intellectual knowledge obtains mystical features, and in the third proof theological predicates are attributed to the Form which was an enabling, a priori condition for empirical knowledge in the second thought process. Knowledge of the Form is an encounter, tied to moral purification, with the most perfect being. The grasp of the unveiled Form after death is community with the divine as a reward for a moral life.

4. SELF-DETERMINATION AND RESPONSIBILITY

112.   The soul is related to immutable being, the Forms, but it is not itself a Form but rather has its place between the changeable and the unchangeable. Thus it is forced to choose its mode of being. Self-determination belongs to its essence. Knowledge and self-determination are indivisible for the *Phaedo*. Each individual person freely chooses her understanding of reality. Whoever turns to the flesh concentrates wholly on it and finds fulfillment in it and its needs becomes a materialist and a hedonist; only what one can touch and see is held to be real. The body is a cage through which the soul observes reality, but the person locks himself in by letting himself be determined by the needs of his body. Through philosophy the soul finds its own essence by liberating itself from desires and fears. That the soul determines itself is also expressed by the picture of reincarnation. The soul that joined itself with the body necessarily searches for a new body after death, that of an animal or a human. It is the expression of the character that the soul gave itself with its way of life (*Phaedo* 81e–83e).

113.   Plato discusses the problem of freedom most fully in the concluding myth of the *Republic* (614a–621d). The souls that return from the underworld back into this life pass by on their way the axis of the heavens, described as a spindle, that goes through the middle of the earth and moves the eight heavenly spheres. The spindle turns in the lap of necessity. Around the spindle sit the three daughters of necessity that symbolize the dimensions of time: Lachesis (past), Clotho (present), and Atropos (future). The middle of the world, thus sketched as the place of necessity, is simultaneously the place of freedom. A prophet calls the souls in the name of Lachesis to *the* basic act of human freedom, that of the choice of a life: "This is the word of Lachesis, the maiden daughter of Necessity, 'Souls that live for a day, now is the beginning of another cycle of mortal generation where birth is the beacon of death. No divinity shall cast lots for

you . . . the blame is his who chooses. God is blameless"
(617de). The choice of a life is the only act of human freedom. It occurs outside time determined by necessity. It is
only after the choice that the soul enters into time. It is the
choice of a demon, of the character that determines the person's particular decisions. Lachesis joins the chosen demon
to the particular individual as the shepherd of his life and
executor of his choice. Plato emphasizes that after this choice
human beings are subject to necessity.

5. THE WORLD-SOUL

114. According to the *Phaedo*'s fourth proof of immortality the soul is the bearer of life. However, life expresses
itself in motion. The *Phaedrus* takes over here (245c–246a).
As the principle of life the soul is the origin of motion and
immortal as such. The argument distinguishes two kinds of
the moved or mover: what is moved by another and moves
a third in turn and what moves itself. As a self-mover the
soul is the first cause of every motion and as such uncreated
and imperishable. The first cause cannot in turn be caused
if one does not want to be involved in an infinite regress.
The soul, as a first cause of motion, must be imperishable,
for if the first cause perished, then it could not be brought
about by another cause, and the whole cosmos would come
to a standstill and perish, which is an inconceivable assumption for the Greeks. In contrast to the *Phaedo,* in the *Phaedrus*
the soul is the principle of life not only for human beings
but also for the entire cosmos. This teaching of the World-
Soul is developed especially in the *Timaeus* (27c–37c) and
in the tenth book of the *Laws* (see also *Philebus* 28d–30e).
The World-Soul of the *Timaeus* serves to explain the regularity and teleology of nature. The Demiurge, the genesis
myth reports, was good and free of ill will. Thus he wanted
that the world be as similar to him as possible. In order to
make it as perfect as possible, he led it from the condition

of chaotic to that of ordered motion and bestowed a soul and reason upon it. The movements of nature, especially of the heavenly bodies, have an intelligible, mathematical structure. For this reason, the myth claims, they can only be explained by a cause that can recognize mathematical laws, namely, by a spirit. But a spirit can only be, according to Plato's conception, in a soul.

The genesis myth proceeds from an ontological dichotomy between eternal being that never becomes and the eternal becoming that never is (27d). To which of these realms does the World-Soul belong? Apparently the *Phaedrus* places it with eternal being by characterizing it as "uncreated" (245d1), whereas the *Timaeus,* on the contrary, attributes it to becoming by letting it be created by the Demiurge. The solution to the contradiction lies in the insight that the soul does not fit into this dichotomy; it participates in both realms. Its creation by the Demiurge is described as a mixture of the components of indivisible, unchangeable being and becoming, changing being. The tenth book of the *Laws* relates the World Soul and the Greek's religious concept of god. Plato attacks the denial of the existence of the gods, the deistic thesis that the gods do not concern themselves with humans, and the claim that they can be bribed. Against materialistic-mechanistic theories that see the world as the result of chance and necessity, Plato argues for the priority of the soul over matter. The soul, defined as "the motion that can move itself" (896a), is the first changing being. The ordered, perfect movement (circular motion) can only be explained by a soul endowed with reason (897b). The World-Soul of the *Laws* has personal features. Ascribed to it are wants, deliberation, care, and moral virtues. It is not only the principle of the regular movement of the cosmos but also providence that steers the fate of human beings. Plato identifies it with the divine (899b).

V. The State

1. THE *REPUBLIC*'S IDEAL

115. In one of the ancient sources the *Republic* bears the name "The State or on the Just." The connection of these themes is drawn in a preliminary, methodological remark made by Socrates which is important for the composition of the work (368c–369b). If we were given the task of reading small letters from a distance and discovered that the same letters in larger print can be found elsewhere, we would begin by reading the large letters and then look to the small letters to see if they were in fact the same. "Just" is attributed to both the individual human being and the state. For this reason Socrates wants to start by observing justice in the state and then ask whether a corresponding justice can be found in individual human beings. A dominating moment in the *Republic*'s conception of the state is revealed by this comparison: unity. The state is conceived, corresponding to humans, as an organism. The state's classes correspond to the soul's faculties. The individual human is an organ of a comprehensive whole. She has a function for the whole, and she relies upon the whole for her survival, moral perfection, and happiness. The comparison allows the much-discussed question (initiated especially by Karl Popper) whether Plato was the spiritual father of totalitarianism.

116. Plato sees the state's origin in man's inability to sat-

isfy his various needs without the help of others. He initially sketches a state that has an exclusively economical function (369b–373e). At this level already he attacks the individualistic-egoistic picture of human beings that underlies the Sophists' contract theory which Plato uses as the starting point for the conversation (358eff.). As a being with needs, man is already a social being; the other is not an opponent, but rather a helper. The facts that every human has different capacities and that specialization contributes to the quality of work lead to a society with divided labor. Human beings are moderate; they are content with simple nutrition and do not produce more children than their property allows. This picture is, however, unrealistic, insofar as it overlooks the dynamic and differentiated character of human needs and wants. For this reason, after the healthy state Socrates sketches the "bloated" state characterized by superfluous, luxurious expectations. Growing needs are the cause of external and internal conflicts. They let the number of jobs and thus denizens increase and hence force the state to attempt to acquire a neighbor's territory; war results. The principle of a labor-divided society requires its own class for this purpose: the guardians (373e–374e). It is divided into commanders and subordinates. The criteria according to which the leaders are chosen (412c–414b; 484a–487a) reveal another basic feature of the state: intellectualism. The guardians are to protect the state in the comprehensive sense that they are to guard the leaders from downfall. For this they must love the state, which in turn requires the insight that they themselves will only do well if the state flourishes. Only knowledge of the truly Good that abrogates the difference between egoism and altruism enables the rulers to fulfill their task. With the introduction of the guardians the economic division of labor is complemented by the political division between rulers and the ruled. Until then the economic class was left to itself. Now there is a higher resort that can rule on conflicts and thus preserve unity.

117. Plato prescribes a strict division of the guardians

from the economic base (414a–417b). The most important reason for this is the functional point of view that determines the entire state. The guardians can only fulfill their tasks if they do not follow their own economic interests. Otherwise they would be corrupted by their inclinations. If they "acquire for themselves land of their own and houses and coin, they will be householders and farmers instead of guardians, and will be transformed from the helpers of their fellow citizens to their enemies and master, and so in hating and being hated, plotting and being plotted against, they will pass their days fearing far more" (417ab). In this manner Plato comes to prohibit guardians from having property and family. They are to be sustained by other citizens: dwelling, meals, women, and children are common to all. Interpreters dispute how these traits so foreign to reality are to be understood. One hardly does Plato justice if one takes them to be literal provisions for a concrete state. They have a primarily critical function. Plato posits the other extreme as provocation in contrast to the current unfavorable conditions and nepotism. The *Republic*'s state is an ideal pattern whose capacity for realization Plato leaves open (592ab).

118. The state has been founded, and Socrates returns to the original question about justice (427d–434c). The perfect polis must possess the four cardinal virtues that Plato takes over from the tradition: wisdom, courage, temperance, and justice. Wisdom, the virtue of the rulers, is the comprehensive knowledge of the Good that extends over and directs the individual arts, knowledge which advises the state about itself as a whole. Whereas wisdom is knowledge, courage depends on mere opinion, taken over from the rulers, about what is good for the state. The subordinate guardians are courageous when they hold steadfastly to this opinion despite pain, fear, and desires. Temperance is the ordering of desires according to reason. As a political virtue it is the agreement of all classes of the state as to who should rule. The economic base is temperate when it is convinced that it is in its own interest to be ruled by the intellectuals. The

concept of justice formulates the demands of specialization that was already decisive for the founding of the preliminary state (par. 116). Just is whoever does what is proper to him and does not get involved in foreign tasks. Justice is the cause of the other virtues. They arise when a class (or faculty of the soul) dedicates itself exclusively to its specific function. It leads to an extreme separatism and simultaneously to an extreme unity. Only the uppermost class is capable of and authorized to make a political decision guided by reason. The lower classes cannot and may not influence the government. Specialization leads to an extreme interdependence. The individual is an organ that both functions for and depends upon the whole.

119. The *Republic* maintains an intellectual conception of politics that presupposes the Socratic optimism of the motivating power of insight into the Good. When Plato demands that the philosophers should rule, he is not demanding single class rule but rather a politics that is oriented toward the interests of all and according to reason. With the Sophist's enlightenment he is of the opinion that politics is to be oriented toward reason and not norms only established by tradition. Rule may not, and this is the point behind the separation of the guardians from the economic basis, be determined by interests or desires: it is to serve the good of the whole exclusively. If one assumes that self-interest is essential for the concept of a societal class, the *Republic*'s state is no class-state. Here the portrayal of the ideal state is to be complemented by its counterpart, the four forms of decay (543c–576b). They are forms of class rule. Timocracy is rule by the military, and oligarchy by the rich. The cause of decay is failure in education. Both of the soul's lower faculties are removed from reason's rule. The man of timocratic rule is determined by ambition. In an oligarchy competency does not determine who rules the state, but rather the size of one's income does so. The ruling class wants to secure its power through its educational policy. Young persons are misled to licentiousness and waste and thus lose their property and

political influence. A division of the state into the rich and the poor ensues. A proletariat arises that has no interest in the state and becomes a danger to it.

120. Plato assumes that human beings are naturally unequal. Proportional equality underlies the *Republic*'s concept of justice. Each person should attain the level of realization possible and receive what is deserved. The critical question is whether Plato derives unequal political rights from the different natural talents. Is the principle of specialization illegitimately carried over from the economical-technical level to the political level? The answer depends on the weight one gives to his statements about temperance. Such statements can be interpreted in the sense that the consent of the ruled is an essential moment in the state. An equality of political rights despite different talents would be expressed by the governed being able to either give or withhold consent as well. But even a charitable interpretation must admit that the consensus in the *Republic* is not institutionalized. The accusation that Plato defends intellectualistic absolutism is not easily thwarted.

121. The state's goal is to educate the individual to be virtuous and thus free. Human beings should gain rule over themselves and be in harmony with themselves (443c–e). Especially in his criticism of Democritus (555b–562a) Plato attacks a false understanding of freedom. It is not to be conflated with arbitrariness or caprice in which the individual surrenders to his momentary moods and desires. Politically, extreme democracy turns into tyranny. Plato places his own, Socratic understanding of freedom in opposition: whoever can do what she *truly* wants is free. Whoever does what he thinks to be good without it being good is not doing what he truly wants. Freedom is self-determination by reason that alone can know the Good. This knowledge presupposes, however, an order of the soul given by justice. The pathology of the forms of constitutions shows that political freedom decays as does the individual's virtue. It can only be preserved with correct education.

2. THE RULE OF THE LAWS

122. For the *Statesman* also rule that depends on knowledge is an ideal. Only a state that is governed in this manner
is a true state, whereas all others are imitations. The art of
the true statesman is superior to the laws. Like the doctor
or the tax collector, he can do justice to the differences in
human beings and situations, whereas the law is a rigid rule
that can only consider the average conditions (293c–296a).
The true statesman in the *Statesman* also bears absolutistic
features. If he intends only the best and can attain it, he need
not rely upon the citizens' consent (296a–297b). However,
Plato sees more clearly here than in the *Republic* that we
must content ourselves with an imitation because the true
state can never be realized. There is no knowledgeable and
just politician who does not misuse his power. For this reason the state must be governed according to written laws
(301c–302b).

123. In the same way *The Laws* continue to maintain that
reason as the principle of freedom ought not to be subordinated to laws. However, Plato's appreciation of laws has
grown with his knowledge of human nature. Human beings'
lives must be regulated by laws because otherwise they would
be no different than wild animals. Plato thinks the reason
for this lies in the weakness of knowledge and character. Even
when the statesman knows that the general welfare is superior to individual interests, he will not have the will power
to hold onto this insight against his selfishness (874e–875d).
Unity and knowledge of the Good are basic values for *The
Laws'* state as much as for the *Republic*'s. A community of
women and goods is referred to as an ideal (739b–e). But
The Laws aspire to set up laws for a state that can be realized. Unity is to be attained, not by rigorous limitation to
functions, but rather through friendship. The citizens should
get to know each other. For this reason the number of land-
owners and propertyless people is limited to 5040 (737e).
Unity and friendship are also to be served by justice, which

consists in each person receiving what is deserved despite unequal talents (757d) and by structuring the order of the proportion of estates in a manner that avoids unreasonable differences between the rich and the poor (744b). In addition to insight and friendship political freedom arises as a third basic value (693bc). The realization of these basic values requires a mixed constitution with which Plato creates the foundation for the later theory of the division of powers.

All constitutions stem from two "Mothers" (693d): monarchy, which realizes the value of insight at the cost of freedom, and democracy, which realizes the value of freedom at the cost of insight. All citizens of a state ruled by laws have the right to elect their rulers, even if it is differentiated by classes according to wealth. All elected are the executive guardians, the highest military, the council and the local offices that are responsible for the specific provinces (Book VI), and finally (which Book XII adds) the controlling instance of the euthynes, the ten eldest executive guardians, to which all other politicians and state officials must give account for the execution of their offices. The philosopher-king of the *Republic* is encountered again in the highest gremio, which is to ensure the subsistence of the state by watching over the latter's spiritual foundations. The "nightly meeting" introduced in Book XII embodies the statesmanship's reason and experience. It consists of the euthynes, those who have become acquainted with other states in the name of the state, and an equal number of men of a younger generation. Like the *Republic*'s ideal state the legal state has virtue as its goal. According to the conception of *The Laws* it is not possible without belief in the existence of the gods. The foremost task of the "nightly meeting" is thus to uphold the religious convictions that form the state's foundations. Two supporting theological theses are the priority of the soul over matter and that the order of the cosmos can only be explained by a divine reason.

The conclusion of *The Laws* alludes to Plato's conception of the unity of the sciences (see *Republic* VII). Mathe-

matics in its application as astronomy leads to knowledge
of the cosmic order and thus to theology; in its application
as harmonics it motivates human beings to imitate the eternal order in their character and political institutions. The
basic theological aspect of Plato's thought is featured in *The
Laws* as in no other work. "We should keep our seriousness
for the serious things, and not waste it on trifles, and that,
while God is the real goal of all beneficent serious endeavor,
man . . . has been constructed as a toy for God, and this
is, in fact, the finest thing about him" (803c).

VI. The Unwritten Doctrines

124. Until the eighteenth century Plato was interpreted under the influence of Neoplatonism. The dialogs were taken as literary garb for a philosophical system whose core was ontology and philosophical theology. Friedrich Schleiermacher (1804) effected a change by pointing out the unity of literary form and philosophical content. Every sentence "can only be correctly understood in its own place and in the contexts and limitations that Plato gave it." The dialogs imitate Socratic discussion. The reader is to be led to "his own internal creation of the intended thought" or "be forced to admit completely to the feeling of having found nothing" (1855, pp. 14; 16). Despite Schleiermacher's sustained influence the Neoplatonic interpretation has found advocates until recently. This interpretation refers for its authority mainly to Aristotle's and other ancients' doxographic reports on Plato's Lecture on the Good. These reports receive special weight from the *Phaedrus'* criticism of writing (see par. 67) and the seventh letter (341a–344c). Plato did not entrust his actual teaching, it is argued, to the dialogs but rather developed them orally in the Academy. Its residue is found in the so-called doxographic reports.

125. The reconstruction of the unwritten doctrines is due to Leo Robin (1908), Julius Stenzel (1924), and many other scholars, especially Hans Joachim Krämer (1959) and Konrad Gaiser (1963). The concern is a "derived system" according to which all of reality proceeds from two principles, the

One, identical with the Form of the Good, and that of the unlimited dyad (aoristos dyas). Being is divided into three realms. The uppermost circumscribes both principles from above, ideal numbers that are higher than the Forms and from which all Forms are derived, and ideal geometrical constructs. To the intermediary realm belong numbers, geometrical shapes, and the World-Soul. The lowest ontological level consists in moved, perceivable bodies. The One is the origin of unity, knowability, and value for all being. Corresponding to the ontological system is a system of sciences.

126. The authenticity of the doxographical reports is controversial. Do they represent Plato's thoughts or do they rest upon a misunderstanding by Aristotle? If one assumes, along with a large number of scholars, the former, then the question as to the relation between the unwritten doctrines and the dialogs arises. Does a lecture that is to be dated around Plato's last years constitute the essential content, or does the Lecture on the Good's ontology underlie, even if not in a worked-out form but only in its basic features, the early dialogs as Krämer's far-reaching thesis claims? Do the dialogs have an independent value, or are they mere "protreptic advertisement works" (Krämer, 1964, p. 80) for the Academy which are limited to alluding to Plato's esoteric dogmas in pithy intimations?

The unwritten doctrines represent a phase of Plato's later philosophy. It would be mistaken to see in them the systematic background of the entire written corpus and to attribute to them a higher value than the dialogs. They do not attain in philosophical content the dialogs' breadth of phenomena, consciousness of problems, analytic potential, and differentiated complexity. Without doubt the origin of Neoplatonism is to be sought in Plato, but the development occurs via a narrowing of the thematic variety of the dialogs. One would succumb to the same narrowing if one were to see in the unwritten doctrines the whole and proper Plato. Schleiermacher's hermeneutic principles have not lost their validity to this very day.

VII. The Older Academy

127. Plato's successors in leading the Academy (par. 61) are his nephew Speusippus (until ca. 339 B.C.), Xenocrates of Chalcedon (until ca. 314 B.C.), Polemon of Athens (until ca. 275 B.C.), and Crates of Athens (until ca. 268 B.C.). Relying upon Plato's unwritten doctrines, *Speusippus* develops a mathematical ontology. Its principles are the One that stands beyond being and the Many that populate the beings. The realms of being are the mathematical numbers, the mathematical shapes, the soul (World-Soul), and the perceivable bodies. They are created when the One determines and limits the Many. The One and the Many are to be seen as analogous but different principles on each level. Speusippus ordered the entire reality according to the relation of genus and species, applying Plato's method of collection and division (par. 96f.) consistently. Happiness consists in perfect behavior with respect to the naturally given goods; pleasure is valued negatively.

128. *Xenocrates* exercised great influence on the further development of Platonism and the Stoics. He was the first one to order philosophy into physics, ethics, and logic. In addition to the teaching of correct thought logic circumscribes rhetoric, linguistics, and grammar. Like Speusippus his ontology is oriented toward Plato's unwritten doctrines. The Form-numbers, the mathematical, the realm of the stars, the soul, and finally the perceivable bodies underneath the moon follow the principles. The soul as "number moving itself"

is the principle of motion and knowledge of the mathematically ordered world. Taking off from the *Timaeus,* Xenocrates distinguishes three cosmological causes: the Forms as original patterns, the demiurge, and matter. Via allegories he combines the philosophical worldview with mythical religion.

Polemon prepares for the Stoic ethic. He sees the highest good in life according to nature, that is, in the use of naturally given goods as determined by virtue. But even without the bodily and external goods virtue alone can suffice for happiness.

129. Together with Xenocrates *Heraclides of Ponticus* (ca. 390–310 B.C.) ran as a candidate for the position of Scholarch. He assumed a spiritual material. His astronomical theses are important: the earth's daily rotation around its axis and, anticipating Aristarchus' heliocentric worldview, the earth's annual rotation around the middle of the world. Plato's student *Philippus of Opus* is reported to have published Plato's *Laws* posthumously and written himself the *Epinomis. Exodus of Cnidus* (ca. 400–347 B.C.), mathematician, astronomer, geographer, doctor, and philosopher, had close contact with the Academy. He attempted to explain the motion of the five planets, the moon, and the sun with a system of homocentric spheres rotating around the earth. He maintained an hedonistic ethic. *Crantor,* a member of the Academy under Polemon, was the first person to compose a coherent commentary on the *Timaeus.*

D. Aristotle

Life

130. Aristotle was born in Ionia around 384 B.C. in Stageira
on the east coast of Chalcidice. Both parents stemmed from
doctors' families; his father, Nicomachus, was a physician
for King Amyntas III, the grandfather of Alexander the Great.
In 367, during Plato's second trip to Sicily, the seventeen year
old began his studies at the Academy. According to the biographical tradition Aristotle was dubbed "the clear head of
the school" and "the reader." For twenty years he worked
as a student of Plato, as a researcher and teacher at the Academy. In 347 Aristotle left Athens for political reasons, either
before or after Plato's death. As a result of Olynthus' being
conquered and plundered by Philip of Macedon, the influence of the anti-Macedonian party in Athens, led by Demos-
thenes, had gained force and endangered Aristotle's life as
he was pro-Macedonian. He thus took up an invitation ten-
dered by a ruler in Assos, namely, Hermias, ruler of Atar-
neus, to go there. Aristotle moved to Mitylene in Lesbos approximately two years later. It was there that his lifelong work
with Theophrastus (born ca. 370) began. In 343/42 King
Philip invited him to take on the education of then thirteen-
year-old Alexander. Due to the destruction of Thebes in Oc-
tober 335 the resistance against Macedon was crushed, and
Aristotle could return to Athens. He taught in the Lyceum,
a public school in the northeastern part of the city. After
Alexander's death in 323 animosity toward the Macedons
broke out again, and Aristotle was forced to leave the city

a second time. He retired to his mother's home in Chalcis at Euboea, where he died of an illness at the age of 63 in 322. After the execution of his friend Hermias by the Persians 341/40 Aristotle married Pythias, the former's sister or niece. Aristotle and Pythias had a daughter, also named Pythias, and a son, Nicomachus.

I. Works

1. THE TRADITION

131. In Aristotle's works one must distinguish the literary, worked-out (exoteric) writings that were published by him (especially dialogs) from the pedagogical notes (esoteric writings) that were to be used for lecturing. The exoteric writings have been lost, whereas the esoteric writings have a varied historical tradition. Theophrastus was the heir to Aristotle's library. After the death of Theophrastus (288/85) it went over into the hands of his fellow student Neleus, who took it with him to his home city of Skepsis in the Troad, where the written works were stored untouched for approximately 200 years. In the beginning of the first century B.C. they were discovered by Apellicon of Teos and brought to Athens, where in 86 B.C. they fell into the hands of Sylla, who had them worked through by the grammarian Tyrannion. His student, Andronicus of Rhodes, collected the writings according to subject matter, as Porphyry reports (*Vita Plotini* ch. 24), into groups ("pragmaties") and thus created an edition that gave occasion to an intensive study of Aristotle. He did not include the exoteric works in his edition. Thus they fell into obscurity. The passages on the use of the pedagogical works prior to Andronicus are sparse. With his edition Andronicus provided a reason for an interpretation that has dominated into the twentieth century according to which Aristotle's philosophy is a closed, unified system. The ancient

commentating activities divide into two periods. The first, orthodox period presumes a difference between Aristotle and Plato. Alexander of Aphrodisias (around 200 A.D.) was most influential. Porphyry initiates the series of commentators who interpret Aristotle from a Neoplatonic perspective. They achieve their apex in Ammonius Hermeiu and his school (5/6 A.D.), whose most significant figure is Simplicius.

2. THE DEVELOPMENTAL INTERPRETATION OF ARISTOTLE

132. The calling into question of the picture of Aristotle suggested by Andronicus' edition is the honor of Werner Jaeger (1923). For him Aristotle is the "creator of developmental thought in the humanities," and he applies this mode of observation to its originator. Since then researchers have been discussing his developmental hypotheses. Jaeger's thesis maintains that Aristotle develops from being a Platonic idealist to a sober empiricist. He distinguishes three periods. 1. The period of the Academy. Aristotle is a convinced Platonist, as the dialogs that can be dated to this period show. He maintains the doctrine of the transcendental Forms. 2. The traveling years (347–335). Aristotle criticizes Plato's theory of Forms and develops his own metaphysics that is determined, as was Plato's, by the question about the transcendental. The first drafts of his great works are written: the protometaphysics, the protoethics, the protopolitics, and the speculative foundation of the physics and cosmology. 3. The master period, or the second Athenian period. The emphasis lies on empirical research (collection of 158 constitutions, of the material for the biological works, etc.). Metaphysics queries, not about supersensible being, but rather about the principles of particular substances that are perceivable by the senses.

133. The critical response to Jaeger was that his development of Aristotle was constructed a priori according to a

Romantic scheme. The reports about, and the dating of, the dialogs are too uncertain to support the claim of an early Platonic period. The places mentioned in the biological works refer especially to Lesbos and its surroundings. Thus Aristotle had probably already collected this material around 345–343 and not after 335. According to Dirlmeier's programmatic article (1950) Aristotle was an empiricist and a Platonist in the beginning as well as in the end. The interest in natural science brought with him from his parents' house could develop in the Academy, where, as the *Timaeus* reveals, research into nature occupies an important place. At the other end of his development there are distinct intimations of Plato in, for example, Book X of the *Nicomachean Ethics,* which is given a late date: the authentic self is the divine nous in human beings. Jaeger's method has proved to be fruitful insofar as we cannot view the particular pragmaties uncritically as unified works; rather we must ask about the dating of their constituents and count on later inserts, duplications, and reworkings by Aristotle (or a later editor). This question is to be distinguished from the one whether the diversely dated texts allow a philosophical development in Jaeger's sense. The supposition of a development can also be an avoidance of the text's difficulty with repect to its subject matter. Since Dirlmeier (1950) researchers tend on the whole to emphasize the "inner unity and closedness of Aristotelian philosophy" (Düring, 1966, p. 29; see Moraux, 1968, p. 94). Düring's work from 1966 (see the short and complementary presentation from 1968, and Flashar, 1983, par. 13) is the authoritative work for the present state of the dating discussion.

3. THE WORKS

Our short overview follows the ordering of Immanuel Bekker's edition (1831), according to whose pagination the corpus aristotelicum is quoted.

a) The Organon

134. Andronicus collected the *Categories, De Interpretatione,* both *Analytics,* the *Topics,* and *On Sophistical Refutations* into a group and placed them at the beginning of
his edition. Its designation "organon" (tool of thinking) may
derive from him as well. All of these writings stem from Aristotle's time at the Academy. The central chapters 4–9 of the
Categories (Categoriae) investigate what the expressions out
of which a simple assertoric sentence is composed designate.
The *De Interpretatione* concerns (the nature of) propositions
and judgments. The *Prior Analytics (Analytica priora)* contain Aristotelian syllogistic. The scientific syllogism or proof
that has evident, true propositions as premises is treated in
the first book of the *Posterior Analytics (Analytica posteri-
ora);* the subject matter of the second book is scientific definition. The *Topics (Topica)* concern dialectical syllogisms
whose premises are propositions that are only generally held
to be true. An elenchus (refutation) is a syllogism that proves
the contradictory opposite of an opponent's claim. The theme
of the *On Sophistical Refutations (Sophistici elenchi;* also
Top. IX) is the Sophist's misuse of these syllogisms.

*b) Works on Natural Philosophy, Biology,
    and Psychology*

135. The comprehensive subject matter of Books I–VI of
the *Physics (Physica)* is change. Change consists in a substrate losing one determination and gaining an opposing one
(I). In contrast to artificial or man-made products, natural
constructs have the source of change in themselves. The four
causes of change are material, formal, efficient, and final (or
end) (II). Change is the actualization of a possibility. The
kinds of change are those of quality, increase and decrease,
coming to be and passing away, and change of place (III, 1).
It is continuous. The concept of continuity (VI) contains that
of the infinite (III, 4–8), and change is not possible with-

out place, void, and time (IV). Whereas *Phys.* I–VI originate between 355 and 347, *Phys.* VIII stems from the second Athenian period (Düring, 1968, Sp. 333–335); it proves the existence of a first unmoved mover.

136. Books I and II of the early work *De Caelo* (or *On the Heavens*) sketch a picture of the astronomical world. The heavenly bodies are composed of the fifth element, ether, whose sole change is circular motion. The cosmos consists in a series of concentric empty spheres whose outermost sphere is the finite sphere of the "first heaven"; the relatively small, ball-shaped earth rests in the middle. The (ball-shaped) stars are tied to spheres that are moved by the eternal and continuous motion of the first heaven. *De Caelo* II and IV deal with the four elements of the sublunar realm (earth, water, fire, air) and their natural movements. This theme is developed further in both books of *On Generation and Corruption* (*De generatione et corruptione*), which were probably also written at the Academy. Every element consists in the composition of prime matter with two of the opposing qualities warm/cold, dry/wet; the change of these opposites causes their coming to be or passing away. The materials out of which the organs of living beings are formed, for example, muscle, bones (homoiomeries), arise through the mixture of the four elements. The fourth book of the *Meteorology* (*Metereologica*), whose authenticity is questioned, considers the effects of the four basic qualities and the homoiomeries. Books I–III explain physical phenomena in the atmosphere and on earth: falling stars, comets, the Milky Way, fog, clouds, the various types of precipitation (I); ocean, wind, earthquakes (II); the halo around the sun and the moon and the rainbow (III).

137. The *De anima* (or *On the Soul*), dated in the second Athenian period, connects the biological works with Books VII–IX of the *Metaphysics* (see par. 168). Book I reports and criticizes the predecessors' teachings. The definition of the soul as the "first reality" (essence or form) of an organism is central (II, 1). It is developed in the description and on-

tology of the various faculties of the soul: the vegetative faculty, the sensitive faculty coupled with the faculty of desire and the intellect that is not tied to the body (nous) (II–III). The seven smaller works on psychophysical phenomena (perception, memory, sleep, dreaming, length of life, warmth of life, and breathing), which have been collected under the name of *Parva naturalia* since the thirteenth century, can be seen as supplements to *De anima*. The *History of Animals* (*Historia animalium*) provides the factual material for the following, more speculative zoological works. Books I–VI form a unity. Books I–IV contain a general anatomy and physiology. Aristotle proceeds from the most perfect (human beings) to the least perfect living organisms. Books V–VI concern reproduction and development; here he climbs from the lowest to the highest living parturient animals. Book IX describes the nourishment and other life habits and illnesses of animals. The names of places allow one to infer that Aristotle collected the material for the *History of Animals* during his stay in Mitylene. *On the Parts of Animals* (*De partibus animalium*) describes three levels of composition: that of the elements out of the basic powers; that of the homoiomeries and that of the organs. Book I comments on methodological questions of zoology; it was pieced together in the second Athenian period partially from older texts (Düring). The special treatment *De incessu animalium,* which diverges widely from teleological observation, is a complementary work to the *History of Animals. On the Movement of Animals* (*De motu animalium*) treats a borderline question of psychology, physiology, and physics: How can the physical act of striving move the body? The solution claims that the faculty of striving is a physical organ and is to be assigned to the "innate pneuma." The latest and the most speculative of the zoological works is *On the Generation of Animals* (*De generatione animalium*). In Books I–III Aristotle explains reproduction with the help of his principles from natural philosophy. The male sperm is the form, the menstrual blood the matter. Book V explains nonteleological, secondary properties, for example, the color of the eyes and differences in hair growth.

c) The Metaphysics

138. The order of the *Metaphysics'* 14 books that we possess from the tradition is from Andronicus of Rhodes. The title also does not derive from Aristotle but rather stems from the first century B.C. Aristotle quotes the pragmaty as "first philosophy" (*De motu anim.* 700b8). According to widespread opinion the title "Metaphysics" (ta meta ta physika) was originally a librarian's designation for the works that followed the works of natural philosophy in Andronicus' edition. Simplicius was the first to interpret the word as a name for the science of what lies beyond nature (Zeller II 1, p. 80). That is correct as long as one does not overlook that the librarian's order follows that of the lessons, and "this order is grounded in the nature of our knowledge and is thus conditioned by it" (Reiner, 1954, p. 219). The unity of the *Metaphysics* is especially a problem because apparently diverse concepts of metaphysics can be found in it. The discussions about the authenticity, relative chronology, and original order of the works and the attempts to distinguish various levels and projects within the *Metaphysics* extend back before Jaeger (see the overview in Bonitz, 1849, pp. 9–35). What is new in Jaeger is his developmental hypothesis. The following overview of the contents will prepare the way for a philosophical interpretation (par. 147ff.).

139. *Met.* I (Alpha): Metaphysics, called "wisdom" (sophia), is the science of the highest causes or principles. Its origin is the natural human desire for knowledge. Aristotle criticizes the theories of causes from Thales to Plato. *Met.* II (Alpha elatton) is a short introduction to the study of metaphysics that is now called the "investigation of truth." *Met.* III (Beta) formulates 14 aporias whose solution is the task

of the desired science. *Met.* IV (Gamma) defines metaphysics as the science of being qua being. The investigation of principles (the principle of noncontradiction, the principle of excluded middle) is also its task. *Met.* V (Delta) is a dictionary that defines the various meanings of 30 philosophical terms. *Met.* VI (Epsilon) considers being qua being. It poses the question, central to the history of interpretations of the *Metaphysics,* how the science of being qua being is related to that of divine being (theologic), and distinguishes (as does V, 7) four meanings of "being." *Met.* VII–IX (ZHΘ; Zeta, Eta, Theta) (the "books on substance"): The question about being qua being leads to what is the perceivable substance (ousía), being in its proper sense. It is explained with the help of the concepts matter and form, potentiality and actuality. *Met.* X (Iota) is an independent lecture on the concept of the one and the related concepts of identity, diversity, similarity, and opposition. *Met.* XI (Kappa) is probably a post-Aristotelian compilation of *Met.* III, IV, VI and *Phys.* III, V. *Met* XII (Lambda) is a self-contained work. Chapters 1–5 treat perceivable, mutable substances, whereas chapters 7–10 consider the immutable, divine substance. *Met.* XIII (Mu) also asks whether in addition to the perceivable substances there is an unchanging, eternal substance. In connection with this the theory of Forms and the Pythagorean-Platonic claim that numbers are substances are discussed. The treatment ends chapter 9, 1086a18. *Met.* XIV (Nu) (as of XIII 1086a18) criticizes Plato's theory of principles and ideal number theory (see par. 125).

140. With respect to the relative chronology of the *Metaphysics*'s books, there are "as many views as there are scholars of Aristotelian metaphysics" (Düring, 1966, p. 593). For the following interpretation I assume that Lambda is an early attempt of the entire first philosophy and that the books on substance belong to the second Athenian period. There is wide consensus on these points. I agree with Düring's (1968, Sp. 335) claim that Gamma and Epsilon are to be dated to the same time as ZHΘ.

d) Works on Ethics and Politics

141. There are three treatments of ethics handed down under Aristotle's name: the *Nicomachean Ethics* (*Ethica Nicomachea*), the *Magna Moralia,* and the *Eudemian Ethics* (*Ethica eudemica*). Book I of the *Nicomachean Ethics* develops a concept of happiness and a psychology that distinguishes between the rational and the striving (desiring) faculties of the soul. The central point of Book II is the definition of moral virtue, that is, of virtue for the faculty of desire. *EN* III, 1–7 concern the culpability of actions. *EN* III, 8–15 and *EN* IV describe individual moral virtues. It is controversial whether books V–VII of the *EN* originally belonged to *EN* or *EE*. V treats justice, *EN* VI the dianoetic, intellectual, or rational virtues. *EN* VII concerns the weakness of will and provides a first discussion of pleasure. The subject matter of *EN* VIII and IX is friendship. *EN* X begins with a second discussion of pleasure in order to then provide a concluding answer to the question about happiness. The most important themes of the *Magna Moralia* are virtue, distribution of goods, culpability, description of individual moral virtues, justice, dianoetic virtues (Book I), weakness of will, pleasure, friendship (Book II). The *Eudemian Ethics* treats happiness (I), moral virtue in general and culpability (II), the particular moral virtues (III), friendship (VII), happiness in the sense of a fortunate or lucky fortune (eutychıa), and the comprehensive ethical ideal of goodness (kalokagathıa) (VIII). The controversial Books of the *EN* V–VII count as Books IV–VI.

142. According to widespread opinion *EN* is the most mature of the three pragmaties. Its authenticity is undisputed. The *MM* and *EE* were considered inauthentic in the nineteenth century. Since Jaeger (1923) the claim that the *EE* is Aristotle's, albeit prior to the *EN*, has become more popular. The authenticity of the *MM* is still controversial. Is it a post-Aristotelian compilation (Jaeger) or Aristotle's earliest ethics (von Arnim, Dirlmeier, Düring)? The evaluation

of *EN* and *EE* cannot be separated from the problem of the controversial books. Dirlmeier (*EE*, pp. 361–365) attributes them to *EN,* whereas Kenny (1978) ascribes them to *EE.*

143. The *Politics* begins with a question about the difference between a polis and other human societies (I, 1f). A polis consists in house societies (oikos). Thus Aristotle considers the running of houses (oikonomia) in great detail (I, 3–13). A discussion of contemporary political theories and existing constitutions follows (II). Points of emphasis are the criticism of Plato's republic and Sparta's constitution. Book III is a general political theory. It asks about the concept and virtue of a citizen (1–5). Aristotle distinguishes three forms of constitutions and their corruptions: monarchy, aristocracy, polity; tyranny, oligarchy, democracy (6–8). The fundamental principle of a constitution is justice, which consists in equality. But according to what criteria is this to be determined and are the rights of the various groups in the polis to be ascertained accordingly (9–13)? III, 14–18 deal with kingship. Books IV–VI analyze the existing democratic and oligarchic constitutions. One must distinguish the question as to the best possible constitution from the one as to the best constitution that can be realized under the given circumstances. The best possible constitution is the one in which the middle class is most influential. Aristotle distinguishes between the legislative, executive, and judicial powers and describes how these powers are divided in the various constitutions. He investigates the causes of revolutions. The *Politics* closes with a projection of an ideal state (VII–VIII). The question about the best polis assumes an answer to the question about the happiness of individual human beings, so that the interconnection of politics and ethics is evident (VII, 1–3). Aristotle states the external conditions for the ideal polis: the number and natural capacities of the inhabitants, size and location of the territory, location and capabilities of the city, required professions and classes (VII, 4–12). An emphasized point is the detailed guidelines for education (VII, 13–VIII, 7).

The *Politics* is also not a unified work. Nonetheless, the question about the best constitution connects the individual treatments into a certain unity. But this question is posed in different senses and is answered with various methods. The earliest components are books VII and VIII. They show close proximity to Plato, especially to the latter's second-best state in Book V of the *Laws*.

e) Rhetoric and Poetics

144. The *Rhetoric*'s three books circumscribe two works that are both to be dated in the time of the Academy: the *Ars rhetorica* proper (I–II) and the treatment *On Prose,* as Düring (1966, p. 149f.) renders the traditional title Peri lexeōs (III). The latter is concerned with style (1–12) and the parts of speech (13–19). Rhetoric is the art of convincing an audience. The means to this are the speaker's character, the capacity of influencing the audience's emotions, and the strategy of argumentation (1, 2). One needs to distinguish between the advising, or political, speech whose goal is the useful and harmful (4–8), the ceremonial address which is concerned with the beautiful and the ugly (9), and the legal speech whose end is the just or unjust (10–15). Book II discusses the particular means of convincing an audience. The speaker must give the impression of a smart, reflective man with integrity (1). The analysis of the emotional states (2–11) and the description of the properties of a person's character (12–17) serve to direct the emotions of the public. The means of argumentation in rhetoric are examples and enthymemes, that is, the rhetorical syllogism, which in contrast to the proof (see par. 134) works not with necessary but rather only with probable premises (18–26).

145. The *Poetics,* which must have originated at the same time as the *Rhetoric,* is based upon a comprehensive knowledge of the ancient and at that time contemporary literature. Aristotle defines poetry as mimesis (imitation, representation). Its origin lies in human beings' joy in imitating

and the imitated. He provides an overview of its development from its beginnings to his time (1–5). The definition of tragedy is one of the most commentated passages in his entire corpus. Tragedy "is the imitation of an action that is serious and also, having magnitude, complete in itself; in language with pleasurable accessories, each kind brought in separately in the parts of the work; in a dramatic, not a narrative form; with incidents arousing pity and fear, wherewith to accomplish its catharsis of such emotions" (6, 1149b24–28). After tragedy (6–22) Aristotle speaks of the epic, whose great master for him is Homer and compares both types (23–26).

f) Fragments

146. At DL V, 20–27 there is an ancient listing of Aristotle's works. We possess fragments of several of the works listed there but not preserved in their entirety. The dialog *On Philosophy (De philosophia)* (around 350; DL No. 3) discusses Plato's teaching on the principles, ideal numbers, and Forms. He provides an early, theologically oriented cosmology that is close in content (and time) to *Met.* XII. The *Protrepticus* is an advertisement that indicates the necessity of philosophizing for one's life. The dialog *Eudemus* (shortly after 354; DL No. 13) deals with the immortality of the soul. The work composed around the time of Plato's *Parmenides* entitled *On the Forms (De ideis)* forms the background for the *Metaphysics'* discussion of the theory of Forms. Aristotle had begun an extensive collection of materials. Of the 158 "constitutions of the poleis" (between 329 and 322; DL No. 143) only the *Constitution of Athens* is preserved.

II. First Philosophy

1. THE VARIOUS SENSES OF "BEING"

147. What are the works asking about that have carried the title "Metaphysics" since Andronicus and that Aristotle himself called "first philosophy"? On the face of it they concern four different objects. According to I, 1–2 the first causes and principles are at issue. IV, 1 defines metaphysics as the science of being qua being, that is, as general ontology. VII–IX are concerned with perceivable, mutable substance. A fourth concept appears to be found in VI, 1 and XII, 6: the desired science is theologic, that is, it concerns the immutable, invisible, divine substance. How are these various concepts related to each other? The key is the sentence "The word 'being' is said in various senses" (IV, 2 1003a33). Behind this sentence stands the great father figure of Greek philosophy, Parmenides. What he means by this sentence is explained in V, 7, where four meanings of 'being' are distinguished.

148. a) Being in the accidental sense. The Greek word 'symbebēkos', which is rendered as 'accidens' in Latin, means literally "gone together." Being in the accidental sense is a being that is only there because it "goes together" with a being that is per se. Consider one of Aristotle's examples: "The just (man) is musical." "The just (man)" is not a simple expression as "man" is but rather is composite. It signifies a man who is just. Only because a man is there can the just

(man) exist. In the proposition "The just (man) is musical" the word 'is' means that we can ascribe to one being per se two properties of which we can only say that they are because they go together with the one man who is per se.

149. b) Being or being per se. Postpone for the moment the question what "per se" means here. Within being per se there are still several meanings to be distinguished according to Aristotle. They correspond to the "types of judgment" (katēgoria). For every type of judgment there is a distinct meaning of 'is'. Aristotle has in mind propositions in which a general term is predicated of a singular term. Consider the following examples:

(1) Socrates (or: this) is a man.
(2) Socrates (or: this) is a living organism.
(3) Socrates (or: this; or: this man) is pale.
(4) Socrates (or: this; or: this man) is bald.
(5) Socrates (or: this; or: this man) is Xanthippe's husband.

In these examples two things deserve special attention in this context: 1. The sentences answer to different types of questions. (1) and (2) answer the question "What is Socrates?" (3) and (4) answer "What is Socrates like?" and (5) answers "How is Socrates related to Xanthippe?" The general terms of the propositions stand in different relationships to each other. The concept "human being" is subordinate to the concept "living organism." A common concept can be found for the concepts "pale" and "bald," namely, "is such and such" or quality. Taking both criteria into account, it follows that (1) and (2) as well as (3) and (4) belong to the same types of judgment, whereas (1), (3), and (5) all belong to different types of judgment. What is decisive in the present context is that the meaning of the word 'is' is distinguished according to the types of judgment. From this it follows for his concept of being: 1. The word 'being' has no meaning in isolation. It designates a synthesis that can only be known through the terms that this word combines together (*De int.* 3, 16b23). 2. "Being" is not a genus (see *Met.* III, 3 998b22). The highest generic concepts are those which allow the predicate concepts of judgments to be subordinated under them, for example, "is such and such," "to such a degree," and "in such a relation to that." When we combine these terms with a copula, we have expressions that signify modes of being. These modes of being are traditionally called "categories" and are designated with abstract singular terms, for example, quality, quantity, relation, passive, and active (see *Top.* 1, 9; *Cat.* 4).

This interpretation also answers the question why Aristotle calls this meaning being "per se." The discussion of accidental being observes a relation: something is because it can be ascribed to a being. Now this relation is abstracted from, and the mode of being that is expressed by the predicate expression—that is, the terms joined by the copula ('. . . is bald')—is observed "per se," that is, isolated from the substrate to which it is attributed. Thus the difference between accidental being and being per se is one in the modes of observation of the very same judgment. Examples (3) and (5) express accidental being as well as being in itself. When Aristotle speaks of being in itself, he is limiting himself to what is said, the predicate expression, and abstracts from what it is said of in that case.

150. c) Being as truth. The word 'is' means "is true." We can, for example, reformulate (4) as follows:

(4a) It is true that Socrates is bald.

(4a) only says explicitly what was already said in (4). The metaphysical investigation does not need to take this third meaning into consideration. "For the false and true do not lie in the things . . . , but rather in thought" (*Met.* VI, 4 1027b25). True and false are properties, not of things, but rather of statements that we make about them.

151. d) Being possible and actual. This distinction relates to being in itself. ". . . is seeing" can mean ". . . is really seeing at this moment" or ". . . is capable of seeing." The meaning of all predicate expressions is to be distinguished in similar fashion.

2. THE SCIENCE OF BEING AS BEING

152. We have seen that four different concepts of the desired science can be found in the *Metaphysics* (par. 147). Two of these concepts are connected in the first sentence of Book Epsilon: "The principles and causes of being and insofar as it is being are the object of this investigation" (1025b3). The science of being as being (IV, 1) is precisely determined so that it investigates the first causes of being as being. Let's first ask what the expression "being as being" (on hē on) means. Aristotle explains it by working out the difference between the desired science and other sciences (VI, 1 1025b4–18).

153. Every science inquires into causes or reasons. There is no difference in this point between the desired and the other sciences. Aristotle maintains a deductive concept of science. We know a state of affairs in the proper sense of the word when we can derive it from highest, necessary, self-evident principles, so that the state of affairs itself is shown to be necessary (*Anal. post.* I, 2). Other sciences are subject to certain limitations and make certain assumptions. Metaphysics does neither. 1. Each one of the other sciences has a limited genus of beings as its topic. It is thus limited to one of the categories or an area within one of the categories. Physics, for example, is limited to the category of substance. It is concerned with perceivable, mutable substance. The object of mathematics is the quantitative. It observes being that is countable *insofar as* it is countable. Metaphysics, however, is not limited to the realm of one category. The concept of being spans the categories which are modes of being. Its object is being simpliciter, the entirety of being. It investigates being *as* being, that is, not insofar as it is a such and such, but rather insofar as it is. Sciences inquire into the reasons for certain states of affairs, for example, for the fact that the sum of the angles of a triangle is equal to two right angles. Metaphysics inquires, not into the content of particular states of affairs, but rather into beings' existence.

2. Each of the other sciences makes assumptions that they cannot question (*Anal. post.* I, 10). First, there are definitions of the basic concepts with which they work, for example, in mathematics the concept of number. Second, it must presume the existence of its subject matter; the mathematician, for example, must assume that there are numbers. The mathematician does not ask how the concept of existence differs when we are talking about, for example, the existence of numbers as opposed to that of organisms. These questions constitute the task of metaphysics, which thematizes the modes of being of the various categorial realms.

154. Can there be a science of being as being at all (IV, 2 1003a33–b19)? Every science is concerned with a genus, whereas being is not a genus. Until now we have worked out the various meanings of "being." Now we need to ask about the unity of these meanings. 'Being' is not used as a homonym. Rather there is a connection between the various meanings such that there is a primary sense upon which all the others are dependent (pros-hen, unity). Aristotle illustrates this unity of meaning with the example of the word 'healthy'. We designate various things as healthy because they stand in a particular relation to health, for example, clothing because it protects health, medicine because it restores health, and complexion because it is a sign of health. Correspondingly, everything that is said to be depends on a more primary thing or principle. This secures the unity of the science of being. The example of medicine as a science of health shows that the unity of the subject matter need not be that of a genus; it can also be the unity of a relation to a primary thing. Such a science will, however, place emphases within its topic. It will be especially concerned with its primary object. What is, however, this primary object for the science of being? IV, 2 only provides a hypothetical answer: if it is substance, then the philosopher must search for the principles and causes of substance. VI, 1 1026a23–32, which stands in a close thematic relation to Gamma 1 and 2, explains this answer more fully. If there is only perceivable,

mutable substance, this would be the primary object of the science of being; if, however, it can be shown that there is also an immutable substance, it would be the principle of being. In this context Aristotle formulates the problem whether first philosophy is the universal science of being as being or a special science that has a genus of being as its subject matter. He illustrates the relational unity of the subject matter of metaphysics by denying this alternative as false. First philosophy is a science of a particular genus of being, the immutable, divine substance. It is the science of being as being because it is the science of the primary being and as such reveals the relation of all being to the divine substance.

3. OUSIA

155. The science of being as being must in any case investigate the causes of perceivable substance. For only in this manner can it answer the question whether this or the divine substance is the primary thing of the relational unity. The most important passages in the *Metaphysics* for this question are the early attempt XII, 1–5 and the worked-out theory VII–IX which we shall follow here. VII, 1 proceeds from being per se in V, 7 (par. 149). Within this categorial being the "is" from judgments that answer the question "What is x?" receives primacy; it designates the mode of being of ousia. What is ousia? Aristotle often uses for it the expression 'this something' (tode ti; VII, 1 1028a3; Bonitz, Index 495b44). Thus ousia is, first, something we can point and refer to using a demonstrative pronoun. Although English does not show this, it, second, points toward a type of judgment. The demonstrative pronoun ought to be supplemented by a general term that tells what the individual is. A sortal term, for example, 'human being', ought to be inserted after the 'this'. Ousia (in this sense it has been traditionally translated as 'substance') is primary with respect to the other categories in three senses:

a) In time. It is what remains in processes of change. Even when it changes its size, place, qualities, and so on, it remains (numerically) the same thing, and it remains what it is. It is "separate" (1028a34): that is, a perceivable substance is not conceivable without the other categories; a human being is always in a particular place, has a particular hair color, and so on. However, it does not cease being this human being when these determinations change. Conversely, the other categories cannot be separate. This particular spot of color can only be found in this particular individual thing.

b) In definition. For the properties that can be ascribed to an individual thing we can ask, "What is X?" for example, "What is color?" Priority in definition consists in the answer containing the concept of ousia. Color, for example, is the quality of a particular thing that can be perceived by the eyes. Sitting is a bodily situation of a living organism.

c) In knowledge. The various types of judgments that we can make about something mediate knowledge in varying degrees. It results from the concept of knowledge that I only know something in the proper sense when I know what it is.

156. The basic question that motivated Greek philosophy since Parmenides becomes precise with the explanation of the threefold primacy of ousia. "And the question that was posed of old as well as now and forever, and that is always puzzling, that is, what being is, means nothing other than what ousia is" (1028b2). The task now is to fill out this preliminary answer, and to this end Aristotle distinguishes initially four meanings of "ousia" (VII, 3): 1. the essence (to ti hn einai); 2. the universal; 3. the genus; 4. the substrate (hypokeimenon). Meanings 2 and 3 represent Plato's conception which Aristotle rejects (see VII, 13f). We shall not discuss them. VII, 3 proceeds from the meaning "substrate." It is clarified in a first step with the help of predication. A substrate is what everything else is predicated of but which itself can never be predicated of another. It is what we refer to with singular terms that can never be used as predicates. Aristotle distinguishes three meanings of "substrate." First,

it signifies the matter (bronze); second, the form; and third, "the composite" of the two (the statue). With respect to these three meanings the question of priority must be posed again: Which of these is ousia in the primary sense? From the definition of substrate it would seem to follow that priority is to be attributed to the matter.

157. Aristotle obtains the concept of matter here by a process of abstraction. He assumes a correspondence between the linguistic and the ontological level. What something is said (or predicated) of is different from what is said (or predicated). Matter is the something that remains when we abstract from all judgments or ontological determinations. It is thus "that which in itself is neither a particular thing nor of a certain quantity nor assigned to any other of the categories by which being is determined" (1029a20). From the concept of matter clarified in this manner, however, it follows that the claim that matter is ousia in the primary sense is untenable. It is inconsistent with two characteristics of ousia: that it is separate and a "this." The example of bronze shows that both of these concepts only apply to something that has form. There is no bronze as mere matter; it always has a certain shape, for example, as a lump or as a part of a rock mass. Thus only two candidates remain for the title of ousia in the proper sense: "the composite" and the form. The former is eliminated because it is dependent upon form and matter as its causes and is thus secondary in this sense. The ontological investigation therefore turns to form.

158. Instead of the word 'form' (eidos) Aristotle uses the artificial expression to ti ēn einai, which means literally "what-it-was-to-be." According to *Top.* I, 5 101b21–38 the phrase stands for the meaning of a definition. The linguistic form of the expression becomes intelligible when one considers that the proposition

(1) Socrates is just.

can also be formulated as follows:

(2) Being just can be attributed to Socrates (see *Top.* 109a13–26).

Accordingly, asking for the definition of this predicate can be posed with two formulations:

(3) What is the Just?

(4) What is being just?

The danger of formulation (3) that Plato falls into according to Aristotle's criticism lies in objectifying predicates. The danger is reduced for (4) since the expression 'being just' makes it clear that a predicate is being formed from a copula and a general term. The difference between it and an object becomes clear because 'being just' points toward the incomplete expression 'is just', which as such cannot signify an object but rather depends upon supplementation by an object. The expression to ti ēn einai is thus the substantiation of the question for a definition. In contrast to (4), however, the general term is missing in it. Still, that is no objection to the present explanation because there is a formulation in which an empty place for the general term is marked out: the "what is was to be a such" (*Met.* VII, 4 1029b20; see Bonitz, *Index* 764a60). What is especially controversial is how to explain the 'was' as opposed to the 'is' that one would expect. One possible solution is that it expresses an atemporal, necessary being.

159. The claim of Book Zeta reads: the form (eidos; essence) is being in the primary and proper sense. That is a simplified and imprecise formulation, since the eidos or form is objectified, which is precisely what Aristotle is trying to avoid by introducing the artificial expression 'what was essence'. A large part of the book is concerned with the relation between the essence and definition and the criticism of the Platonic theory of Forms. We cannot go into that here. I will limit our discussion to the chapters that show the primacy of the eidos by revealing its causality. Chapters 7–9 show its causality for coming to be, and chapter 17 for the being of substance.

4. THE CAUSALITY OF EIDOS

160. The first sentence of chapter 7 provides an extremely condensed description of becoming (or change) (gignesthai). (Aristotle also uses the words 'motion' (kinēsis) and 'change' (metabolē); *Phys.* III, 1.) "Of things that come to be, some come to be by nature, some by art, and others spontaneously. Everything that comes to be does so by something and from something and becomes something. And the something I say it comes to be I mean according to every category. For it may come to be either a certain "this" or of some size or of some quality or somewhere" (1032a12–15). Every becoming or change occurs within a certain category. Under this respect we can distinguish four kinds of change: something can change the form that makes it what it is (coming to be and passing away); a particular thing can change its size (growth and decay); it can change its condition (change in quality); it can change its place (locomotion) (see *Phys.* III, 1). The questions by what and from what something comes to be lead to the principles of becoming.

161. The question "From what does something come to be?" is ambiguous (VII, 7 1033a5–23). Consider the following examples:

(1) A ball comes to be from a stone.
(2) The sick (person) becomes healthy.
(3) This ball is of stone.
(4) A human being becomes healthy.

Aristotle calls the original position of change described in (1) and (2) "privation" (sterēsis, or literally "robbed"). It consists in something not having a perfection or determination that it could (as in [1]) or should (as in [2]) have (see *Met.* V, 22). Conversely, (3) and (4) speak of the matter in which the change takes place. The proper answer to the question "From what does this come to be?" is the privation. The reason for this is that we cannot say of the sick person that he is healthy, whereas this is possible for human beings. "Human being" does not stand in opposition to "healthy human being"; to this extent it cannot, as opposed to "sick human being," serve as the starting point of change. Human beings are beings that can be healthy and sick, and only insofar as they can be subject to both of these can they be the matter of the change in question. As Aristotle proceeded in VII, 3 from predication to the concept of matter (hylē) (par. 157), in VII, 7 he introduces the concept of matter as one of the principles of change. "All changing things are capable of both being and of not being, and this capacity is the matter in each" (1032a20–22). Matter is the principle of an individual thing due to which it can be and not be. "Being" here is to be understood as being per se in all categories. The matter explains why an individual thing can gain or lose a determination. "Matter" is used in various senses. It is distinguished correspondingly to the categories. The matter for being healthy and being sick is the human being or the living organism, the matter for locomotion is a body of any given shape, the matter for a bed is wood, and that for a statue is bronze. Analogously we must assume a matter that explains that natural things (animals, plants, the four elements fire, water, air, and earth) can receive and lost their essential determinations, that is, come to be and perish (*Phys.* I, 191a7; 192a31; *Met.* VIII, 1042a27). This matter is traditionally called "prime matter" (materia prima).

162. The principles through which the individual comes to be are nature and art. "Nature" (physis; *Phys.* II, 1; *Met.* V, 4) means in one sense matter. More important in our context is that it can also signify the eidos or form insofar as it is the cause of change. The nature is the particular organism's (and element's) own cause for changing or staying the same. It causes growth and decay, change of quality and locomotion. The phrase often used by Aristotle "man begets man" says that the eidos as nature is also the cause of coming to be. The eidos of reproductive living organisms brings forth the reproduced eidos. A corresponding causality is present in the eidos in the other kind of production, namely, art, or man-made products. Just as man begets man,

health arises from health or a house from the eidos of house. The cause here is the form in the mind of the producer. It is the definition and the (applied) science. Aristotle illustrates this with the example of health. A scientific definition cannot simply state what we understand by the word 'health', but rather it must also provide the cause of health (*Anal. post.* II, 10). It is the homogeneous condition of the homoiomeries (par. 136). This procedure is to be continued. We must inquire into the definition of the homogeneous condition in order to find its cause and so on. This analysis is continued until we come to something that can be produced here and now. The process of knowledge has thus reached its conclusion, and the process of production (poiēsis) can set in.

163. Eidos, as we saw, has priority in two respects. It is the efficient cause for the coming to be of an individual thing, and it has an existential priority over the matter which as such has no reality at all insofar as it is indifferent between being and not-being. A third priority (VII, 8 1032a24–b19; 9 1034b7–19) consists in the eidos' mode of being being different than that of the individual thing. The latter is subject to coming to be and passing away, whereas the eidos does not come to be or pass away. The producer bestows a form to matter, for example, the shape of a ball to the bronze or the form of health to the human being. But the producer cannot produce either the form or the matter. That health depends upon the homogeneous condition of the homoiomeries cannot be produced by the doctor but rather must be discovered. With the help of a regress argument Aristotle shows that the immutability of the eidos is valid for every kind of change, for natural as well as artificial production, and this in all of the categories. If the eidos were to come to be, it would presuppose a matter and a form and so on ad infinitum.

A natural objection would be that the claim of the immutability of the eidos relies upon an outdated conception of natural science, the constancy of species that is proved false through the theory of evolution. If, however, one accepts the Aristotelian analysis of change, the regress argument is valid. The Aristotelian conceptual framework is suited to describe evolution. For even in evolution I must be able to state a starting point and the point reached so far. X was an ape and is now a human being. This description presupposes that there is a difference between being an ape and being a human being. It is not the case that being an ape became being a human being, but rather that from the class of apes came the class of human beings. It is not the qualities of the classes that changed but rather the members of the classes—whose identity must be fixed according to other criteria, for example, genealogical connection—acquire a different determination.

164. Until now it has been shown that the eidos is the cause for the coming to be of a perceivable individual substance. VII, 17 shows that, and in what manner it is the cause of its being. The chapter intends to prepare the way for an imperceptible, immaterial substance. This occurs when Aristotle argues for the immateriality of the eidos. It remains open, however, whether the eidos, immaterial per se, can exist without matter.

165. The starting point of the investigation is that eidos is a principle and a cause. When do we ask for a cause? (For the following see *Anal. post.* II, 1; 8; 10.) It is to explain a fact, for example, that it is thundering or that the moon is eclipsed. A fact has a predicative structure: something is ascribed to something else. In order for the question for an explanation to be intelligible, the terms must be distinct from each other. Tautologies need no explanation: for example, the question why human beings are human beings is nonsense. The question for a cause or explanation must thus read: Why does the one thing pertain to the other, different thing? The fact to be explained must itself be undisputed, for example, that the moon is eclipsed; only under this assumption can one sensibly ask for an explanation. An explanation proceeds such that we refer to a third thing that

connects the two determinations. Why, for example, is there noise in the clouds? Due to the putting out of the fire. In VII, 17 Aristotle is concerned with examples that do not appear to have this kind of structure. One example is the sentence 'A human being exists' that we would interpret today as an existential sentence. It is apparent that we are not predicating something, since there is no predicate term in the sentence. The questions "Why does a human being exist?" "Why does a house exist?" thus appear to be nonsense. Aristotle views these sentences as obscure. In a precise and clear formulation they read: "Why is this a house?" "Why is this a human being?" In this formulation it becomes clear that they too have a predicative structure, even if they differ from the above examples. This structure asks for the cause of the matter being something determinate. The concern is the cause of being, not of coming to be. Thus we cannot answer by referring to an architect. The cause for this being a house is rather being-a-house. But isn't that a tautological, uninformative explanation?

166. In order to clarify this explanation Aristotle proceeds from two possibilities of how several components or elements can be combined with each other. The entirety of the components can form a pile, but they can also be a whole, a unity, as, for example, a syllable or meat. The syllable *ba* consists of the letters *b* and *a,* but the two letters alone do not constitute a syllable; the sole material components of meat are fire and earth, but fire and earth alone do not constitute meat. Thus the whole is not the same as the sum of the parts. When the whole is dissolved, the sum of the parts remains. Both letters or the fire and earth still exist, but the syllable or meat do not exist any more. Therefore, the letters or elements do not suffice to explain the syllable or meat. For this we need something else that is the cause of the determinate order. What can we say about it? It cannot itself be an element, but rather it is to be distinguished ontologically from the elements. A reductionist theory could assume that it is itself an element or consists in elements, but if it

were an element, an infinite regress would result. That it is an element means that it remains after the destruction of the whole. Thus we have only added the sum of elements by one member without having explained the whole. If it were constructed from elements, the same problem we encountered with the meat and the syllable would recur. Thus a materialist, reductionist explanation of this other thing that causes the order is not possible. What can be said positively about it is that it is the first cause of the thing's being and unity (VIII, 6 1045a8–11). It is the first or ultimate cause for this thing (the letters; the fire and earth; the stones), which as such is a chaotic pile, to be a syllable, meat, or a house. It is that through which what is is what it is, whereas the elements are only that from or out of which it is.

5. POTENCY (POTENTIALITY) AND ACTUALITY

167. In several passages Aristotle equates form with reality (energeia) (*Met.* VIII, 2 1042b10; 1043a6.20.28; 3 1043a30–33). We want to follow up this connection and ask how the concept of form is further developed by this connection and how the investigation of the principles of being qua being is furthered in the process. First consider the method with which Aristotle acquires the concepts "potency" (dynamis) and "actuality." The words 'potency' and 'actuality' cannot be defined. We must learn what they mean through examples by seeing the common thread in them. The concepts must illuminate each other. "Actuality consists in the existence of a thing not in the way we express by 'potentially'" (IX, 6 1048a30–32). Examples are: a waking to a sleeping person, a seeing person to one who can see, but whose eyes are closed; the architect who is building a house to one who can but is not practicing the art; the figure that is carved out of the block of wood to the uncarved block of wood. The examples illustrate a proportion. The first member stands in the same proportion to the second as an

actual being stands to a potentially existing being. This relation is not, however, univocal, but rather analogous. The examples reveal two different forms: 1. the relation between capacity and activity. Such capacities are vision and architecture; the corresponding activities are seeing and building. 2. The relation of matter and form. It is illustrated by the example of the statue carved out of the block of wood.

168. These two relations are explained more fully with the help of *De anima* II, 1, where Aristotle develops a definition of the soul with their help. The decisive contribution that this chapter makes toward the question about the form consists in it showing that the form is the capacity for an activity. The soul is the form of a living organism, and it is compared with the functional capacity of an ax and the eye's capacity for sight. Aristotle distinguishes between the composite ousia (an animal), the form (the soul), and the matter (the body). The eidos is equated with actuality (entelecheia). More precisely, the eidos is the first actuality which is distinguished from the second actuality. The first actuality of the eye is the faculty of sight, whereas the second actuality is the exercised activity of seeing. Like the eye, the whole organism exercises an activity: life. Life is defined as "nutrition, growth, and decay by itself" (412a14). The eidos or the first actuality is thus the capacity of a plant or an animal to exercise its activities in life, which are its second actuality. That the eidos is a faculty of exercise illustrates again its ontological priority with respect to matter. One of the examples in which *De anima* elucidates the concept of the soul or the eidos is that of the ax. The eidos of the ax is being-an-ax, that is, its capacity of splitting wood. It determines the matter from which the ax is made. This primacy is also evident in the definition of the soul as "eidos" or "first actuality of a natural body that can have life" (412a20.27). It is difficult to comprehend what Aristotle means by "body" in this definition. Is not the characterization that he provides for it accurate for the whole, the animal, as well? The difficulty becomes more acute when Aristotle writes: "not that

which has lost the soul it once had is 'potentially capable of life', but rather only what still retains it" (412b25). Matter and form are, not principles of becoming here, but rather principles of being. The body is matter combined into a functional unity by the form. The body is determined by the eidos as the matter, and shape of the ax by its capacity to function. The difference between body and animal becomes clear when we take into consideration the difference between capacity and possibility. An animal *has* the capacity for its activities in life; it is characteristic for the body that it can have the capacity potentially, that is, that it *can have* the capacity. But since the body is an animal's principle of *being,* this possibility is realized. Insofar as it is realized, the body is not distinguished from the whole. Nonetheless, the body is the principle of the whole and as such distinct from the whole, because the whole can lose the form and thus perish. Body as the material principle has potentially the capacity for its life acts in the sense that it is indifferent as to whether or not it has the capacity.

169. The investigation of the books on substance concludes with the claim made in IX, 8 that actuality has a three-fold priority over potentiality.

a) In definition and in knowledge. The definition of a certain capacity or a certain potentiality presupposes the definition of the corresponding activity or actuality. Whoever does not know what "to see" means cannot understand either the word 'faculty of sight' nor the word 'visible'. That something can see or is visible can only be known if it actually sees or is actually seen.

b) In time. If we observe a particular individual or a single activity, a potential being is earlier than what exists in actuality. However, if we observe the species, the order is reversed. For the birth of an individual organism the sperm, a potential being, is temporally earlier than the fully developed individual. But the sperm can only be created by a fully developed individual of the same species, for "man begets man." Whoever desires to play a piano sonata must be able to play the piano; the faculty is temporally prior to the exercise of it. However, this capacity is only obtained through practice and the help of someone that can play. In this sense the activity is temporally earlier than the faculty.

c) In ousia. The word 'ousia' is a substantiation of the Greek infinitive for "being" (einai), and it must be understood in its original meaning here. What is earlier with respect to ousia *is* in a more proper sense, and this primacy is revealed by its causality. What is in a distinguished sense and is a cause can only be conceived of as actuality. Aristotle raises two considerations in support of this claim. The first shows that being in the sense of actuality is the goal of all being. The second makes clear that the imperishable and necessary can only be conceived as actuality.

170. We encounter in IX, 6 (par. 167) the relationship between potentiality and actuality in two forms, as the relationship between a faculty and its exercise and as the relationship between form and matter. From *De anima* II, 1 (par. 168) a unity of these two relationships becomes clear: the eidos too is a faculty. Now the relationship between faculty and exercise is determined more precisely. The exercise of a faculty is the goal of the faculty. The faculty is for the sake of its exercise, and in this sense the exercise is the cause of the faculty. The concept of the goal or end is taken from the life-world of human beings, and the claim is justified by reference to life-world phenomena. What is problematic is how its application to nonhuman nature can be justified. We have the faculty of sight in order to see and not vice versa. We acquire a capacity in order to exercise it, but the mere possession of this capacity is not a desirable goal. In a further step Aristotle distinguishes two kinds of activity or actuality (see VI, 6 1048b18; *EN* X, 3). Examples are building and seeing. Building is directed toward a goal distinct from itself, the house. If it is accomplished, the process of building is complete. The actualization of the goal is also the temporal end of the process. Thus it has its goal outside itself. In this sense it is incomplete per se. The activity of building takes place in a substrate distinct from the (activity

of) building. It is not the builder who has changed (except accidentally), but rather the building material. The activity has a product that is distinct from itself and the builder. The builder causes a change, not a being. Its activity has an actuality distinct from it as its goal (par. 168): the eidos of the house actualized in the material. Aristotle calls this kind of activity movement or change (kinēsis; see par. 160). The other kind of activity of which seeing is an example has no goal distinct from itself. It does not bring about something different than itself but is rather a life activity of the agent itself. Its goal is also not its (temporal) end. Rather it contains its goal in itself every moment, for it has nothing other than itself for its goal. In contrast to building we cannot distinguish any phases in seeing, but rather the act of seeing (in contrast to viewing) is given as a whole in every moment. Since seeing has neither phases nor a goal distinct from itself, it cannot occur slowly or quickly. In this sense it is atemporal or timeless. Aristotle calls this kind of activity activity in the narrow sense (energeia).

171. The exercise of a faculty is ontologically prior to its goal. The distinction between movement and activity in the narrow sense has resulted in a further ontological priority. Movement is incomplete, whereas activity in the narrow sense is complete. But this activity is, to the extent we know so far, the second actuality (par. 168) of a substance that comes to be and passes away. As such it cannot be without substance. Thus we are confronted with the following aporia: activity, as the goal of a faculty, is being in the proper sense, whereas as second actuality it is dependent upon substance and thus cannot claim absolute priority. How is this difficulty to be resolved?

6. THE UNMOVED MOVER

172. Aristotle begins a new line of thought (IX, 8 1050b6). Actuality is ontologically prior to potentiality in an even more proper sense than was shown so far. The eternal is ontologi-

cally prior to the perishable. But nothing that has potentiality is eternal. That something exists potentially means
that it is indifferent to being and not-being. This is also true
for realized potentialities. What can also not be is perishable. We must distinguish between perishability and change.
A being is perishable if it is potentially, that is, it can either
have or not have its essential form. According to this consideration the eternal is also the necessary. As such it is the
ontological first or primary being, for if there were no necessary being, there would be nothing (1050b19). A proof for
the last sentence is only quickly mentioned: "In time one
actuality always precedes another back to the original prime
mover" (1050b4). A regress argument is at issue. Organisms
come to be and perish. Every organism is brought forth by
another one that is in turn brought forth. This series cannot
go on to infinity. We must arrive at a cause that is not itself
caused and cannot perish. It cannot be potentially, that is,
it cannot be composed of matter and form.

173. This "original prime mover" is treated in more detail in the early book Lambda (XII). Aristotle presumes (XII,
6) that the other categories only exist due to the first one
(see par. 155). The perceivable substances surrounding us
are, however, perishable. If they were the only substances,
all being would be perishable. But that is unacceptable for—
the proof assumes that—movement and time cannot come
to be nor perish. The two stand in a close relationship to
each other; as XII, 6 intimates, they are either the same, or
time is a property of movement (see *Phys.* IV, 10–14; VII,
1–3). The only continuous movement is locomotion and
more specifically circular motion. It alone can occur without beginning or end. But motion is a mode of being of substance. Thus an eternal motion is only possible if there is
an imperishable substance. This is the first heaven, or the
sphere of fixed stars. It moves all else but is itself moved.
The first mover must be such that it guarantees the eternal
continuous motion of the sphere of fixed stars. For this reason it cannot be composed of matter and form, for if it were,
it would be perishable. It also cannot be conceived as a be-

ing that has the capacity for an activity, because then it could also be inactive. Therefore, the first mover must be pure activity. Since it excludes as such any potentiality, it is necessary and immutable. This necessity is its highest freedom, for since it cannot change or be changed, nothing can happen to it that could influence it in its own act of life (see XII, 7 1072b4–13).

174. But how can something that is not moving move something else? Aristotle refers to striving/desire and knowledge. The object of desire or knowledge moves without itself being moved. The unmoved mover as the most perfect being is also the most perfect good. "It moves as being loved" (XII, 7 1072b3). But isn't it just an unacceptable anthropomorphism to describe cosmic processes with the help of psychic categories? In *De anima* II, 4 Aristotle speaks of the reproductive capacities of living things. The most natural achievement of a living thing is to bring forth a being of the same species, "an animal another animal, a plant another plant, so that they can participate in the eternal and the divine insofar as possible. For everything *strives* for the latter, and all living things do what is in accord with their natures for the latter's sake" (415a28). The living cannot, however, participate in the eternal and divine in such a manner that it possesses eternal existence as the divine does, for no perishable being can subsist eternally as numerically the same. For this reason it participates in the eternity of the divine in the manner possible for it. Since the individual cannot be imperishable, it strives to preserve its species eternally. The unmoved mover moves as a pure actuality that is imperishable as such. Plants and animals strive for its mode of being by developing and securing the eternal duration of their species through their lives' activities. That the unmoved mover moves as being loved is to be interpreted with an analogous concept of striving. All living things strive when developing and preserving themselves. According to its level of life a being is either aware of this striving only as a desire or not at all. Its potentiality is fulfilled only in actuality, and in this sense it "strives" for actuality.

175. The god of Aristotelian metaphysics is a self-think-
ing thought (noēsis noēseōs; XII, 9 1074b34; see XII, 7
1072b14–29). Let's try to penetrate at least somewhat into
this statement with the help of *De anima* III. The following
considerations circle around the relationship between the
form and mind (nous). "The soul," so it is called in the beginning of *De anima* III, 8, "is in a sense all existing things.
For an existing thing is either perceivable or intelligible;
knowledge is in some sense the knowable, and perception
the perceivable" (431b21). Two comparisons explicate these
sentences: "Thus the soul is like the hand; for as the hand
is the tool of tools the mind is the form of forms" (432a1).
De anima III, 5 compares the active mind (intellectus agens)
with light, "for in a sense light turns colors that are only
potentially into real colors" (430a16). Both comparisons work
with the conceptual pair of potentiality and actuality. Only
a hand can use a tool and thus turn it into its proper actuality. Only through light can colors become true colors. Correspondingly, only the mind can bring the eidos into its own,
full actuality. Being is not to be understood as reality. Rather
being is actuality, and "actuality" comes from "acting" and
"being-at-work." The full actuality of a tool is being-at-work.
The being of organisms is their lives' acts. "Life is being for
the living" (*De anima* II, 4 415b13). Only by achieving its
life's acts does a living being obtain its unity. Nonetheless,
a being's causality (or "action") does not find its ultimate goal
in its preservation. The word 'eidos' alludes to the fact that
for Aristotle as for Plato the concept of being is conceived
in analogy with seeing. Being preserves itself in order to dis-
close itself. The eidos is the visible. The visible as visible
is not, however, being in the proper sense. Visibility is the
potentiality of being seen, and it is only realized by actually
being seen, that is, by the eidos being known.

176. Just as the tool relies upon the hand, the hand relies
upon the tool. The hand can only develop all of its potentialities through the use of tools. Not only does the visible
turn into the seen through sight, but it is also true that
the faculty of sight only becomes an actually seeing things

through the visible. Correspondingly, the mind relies upon the forms for its realization. "Thought thinks itself because it shares the nature of the object of thought. For the mind becomes an object of thought by touching and thinking the objects of thought, so that the mind and the object of thought are the same. For that which is capable of receiving the object of thought and the ousia is the mind. But it is active when it possesses this object" (XII, 7 1072b19–22). The actuality of the mind is none other than that of the form thought by it. "For the forms without matter the mind and the thoughts are the same" (*De anima* III, 4 430a3). The mind is only at home when it is with its objects. Idealism and realism are not exclusive but rather necessarily complementary positions for Aristotle. For only as conceived is reality actual, and only in its reference to reality can thought be active.

177. In the attempt to think the unmoved mover human reason arrives at its limits (see XII, 9). The unity of mind and object of thought in the unmoved mover must be distinguished from the analogous unity in the human process of knowledge. In the latter case the unity is the activity of the mind that can know and of the eidos that can be known. Conversely, the unmoved mover is not a realized potentiality but rather pure actuality. The unity of thinking and thought in it does not depend upon a realization, but rather it is the original actuality simpliciter. Human knowing is always related to a variety of forms, and this is expressly excluded for the unmoved mover. How is what is thought by the unmoved mover related to the plurality of forms in this world? No answer can be found in Aristotle, but Plotinus (par. 272) will pick up on this question.

7. ON THE IMPORTANCE OF ARISTOTELIAN METAPHYSICS

178. The task of an ontology as Aristotle saw it is to develop a framework language that encompasses the various

languages that we use in the different realms of life, for example, in our everyday world, in religion, art and production, and in the various theoretical sciences. The various languages work with the means of assertive propositions in which we use the word 'is', whose manifold meanings are pursued by the *Metaphysics*. As the most comprehensive framework of languages, ontology cannot be judged from a yet higher framework but rather only according to pragmatic criteria. One such criterion is, for example, whether an ontology is capable of creating an overview, that is, of clarifying the connection between different realms of life while at the same time being able to differentiate within this unity, that is, make evident the characteristic elements of each realm. With his teaching of manifold meanings and the relational unity Aristotle does justice to this criterion. We have given a cursory look at the concepts "potentiality," "actuality," "capacity," and "activity." They stand up within the Aristotelian project, for example, with respect to the mind-body problem, philosophy of mind, action theory, and philosophy of nature. As a comprehensive language, ontology claims that its concepts can function as the fundamental concepts in the individual sciences. The language of ontology strives to connect the everyday world with that of the sciences. A further criterion results from this: an ontology must stand up under the problems of the particular sciences and prove to be superior to competing hypotheses. For this to occur, it must be developed through discussion with the particular sciences. Aristotle himself met this demand to a high degree. One could show that, for example, through an interpretation of the *Physics,* of the biological works, or of *De anima.* The critical question, however, is to what extent the Aristotelian ontology is tied to outdated conceptions in natural science. One would have to investigate which of its fundamental concepts can still be used today for the interpretation of scientific results and whether it is superior to other ontologies due to its coherence, its capacity to integrate new things, and its capacity to differentiate. In a discussion with the natural sciences, psychology, anthropology and so on, what is tied to his time would have to be distinguished from what is still valid today.

179. The achievement of the *Metaphysics* for the further history of theology is to be seen in Aristotle conceiving the concept of god with the help of his concept of being. The Aristotelian teaching of god is onto-theology: the inquiry into the meaning of the word 'being' leads to the concept of god. The god of Book Lambda is the necessary being (ens necessarium), the most perfect being (ens perfectissimum), and the uncaused being (ens a se). The relational unity further developed in the scholastic theory of analogy and the distinction between movement and activity enable one to conceive of god as distinct from the world and at the same time the world as dependent upon god. Through the concept of mind thinking itself Aristotle opens a path to god from the metaphysics of knowledge and the theory of mysticism. Aristotle's theologic is meta-physics: conclusion of the physics, that is, the teaching of change (*Met.* XII; *Phys.* VIII). In this lies its importance, because it attempts to find a path to god independent of religious and moral presuppositions. In the form in which Aristotle developed it, the proof rests, however, on assumptions that stem from his philosophy of nature and the current worldview. Whoever wants to use the ontological concepts of the *Metaphysics* for a proof of the existence of god must show that they can be used independently of these presuppositions.

III. The Science of the Good Life

180. In the beginning of *EE* Aristotle quotes an inscription at Delphi: "What is most beautiful is what is most just, but the best is health. What is most pleasurable is to retain what one loves" (I, 1 1214a5). The epigram separates the morally good from the useful and pleasurable. Aristotle objects that there is a good that is the most moral, the most pleasurable, and the most useful, all in one. This criticism can be seen as characteristic for his whole ethics. It thematizes the components of happiness and inquires into their interrelations. The complete good can only be conceived as a whole. It encompasses morality and well-being. It corresponds to reason and inclination. In order to know it, the proper considerations and relevant feelings are required. The good life connects theory and practice/experience. It cannot be realized in the individual without society, so that the contrast between egoism and altruism proves to be temporary.

1. THE TASK, PRESUPPOSITIONS, AND LIMITS OF ETHICS

181. In *Met.* VI, 1 1025b19 Aristotle sketches a taxonomy of the faculty of reason and the sciences that correspond to it. He distinguishes between the theoretical, the practical, and the productive sciences. They differ not only in their realm of application but also in their goal. The goal of the

162

theoretical sciences is knowledge, that of the practical sciences is correct decisions, whereas for the productive sciences the goal is the respective product. Ethics and politics are concerned with human actions not for the sake of knowledge but rather for the sake of the good life. In contrast to, for example, a lecture on mathematics, a lecture on ethics places special demands on the life of a member of the audience. Knowledge of the correct action presupposes moral experience. The audience must know from prior experience what is morally right; only then can the question about the reasons be posed. Finally, ethics is distinguished from the theoretical sciences by its degree of exactness. The ethicist would be ill advised if she took mathematics as her paradigm. Rather the method and exactness must correspond to the various topics. Moral decisions are not conclusions that follow necessarily from necessary premises. Ethics can merely provide a broad outline of morally correct action; its principles tell, not what must always be right, but rather only what is right most of the time.

182. If one reads these remarks on method from the *EN* (I, 1 1094b11; I, 2 1095a30; I, 7; II 2 1103b34; X, 10 1178a33), one might doubt whether it is reasonable to do ethics in the first place. How does this science help if we must already know beforehand what is right and if it does not help us make particular decisions, which is what is important ultimately. This objection makes clear that practical science is to be distinguished from practical judgment (phronēsis) and can never replace it. That we need ethics despite the revealed presuppositions and limits can be shown through the comparison with medicine that Aristotle uses so often (II, 2 1049a9; X, 10 1180b7; 1181b2). Doctors too are always concerned with specific cases. Nonetheless, medicine is a science that works with general laws (*Met.* I, 1 981a5) and cannot abandon them even if knowledge of it does not enable its application. Although the doctor's personal experience is indispensable, she must rely on learning from others, for not everyone can discover all laws anew. Life in a

community requires general norms; ethics strives to help the politician in legislation. The various differences of opinion suggest that morality is merely conventional, on the basis of which the question as to truth and falsity is nonsense (*EN* I, 1 1094b14). Ethics shows that a rational discussion that leads to several fundamental results is possible. The sophists, Plato (*Meno* 70a), and Aristotle (*EN* I, 1; II, 1; X, 10) disagreed as to whether virtue is innate, whether it can be taught, or whether it can only be acquired by habit and practice. The importance of the problem for one's own actions and for political and social institutions is obvious. If virtue is innate, it is nonsense to try to become good (*EE* I, 3 1215a8). Whether and how education (and punishment) is possible depends on this answer.

2. THE QUESTION ABOUT HAPPINESS

183. Aristotle acquires the leading question of his ethics from an elementary life-world phenomenon. Human beings are after a goal in their various pursuits and activities. That is true for the various crafts, applied sciences, and arts; they have a product as their goal. It is just as true for our decisions; they are determined by our lives' plans. Practical rationality as it is revealed in this manner cannot, however, stay with ends that are in turn only desired as means for something else. That is excluded because only an end as such can motivate us to produce means or to decide. For this reason Aristotle develops an initially purely formal concept of the ultimate end (*EN* I, 5). It is the one end that can never be for the sake of another, is always desired for its own sake, and encompasses everything that we could desire for its sake, so that nothing in our lives is lacking if we attain this end. This concept would appear to be a mere construct; it is an idealization of the concept of an end that we use in our everyday technical/practical activities. Is it a meaningful concept? Is the action-theoretical consideration that leads to it

cogent? Or can we object that the various ends are given by our needs and by purely factual decisions that cannot be questioned, so that a final, comprehensive end is unnecessary? Aristotle replies that his concept of the ultimate end only clarifies an idea that is actually found in the lives of human beings. They have a word for it with which they all conceive a general content. Human beings strive for *happiness,* and they mean by it the good life (*EN* I, 2 1095a17). Moreover, there is a science whose task is to coordinate the various human activities such that they serve the common good life, politics.

184. Differences of opinion among people begin with the question in what precisely does happiness consist. Clarification of this question is of great importance not only for the life of the individual but also for that of the polis and its constitution (*EN* I, 1 1094a22; *Pol.* VII, 1 1323a14). Aristotle's own reply reads: happiness is the activity which the soul exercises in its best condition. What this means and how Aristotle arrives at it will be our concern in the next section. Here we shall only be looking at method. Aristotle provides, according to his own testimony (*EN* I, 8 1098b9), a deductive proof. He supplements it by delving into human opinions. *EN* I, 3 discusses briefly the widespread forms of life that express conceptions of happiness: Should one choose pleasure or honor or riches or science as the content of one's life? *EN* I, 9 asks the tradition, the large majority of human beings and famous people, what they view the essential component of happiness to be. Aristotle attempts to show that his deductively developed concept of happiness includes all the discovered elements. This method and its presuppositions are formulated in the *EE* as follows: "For every human being has a contribution to the truth. One must begin with this and somehow show how the matter stands. For from the opinions that are true but unclear, clarity will result in the course of the investigation when one exchanges the usual confused way of speaking with the more insightful way" (1216b30).

3. THE FUNCTION OF HUMAN BEINGS

185. Happiness is, according to general consensus, a way of life. In his "deductive proof" (EN I, 6) Aristotle defines it more precisely with the help of the concept of function (ergon). The goal or good of an artist as such is her product, as, for example, for a sculptor, or his activity, as, for example, for a pianist. In the same way the organs, such as the eye, have a function. The function of human beings as such is to be determined by their place within the hierarchical order of nature. The faculty of reason distinguishes human beings from plants and animals. The goal or end of a faculty is its activity (par. 170). What has a faculty can, as the example of the eye illustrates, be in a good or bad condition. The end or good of human beings lies in the activity that the rational soul of human beings exercises due to its highest capabilities and in its best condition.

186. The argument reveals an essential characteristic of Aristotelian ethics. Happiness consists, not in having or receiving, but rather in being active. Only mental capacities enable human beings to flourish; an animal and a child cannot be happy (*EN* I, 10 1099b32). Happiness requires effort. It is a function that human beings must exercise. The higher the exercised capabilities are the more intensive the experience of happiness will be. The train of thought leads from the concept of happiness to that of virtue, which will be the most important topic up to and including *EN* VI. 'Virtue' is an insufficient translation of the Greek word 'arete' (aretē), whose use is not limited to the moral realm. A tool, an artisan, or an organ can have arete as much as a human being can. The concept is related to that of capacity (par. 168). What has a capacity can, with respect to this capacity, be in a good or bad condition or state. It will exercise its function perfectly or imperfectly accordingly (Plato, *Rep.* 352d; *EN* II, 5 1106a14). Aristotle calls this good or bad condition (hexis) excellence, as one can render 'arete' literally

in its general meaning, or inferiority (kakia) respectively (*Met.* V, 20 1022b10).

187. This proof also provides myriad points for attack. It executes a change in perspective. Until now the concept of happiness was developed from the agent's point of view, whereas now Aristotle is observing human beings from the outside, as that of a natural being. The teleological viewpoint is transferred to human beings as such from the realm of technical ability. Morality is described in the language of technology, biology, and ontology.

Such objections and similar ones run the risk of missing the point of the line of thought in *EN* I, 6. It is without a doubt central insofar as it introduces the concept of arete. Nevertheless, what is at issue is only a first, very rough sketch (*EN* I, 7 1098a20), whose argumentative import should not be overemphasized. The concepts are merely explicated with the help of analogies; they require specification and differentiation. The rough outline must prove itself with respect to the current conceptions of happiness. Similar to the beginning of *EE* (par. 180) Aristotle defends against an isolation of the moral realm. If happiness is a way of living, he is justified in asking how this act of living is to be distinguished from others and how it is to be described ontologically. The accusation of naturalism (see GK 4, par. 55) that underlies these objections loses its very object as soon as one looks more closely at the concept of reason or language (logos). In *Pol.* I, 2 1253a9 the difference between animals and humans is as follows: "Man is the only animal that possesses language. Whereas mere voice only indicates pleasure and pain and is therefore found in other animals, . . . the power of speech is intended to clearly enunciate the expedient and inexpedient and thus the just and unjust. For it is characteristic of man, as opposed to animals, that he alone is capable of ideas of the good and bad, the just and unjust."

188. The relation between morality and happiness is one of the much-discussed topics in ancient ethics. As the defini-

tion of happiness from *EN* I, 6 has been interpreted so far, it might seem that Aristotle identified happiness with the morally good life (par. 186). However, a difference between the two has already been revealed in our evaluating comments. We praise virtue, but we prize happiness (*EN* I, 12). In *EN* I, 6 Aristotle alludes to the difference with an addition: "But we must add: 'in a complete life'. For one swallow does not make a summer, nor does a day" (1098a18). Whether a person is happy depends in part on external goods and conditions that are not under that person's control. Length of life is mentioned as paradigmatic for this. Whoever dies young can be called happy as little as one who suffers a fate like Priam, the king of Troy. Constancy is essential for happiness.

If we grant Aristotle the difference between morality and happiness, can one claim that happiness is the ultimate end of our action if it is not in our power to attain it? Nonetheless, it must be admitted that in all we do we strive for happiness, and in this sense happiness is the final goal of action. Or is the content of the concept of happiness to be criticized? Is there a state of complete contentment that human beings can attain independently of external conditions? Aristotle replies with a distinction within happiness. If this contentment also requires supplementation by favorable external conditions, perfect activity is essential for happiness. If one finds support in it, one will survive blows of fate with honor and composure.

4. VIRTUE

189. Happiness is the activity of the human rational faculty in its best condition. The concept of happiness presupposes the concept of virtue, and in order to clarify and differentiate the latter we need basic knowledge of the human soul. The word 'soul' is not to be understood in the sense of a dualism that downplays the body. Body and soul are

one like a piece of wax and its shape (*De anima* II, 1 412b4).
The soul is the (first) actuality of the body without which
it would not be the body. It is the capacity of human beings
for their life acts (par. 168). If we want to characterize it more
precisely, we must start with human activities (see par. 169).
In this manner *De anima* distinguishes between the vegetative faculty, the faculty of perception, the faculty of thought,
the faculty of desire, and the capacity for movement (II, 3
414a29). An arete corresponds to each of these faculties. Since
ethics asks about happiness of which human beings alone
are capable, its anthropology must only go into the faculties
that distinguish human beings from other living organisms.
The vegetative and perceptive faculties are shared with animals and plants. The faculties of thought and desire remain.
(The capacity of moving one's own body as a mental faculty
is identical for Aristotle with the faculty of desire.) Like Plato
(par. 104) Aristotle develops his moral psychology (*EN* I,
13) with the phenomenon of conflict within the soul in mind.
The incontinent person knows what he is to do; his failure
to actually act according to his correct insight is due to his
conflicting desires and emotions. The continent person experiences the same conflict, but her drives and desires ultimately follow reason. Thus one must distinguish between
reason and striving, but the described phenomena show that
that is not to be understood as if the faculty of desire is irrational or without reason whatsoever. Granted, it is not capable of its own considerations and insight, but it can listen
to reason as a child does its father or one friend to another
friend's advice. Corresponding to the distinction between the
faculties of reason and desire, Aristotle distinguishes between
dianoetic (intellectual) and moral virtues.

a) Moral Virtue

190. The word 'ethical' (ēthikos) comes from 'ēthos', which
is best translated as 'character'. *EE* defines 'ēthos' as the constitution of the nonrational soul that is capable of following

the rational soul (II, 2 1220b5). What is more important philosophically is the etymological connection with 'ethos': 'habit', 'custom', 'mores'. Aristotle sees in it a pointer to the origin of moral virtue. It is not given to us by nature. Although we do have a natural capacity for it, what is all important is that we develop it with the correct habituation. On this point, ethics is best compared with art, which we can only acquire through practice. In order to become just and courageous, we must initially perform just and courageous actions. Moral virtue, according to Aristotle, can thus never be exclusively up to the autonomous individual. He emphasizes the great importance of education and thus of the ruling customs and laws (*EN* II, 1; X, 10 1179b20).

191. Objections already arise at this point. Doesn't this approach lead to an extremely conservative ethics? A human being acts as it was raised; changes and reforms are excluded; moral action is degraded to mere habit. Moreover, we are apparently succumbing to a circle: we are just when we perform just actions, but in order to perform just actions, we must already be just. Aristotle expressly replies to this last objection (*EN* II, 3). Again, the comparison with art is helpful. The apprentice imitates the techniques of the master and creates works under the latter's precise supervision. But the apprentice is only an artist when she has perfect command of the techniques independently of her master and has developed a style of her own. Within moral virtue we can distinguish between legal action ("performing just actions") and moral action ("acting justly"). Whether an action is legal can for the most part be judged with external criteria of behavior. For moral action, however, the agent's constitution is decisive. First, he must know that the action is morally good. Second, he must perform the action for its own sake, that is, he must choose the action because it is morally good. Third, it is not enough if he acts justly only occasionally; rather, acting morally must have become second nature to him. This also provides an answer to the other objections. Habit or custom is a preliminary condition; it has

its own moral insight as a goal. The virtuous person is autonomous in the sense that he has insight into the good and can be responsible for his decision. This theory, however, presupposes the polis as a morally relevant community. How does it stand for the moral insight and responsibility of those who are not raised morally? Would such people have the possibility of emancipating themselves from the conventions of their society and milieu?

192. Moral attitudes are to be derived from manners of behavior. What must these be like in order to form a good character? Here Aristotle develops his well-known theory of the mean. Virtue arises when we are raised to have emotional reactions in a mean or middle area. Virtue becomes active by always hitting the mean. It is the mean attitude between two extremes. Thus, for example, courage lies between cowardliness and daredevilry, generosity lies between prodigality and miserliness (*EN* II, 2; 5–9). Here, too, Aristotle refers immediately to art. When the doctor and the coach want to make an athlete well conditioned, they must prescribe nutrition and daily training in the correct doses. Any amount too much or too little would be harmful. The analogy shows that the mean cannot be calculated through a mathematical formula and be determined once and for all. Rather the individual constitution and the momentary bodily state are to be taken into consideration. Hitting the mean means no more than finding the right thing under the given circumstances. It is really an empty formula that Aristotle consciously uses in order to show that what ought to be done here and now cannot be deduced from principles.

193. The realm in which moral virtue has to meet the mean are the emotions. Common to them all is that they are accompanied by pleasure and displeasure/pain. Aristotle emphasizes the momentous influence that pleasure and pain have on our decisions. Before we ask whether an action is morally good or useful, we spontaneously know whether it is comfortable or uncomfortable. Pleasure and pain are the motives that keep us from doing what is right. They influ-

ence our practical judgment; we tend to believe that what is pleasurable is also good. For this reason ordering these sensations is all important in order to decide correctly. Moral virtue is the disposition or constitution of the faculty of desire that secures the correct decision by securing the correct emotional reaction (*EN* II, 6 1106b36). The word 'correct' in this definition shows that the concept of moral virtue presupposes that of moral knowledge which indicates what is correct in the situation. On the other hand, moral knowledge is not possible without moral virtue. Aristotle fosters the distinction between the moral virtues from the realm of pleasure and pain with respect to which it and the opposing extremes are referred. The emotions of fear and confidence are in the realm of courage; the sensations of pleasure conjoined with eating, drinking, and sexuality are referred to temperance; there are virtues whose object is the correct relation to anger, to honor, to wealth, and so on.

b) The Dianoetic Virtues

194. In the middle of Book VI of the *EN* stands 'phronesis'. Possible translations of this term are 'cleverness', 'moral knowledge', 'moral insight', 'practical judgment', and 'practical reason'. Only the context can show what the word means. For this reason I leave it untranslated. *EN* VI, 2 returns to the anthropology of *EN* I, 13. After the virtues of the striving faculty that can listen to the logos, now the issue at hand is the virtues of the soul that have the logos. For the word 'logos' we again encounter difficulties in translation. They rest upon *EN* VI, 2f dividing up the faculty that has logos into one part with which we observe necessary being and into another part with which we observe contingent being and allocating to this faculty five virtues. Thus, 'logos' is used with various meanings. Aristotle wants to point out the variety of phenomena of reason or knowledge. In order to isolate what is characteristic of practical reason, he places the faculty of logos' other activities next to prac-

tical reason. A further reason why *EN* VI is concerned with the entire faculty of logos is that the contemplation of necessary being belongs to happiness.

195. These two faculties of logos have a common function: truth. In order not to miss it, they require a corresponding good constitution. For the faculty with which we observe the necessary it is science (epistēmē), intuitive reason (nous), and wisdom (sophia). Science uses proofs. We know a state of affairs when we can derive it with the help of a syllogism from necessary, self-evident principles that cannot themselves be proved (see *Anal. post.* I, 2). Deductive proof presupposes inductive knowledge of principles. Such knowledge is the task of intuitive reason (*EN* VI, 6). It is characteristic for the Aristotelian concept of induction that intuitive reason is capable of grasping a state of affairs as necessary due to repeated observation. In *Met.* I, 1 and *Anal. post.* II, 19 Aristotle mentions the following stages of knowledge: We perceive a state of affairs and retain it in memory. A manifold of memories forms experience. Through a process of abstraction we gather from similar experiences general principles that intuitive reason knows as necessary.

The distinction between science and wisdom (*EN* VI, 7) is not very clear, for the demand that the wise man must not only draw the correct inferences but also not err with respect to principles is true for science as well as for wisdom. Yet this is not possible without intuitive reason. If Aristotle thus distinguishes intuitive reason from science, it is a formal, abstract mode of reflection that emphasizes the deductive character of science. Wisdom encompasses both. It is important for ethics that its subject matter be limited. Only knowledge of the highest and most perfect being, and especially of the sphere of fixed stars and the unmoved mover, is wisdom. It lets human beings know that they are not the best in the cosmos. In this manner it influences man's feeling for life. It reminds people of their transience and protects them from overestimating themselves. The practical-political science does not occupy first place since it is only concerned with the good of human beings. The happiness of human beings is not possible without a relation to the most perfect being, the divine.

196. The dianoetic virtues of art and phronesis are assigned to contingent being. ('Art' is the translation of 'technē'. It is to be understood as the substantiation of the verb 'can'; what is intended is production in the broadest sense (as in "artifacts" or "artificial").) This distinction presupposes that between producing and acting. Both are activities directed toward a goal. The manufacturer/producer always makes a determinate, clearly delineated product that represents one good among others, which can in turn be a means to a goal distinct from itself. Action has the good life as such and as a whole as its goal. The agent must have her whole life and other people in mind when making a decision. Production is subordinate to action. Whether I should exercise an art and produce something, whether and how I should use the products of art: that must be decided with respect to my idea of a good life as a whole, that is, as an agent.

197. That art and phronesis are concerned with the contingent requires some clarification through which the essence of these two virtues becomes more intelligible. Like Plato (par. 91) Aristotle distinguishes between knowledge, which is only of necessary propositions, and opinion, which has the contingent as its object (*EN* VI, 2 1139a6; VI, 3 1139b20; VI, 5 1140b25; VI, 13 1144b14). But when we are producing something or acting, the concern is apparently not (merely) our opinion. When we believe (or opine) something, we are claiming that something is the case. In producing or acting, the issue is not what is the case but rather what will be the case, and, more particularly, due to us. When we act and produce, we are not claiming anything but rather asking, that is, deliberating, how we can best attain our goal (*EN* VI, 10). An opinion is true or false; when we express it, its truth value is already determined (except for contingent propositions about future states of affairs: *De int.* 9). On the converse, deliberation is either right or false. What value

it has can only be definitively revealed afterward. Phronesis and art are thus only concerned with the partial set of future contingent states of affairs that are up to the producer or agent as to whether it will be the case or not (*EN* VI, 2 1139a31.b8; VI, 14 1140a13; *Met.* VI, 1 1025b22).

198. Consider now the following examples in order to differentiate the concept of deliberation. 1. A geometer has the task of constructing an equilateral triangle. The triangle on the paper is a contingent construction. Whether it comes to be or not depends on the geometer. He asks himself which operations he must carry out in what order. The answer is provided by the essence of the triangle through which the individual steps are necessarily already traced out. 2. A banker has the task of investing her customer's money as profitably and safely as possible. In contrast to the first example, there is no necessary and sufficient path to be discovered. There are various opportunities for investment. The banker must weigh safety and profit against one another. The possible opportunities for investment have various side effects. They can be a political or an economical nature; they can influence positively or negatively the company's relations, and so on. The banker can rely on rules and experience that promise a successful investment. But they will not provide absolute certainty, because unforeseeable events can always occur. The successful manager of a company to which she has given substantial credit can suffer an accident. Unforeseeable political events can change the overall economic situation drastically.

The two examples stand for two different kinds of questioning of how a goal can be attained. Aristotle only calls the second one deliberation (bouleusis) (*EN* III, 5). In it the contingent receives a greater import than in the first procedure. Not only is the attainment of the goal contingent, but also many or all of the rules whose following is supposed to realize the goal. They are successful most of the time, but not necessarily or always.

199. Phronesis is the virtue that enables human beings

to recognize the correct decision and action. The portrayal of the process of deliberation which is characteristic for it has shown that it is not purely a priori knowledge. Aristotle emphasizes that it presupposes experience and age (*EN* VI, 8 1141b15; 1142a11; VI, 12 1143b11). Still, it is bound to moral virtue and thus to moral practice. Practical deliberation presupposes a principle or a goal, and only the morally good person can recognize it (*EN* VI, 5 1140b11; VI, 13 1144a29; 1145a4). What idea a person has of the good life depends on his life-style and emotional constitution. The essence of avarice, for example, is the fixation on a certain experience of satisfaction. The function of phronesis is knowledge of the correct individual action here and now. According to the presentation in *EN* VI, 12 1143a35 it can only be prepared by discursive, practical deliberation based on experience. Practical knowledge arrives at its goal only in an act of insight. Like scientific knowledge, practical knowledge for Aristotle also relies upon intuitive reason. If it is intuitive reason's task in the former case to grasp necessary principles, in the present case intuitive reason's object is the particular. It sees which of the alternative actions is the right one under the given circumstances.

200. Aristotle explains action again and again with the help of production. This is especially clear in his description of decisions and deliberation in *EN* III, 4–7. The doctor, for example, has a certain goal, not questioned further by her as a doctor, namely, the health of her patient. Her deliberation and decision are related to the means through which it can be realized. Correspondingly, the agent is given a goal through her character; practical deliberation has the task of finding the right means. This model leads to the problem of responsibility for one's actions. How can an agent be responsible for his actions if they are conditioned by his character, which in turn depends on education and social conditions? First, one must ask whether Aristotle is not wrongly applying a distinction from production to acting with the concepts of "means" and "end." He repeatedly points out that in contrast to production, action has no end dis-

tinct from itself; we only act well morally when we are performing the action for its own sake (*EN* II, 3 1105a32; VI, 5 1140b4; VI, 13 1144a16). How is this aporia to be resolved? We must turn to the concept of happiness once more.

5. THEORETICAL AND PRACTICAL LIFE

201. The treatment of happiness at the end of *EN* (X, 7–9) returns to the criteria of happiness developed in the first book. Happiness consists in the most perfect activity of which human beings are capable. It must be characterized by its continuity; by the contentment that it bestows; by its independence from external conditions; by the fact that it is done exclusively for its own sake. Theoretical activity best fulfills these requirements. Aristotle underlines its theological character. It is the contemplation of the most perfect or divine being. Through it human beings activate a superhuman, divine faculty in themselves. The holy life of the gods can consist in nothing other than this theoretical activity. Whoever is dedicated to it will receive the care and attention of the gods.

Next to this perfection there stands a happiness of the second order, the practical life according to phronesis and the moral virtues. The distinction and evaluation of these two forms of life rely upon an anthropomorphic dualism. The mind (nous) which enables man to lead a theoretical life is not the form of the body as the rest of the soul is (par. 168), but is separate from it. Mind is the divine element in a human being and is the latter's proper, better self. On the contrary, human beings live practical lives insofar as they are body and soul united. What kind of relationship obtains between the two forms of life? Do they stand next to one another isolated so that humans can choose one of them? Or are they mere abstractions so that the theoretical and practical life are both always requisite for happiness, albeit in varying degrees?

First, consider the practical life. The moral virtues are

specifically human virtues because they are concerned with human beings as body and soul. They order the emotions, which are psychophysical phenomena (*De anima* I, 1 403a3). Human beings experience emotions prior to their decisions. They are sensations that refer prerationally to the goals of human beings: nutrition and reproduction; survival in danger; social acceptance; validating justified claims; attention that one gives or receives. The task of the moral virtues is to bring the emotions into harmony with each other and with practical reason. The happiness that they cause is the unity of the person on the level of the individual (*EN* IX, 4). The morally bad person lives in internal discord with himself. Because her sensations are in harmony with each other, the morally good person loves herself. She affirms her life and has an unabashed relation to her own past and future. The unity and constancy of her feelings enables her to make and carry out decisions.

202. Without a community of others a human being cannot be happy. This is true initially for reasons of mere utility. Human beings rely upon communal action with others for the preservation of life. Every community, and the polis is no exception, has utility as a goal (*EN* VIII, 11 1160a8). But even if one were to have all goods independent of others, one would never want to live life alone, "for human beings are determined by nature for the community of the polis and for social life" (*EN* IX, 9 1169b18). Without a successful communal life with others there can be no happiness. A community is held together through justice and friendship, neither of which is possible without moral virtue. In the beginning of *EN* V Aristotle distinguishes universal justice from justice as a special moral virtue that is concerned with the equality of nonmoral goods. Universal justice is identical in content with the entirety of all moral virtues. Every moral virtue also has a social aspect. Whoever lets irrational drives take over harms others as well. Virtue is only complete when it serves the human community. The temperate person, for example, respects the marriage of others; the courageous per-

son takes risks unto himself for the sake of the polis. When we view moral virtue in its social respect, we call it universal justice (*EN* V, 3).

With respect to friendship Aristotle distinguishes two imperfect forms and one perfect form (*EN* VIII, 3f). What is common to all is that friends desire good things for each other and do not hide this attitude from each other. They are distinguished by the motive of good will. This can be such that the other person either is useful to me or is enjoyable, likable, attractive, and entertaining, or that the other person is morally good. Only in the perfect friendship of morally good people is good will directed toward the other person for their own sake. It includes the goods of both imperfect forms of friendship. Due to the similarity in character a good person is agreeable to other good persons. At the same time the morally good person is always useful as well. Only the friendship between good people has constancy, for only one who is true to herself is capable of a lasting relationship. The friendship of good people as such includes universal and particular justice, but it is more than this. Aristotle especially emphasizes the importance of a shared life and affection (EN VIII, 6). When two friends are separated from one another, they have a benevolent attitude toward one another. But their friendship is only realized when they share daily life with each other. But that is only possible when they enjoy being with one another. Happiness as perfect activity is not possible without other human beings (*EN* IX, 9). Through a shared life and work with people similar to oneself life increases in constancy and intensity. Awareness is essential for life and activity. But without others a human being cannot come to a full awareness of himself and his worth.

203. Let's return to the question about the relationship between theoretical and practical life. In the sense in which we have considered life according to the moral virtues until now, it is indispensable for the theoretical life. The philosopher, who inquires into the first causes of reality, must be

at one with himself and be capable of living in his community. The relation of the two forms of life is probably held
to be the closest in the *EE*. The task of the moral virtues
is the correct use of nonmoral goods, and this is measured
by a goal. "The choice and acquisition of natural goods,
whether it be bodily or wealth or friends or other goods,
that best enables the contemplative behavior of the god is
the best, and this standard is the most beautiful" (VII, 3
1249b16; see *EN* VI, 3 1145a6). Can the practical life re-
n ounce the theoretical life completely? On the face of it, Aristotle seems to claim this. The most developed form of practical life is that of the politician, and he distinguishes this
life clearly from that of the philosopher. Granted, the concern here is only happiness of the second order. But if one
wanted to affirm the question, one would have to call a life
happy in which no room at all is given to a natural human
desire. The first two chapters of the *Metaphysics* show that
wisdom (par. 195) arises from a naturally given human desire that already influences the latter's perception characteristically. It is intelligible in itself, abstracting from its practical use. It reveals itself in the amazement that humans show
in light of the stars and the whole cosmos when they ask
about the causes of these things. Without a doubt very few
are capable of living the theoretical life in the sense that they
can devote themselves to wisdom as a fully developed science. But perhaps one can distinguish wisdom or metaphysics as a natural capacity from the theoretical science as a
developed science and interpret Aristotle such that these too
must be developed to some degree of awareness in the practical life if it is to be truly human.

Aristotle distinguishes between relaxation and leisure (EN
X, 6). Relaxation is not for its own sake; it serves to prepare
one for new efforts. Conversely, leisure is an end in itself.
Only in it are human beings free from the necessities of life
and there exclusively for their own sake (*Met.* I, 2 982b22).
Leisure presupposes virtue; human beings must be raised for
it; Aristotle calls philosophy the virtue required for leisure

(*Pol.* VII, 15 1334a23). Thus, whether the practical life can renounce the theoretical life completely turns into the question whether a life can be happy that is exhausted in the necessities of daily life and does not know the profound question about the ultimate cause of the whole.

204. In par. 200 it was asked whether Aristotle was not wrongly applying a distinction of production to that of action with the concepts "means" and "end." A first answer is provided by the distinction between How and What. The goal of action as such is not something that we want to attain, but rather what is is the manner in which we act. Human beings have many needs that must unavoidably be fulfilled. What is important are one's constitution and the manner in which these needs are done justice. Nonetheless, the goal does not consist exclusively in the How. Human beings are not mere slaves to the necessities of life, but rather are to experience their lives as free, that is, as independent of anything given. In this respect the How is a presupposition of the What. Aristotle mentions two goals in which human beings are truly themselves and which constitute the meaning of life. Although the inquiry into the ultimate causes of the cosmos arises from the essence of human beings, it is only the task of a few to follow it up in a scientific investigation. On the contrary, daily life that serves the necessities of life can be constantly filled with happiness that is bestowed by contact with good people. It is intelligible in itself, and without it life loses its meaning as well as all other goods their value (*EN* VIII, 1).

IV. The Peripatetics

205. "Peripatos" means literally "colonnade" or "covered walk." Because the halls of the public schools were used for teaching, the word received the meaning of "school of philosophy," and after 285 B.C. it was used as a proper name for Aristotle's school. The school in which Aristotle taught since 335 was named "Lyceum" after the temple of Apollo Lycius, on whose property the school was founded. The typical peripatetic tended to work in the areas of the particular sciences. The empirical element in Aristotle's philosophy dominates. The systematic integration of the various areas of knowledge which Aristotle had achieved especially with the *Metaphysics'* concepts is lost for the most part. "An incomparable openness on the horizon had to be bought here by a premature disintegration" (Wehrli, 1983, p. 464).

206. The most important figure is *Theophrastus* of Eresus in Lesbos (ca. 370–287), who might have already met Aristotle in the Academy. In terms of the breadth of his research he is not overshadowed by his teacher. The table of contents preserved in DL V42 encompasses logic, metaphysics, philosophy of nature, psychology, ethics, politics, rhetoric, poetics, and the history of philosophy (see par. 5). Preserved are two botanic works (*Historia plantarum; De causis plantarum*), the *Metaphysical Fragment,* several smaller works in natural science, and the *Characters.* The *Metaphysical Fragment* reveals Theophrastus as an aporetic thinker who points out inconsistencies and unclarified questions in Aris-

totle. Several of the ethical works are directed to a broad public. The *Characters* are noteworthy for the picture they paints of the reality of daily life. They diagnose human weaknesses and vie for tolerance with a sense of humor.

207. The research areas of *Eudemus of Rhodes* (born prior to 350 B.C.) were especially logic and physics. His relation to the *Eudemian Ethics* is unclear. The anti-Platonic tendency of the Peripatetics becomes clear in *Dicaearchus of Messene* (born ca. 376 B.C.), for whom the soul is nothing other than the proportion of the mixture of the body's four basic elements and is thus transient. His history of culture in the *Life of Greece* evaluates the development of culture as a decline from an early ideal time. *Aristoxenus of Tarentum* (born ca. 376 B.C.) had personal relations to the Pythagoreans. He is one of the great theoreticians of Greek music. His biographies of Pythagoras and his followers picture their lives as models; they are the first philosophical biographies. Theophrastus' successor as Scholarch was *Strato of Lampsacus* (ca. 340–270 B.C.), with the nickname "the physicist." He rejected the Aristotelian eidos and moves closer to the materialism of the atomists. His attacks are directed at the teleology of the *Timaeus,* Aristotle's unmoved mover, and the proofs of the soul's immortality in the *Phaedo.* Soul and knowledge are conceived of purely sensualistically. Strato's student is believed to have been *Aristarchus of Samos* (first half of the third century), who held an heliocentric worldview (prior to Copernicus). The stars and the sun are unmoved, whereas the planets and the earth orbit around the sun while rotating around their own axes. *Sotion of Alexandria* wrote a history of philosophy *Series* (diadochē) *of Philosophers* around 200 to 190 that Diogenes Laertius (first half of the third century A.D.) is considered to have consulted. Philosophers were ordered according to the pattern of teacher-student relations. Sotion distinguished the Ionian succession that leads from Anaxagoras, Socrates, the Academy, and the Peripatetics to the Stoics from the Italian succession that leads from Pythagoras up to Epicurus.

208. A renaissance of Aristotelianism begins (par. 131) with *Andronicus'* edition in the first century A.D. *Alexander of Aphrodisias'* interpretation of Aristotle (around 200 A.D.) is, as those of the earlier Peripatetics, markedly anti-Platonic. The individual is prior ontologically to the universal. The souls of living organisms are nothing other than the power that results from a particular proportion. Human reason is, like the soul, mortal. It only becomes active through the active mind that enters from the outside (nous poiētikos), and this Alexander equates with the unmoved mover.

E. Hellenistic Philosophy

209. Socrates' importance is not exhausted in being the teacher of Plato. Hellenistic philosophy that does not latch onto Plato and Aristotle takes recourse to him. Especially Diogenes Laertius reports on the Socratics who polemicize against Plato and anticipate characteristic features of Hellenistic philosophy. He traces the Stoics' lineage back through the cynical philosopher Crates of Thebes, the teacher of its founder Zeno, Diogenes of Sinope, *Antisthenes,* and finally to Socrates (I, 15). Epicurus' ethics owes important influences to the Cyrenaics, who go back to Socrates' student *Aristippus.* Finally, among the minor Socratic schools, there are the Megarics, founded by *Euclid.* Antisthenes, Aristippus, and Euclid were mentioned in Plato's *Phaedo* (59bc) as Socrates' friends. The doxography places particular importance on the ethics of these three Socratics. Antisthenes is believed to have taught that virtue suffices for happiness and that one only needs the strength of character of a Socrates in order to be virtuous (DL VI, 11). Aristippus is considered to have viewed "movement, softly increasing to sensation" as the highest good (DL II, 85), that is, certain experiences of pleasure. Euclid appears to have ontologized the Good, apparently under the influence of Parmenides, and equated it with di-

vine reason. "He teaches that the Good is One and is named with many names: sometimes insight, other times god, yet other times reason and so on. What is opposed to the Good is rejected, and he claims that it does not exist" (DL II, 106).

210. Especially the attitude toward life that Antisthenes displays along with his students Diogenes and Aristippus, according to Diogenes Laertius' report, can lead to an understanding of Hellenistic philosophy. The critical question of sources, to what extent the ideals of Hellenistic students are already being projected onto these Socratics, must remain open here. Antisthenes and probably also Aristippus were students of Sophists before they became affiliated with Socrates, and the opposition of physis-nomos (par. 57) is unmistakable in them. The highest values are freedom, independence, and a proper relation to oneself. Asked what philosophy had done for him, Antisthenes replied: "The capacity of dealing with myself" (DL VI, 6). Perhaps it was the impression of an autonomous, independent man that occasioned Alexander the Great to say that if he were not Alexander, he would want to be Diogenes (DL VI, 32). The esteem of individual freedom reveals itself in the emphatic contempt of societal values and conventions and even mere rules of etiquette. The philosopher understands himself as an autonomous being. "If all laws were repealed, this would change nothing in our way of life" (DL II, 68). This independence is lived differently. For Antisthenes and Diogenes it is revealed in extreme asceticism and contempt for pleasure (DL VI, 2). Aristippus demonstrates his control over pleasure by showing that he does not deny himself them (DL II, 75).

211. The period of Hellenism lasts from Alexander the Great's death (in 323) to the battle of Actium (31 B.C.), with which the period of the Roman Emperors begins. The new beginning in philosophy is to be explained by several causes. First, there is the state of the schools that pass on Plato's and Aristotle's legacies. The teaching of the Academy under Xenocrates became rigid and a kind of scholasticism. The destruction of Aristotelian metaphysics and the emphasis on

the particular sciences begins with Theophrastus. But political causes should not be overlooked. The battle of Chai-
ronea (338) means the end of the Greek polis as a social,
political, moral, and religious institution. Knowledge of foreign religions was increased greatly by Alexander's campaigns
and led to syncretism and relativism for the educated. The
downfall of traditional religion forced one to look for a new
orientation for one's own life.

I. The Stoics
Personalities and Sources

212. The founder of the Stoic school is *Zeno of Citium* in Crete (ca. 333/2–262/1). Around 311 he went to Athens, where he joined the cynic Crates. In addition to him he is to have listened to lectures by Xenocrates and the Megarean Stilpo. Around 300 he began to teach in the hall (stoa), drawn by Polygnotus across from the Acropolis. The claim that important Stoic teachings were of Semitic origin (Pohlenz) and justified by Zeno's heritage is not currently maintained. Zeno's successors as the leader of the school were *Cleanthes of Assos* (dec. ca. 232) and *Chrysippus of Soloi* in Cilicia (dec. 208/4), who is called the "completer" of the Early Stoic system. The tradition on the Early Stoics relies especially on his works. Important advocates of the Middle Stoics are *Panaetius of Rhodes* (ca. 185–109) and *Poseidonius of Apamaea* in Syria (ca. 135–150), who taught in Rhodes, where Cicero heard him lecture. *L. Annaeus Seneca* (4 B.C.- 65 A.D.), the educator and influential minister of the Emperor Nero, the freed slave Epictetus (ca. 55–138 A.D.) of Hierapolis in Phrygia, and the Roman Emperor Marcus Aurelius (121–180) belonged to the Late Stoics. The typical division of the Stoics into early, middle, and late should not obscure the inner unity of the school. Developments concern ethics especially, where Peripatetic elements are adopted by Panaetius. Late Stoicism is popular philosophy to a great extent; the interest

is less in problems in principle than in moral exhortation and practical wisdom.

213. Only the Late Stoics' works have been completely preserved. They are of little value for knowledge of the Stoic system due to their popular and admonishing character. For the Early and Middle Stoics we possess the following sources: a) A few papyri. b) Literal fragments in ancient authors; the most important is Cleanthes' Zeus-hymn preserved by Stobaeus (SVF II, 537). c) Stoic textbooks that we can reconstruct from ancient authors, for example, the compendium of Stoic and Peripatetic ethics that Didymus, teacher of the Emperor Augustus, put together and Stobaeus used. The very valuable outline of Stoic teachings by Diogenes Laertius relies upon such textbooks as, for example, the dialectic textbook of Diocles of Magnesia (first century B.C.). d) Reports in ancient authors that are often opponents of the Stoics. The earliest is Cicero (106–43); Plutarch, Galen, Sextus Empiricus (par. 251), and the commentators on Aristotle, especially Alexander of Aphrodisias and Simplicius (par. 279), are to be mentioned.

In line with Xenocrates (par. 128) the Stoics divide philosophy into physics, ethics, and logic. The order of these subjects in the lectures varied. It is of less importance because the three elements form an organic unity that the Stoics illustrate with a comparison to a living organism: logic corresponds to the bones and tendons, ethics to the more meaty parts, and physics to the soul (DL VII, 39). The principle of unity is the concept of logos that is central in each of the three philosophical disciplines. Logic is concerned with language and thought. Human reason, which is active in this manner, is part of divine reason which determines natural occurrences, and correspondence with divine reason is the goal of human life (DL VII, 88). The proximity of this concept of logos to that of Heraclitus (par. 33) cannot be overlooked. Cleanthes is thought to have written a commentary on Heraclitus (DL VII, 174).

1. LOGIC

215. Stoic logic encompasses rhetoric, with which we shall not be concerned here, epistemology, and dialectic, which is divided into the teachings of linguistic signs and of the signified (DL VII, 41–43).

216. Epistemology inquires into the criterion of truth. It consists in a certain representation (phantasia); for this reason this concept must be clarified first (DL VII, 42). Diocles (DL VII, 49–53) distinguishes representations, among other things, according to the following respects: a) According to its subject. The representations of reasonless living beings are not rational, those of human beings are rational and are called thoughts; only the latter are intended in the following. b) According to its origin. Sense representations stem from the sense organs; they are conceived as physical changes of the soul. The non-sense representations arise from operations that the understanding undertakes proceeding from the sense representations. Thus, we can, for example, form the concept of the middle point of the earth by analogy with smaller spheres or the concept of (noncorporeal) meaning or of place by transcending sense experience. The representations of the good and the just which we naturally possess count among the non-sense representations. c) According to their epistemic value. Here Diocles distinguishes deceptive from true or, in Stoic terminology, "cataleptic" (grasping) representations. A true representation is an impression that arises from something actually existing. The cataleptic representation is the criterion of truth.

217. The Stoic theory of knowledge can be reconstructed approximately as follows from Cicero's *Acad. post.* I, 40–42 (SVF I, 60) and *Acad post.* II, 144 (SVF I, 66). We are affected by a representation that shows self-evidently that it is caused by something actually existing. Because it enables us to grasp the represented thing, it is called the "grasping representation." Due to its reliability we freely give our as-

sent to it. Through the cataleptic representation and our assent we "grasp" (know) reality. It is only here that Stoics speak of perception. It is the act of "grasping" (katalēpsis) the actually existing. Zeno illustrated this process with a comparison. The cataleptic representation corresponds to a flat hand with its fingers spread apart; assent corresponds to the bringing together of the fingers; and the grasping corresponds to the fist that is grasping the object. According to Diocles' report (DL VII, 54) the criterion of truth was controversial even within the Stoic school. Thus, for example, Boethius of Sido, a fellow student of Panaetius, maintained the position that the criteria are reason, sense perception, desire, and knowledge; others held correct reason to be the criterion. The passages from Cicero reveal that these criteria need not be considered mutually exclusive. They distinguish between true perceptual judgments and knowledge. Zeno illustrates knowledge by the left hand that presses together the right hand which is closed into a fist. We only have knowledge when a perceptual judgment cannot be attacked by any argumentation, that is, when it is ordered into a comprehensive system of justification. The true perceptual judgment stands between knowledge and ignorance. It is, however, the starting point for knowledge, since concepts and principles are acquired from it.

218. The theory of linguistic signs (DL VII, 55–62) begins with the voice (phōnē). It is a vibration of air. Animals' sounds are expressions of mere desire. Those of human beings, conversely, are brought forth and articulated by the understanding. The articulated sound is called 'lexis'. There are 24 elements from which the lexis is composed: sounds designated by letters; among them there are seven vowels and six silent sounds. Speech (logos) is distinguished from lexis by its meaning; a speech always has a meaning, whereas sounds can be meaningless, as "blytyri." The five parts of speech are: address, as "human being"; name, as "Socrates"; verb, as "writes"; conjunctions; articles.

Since the time of the sophists it was discussed whether

the relation between linguistic signs and the reality designated by them was natural or depended on human convention (see Plato's *Cratylus*). According to Aristotle (*De int.*
2) it is conventional. According to the Stoics, however, words
picture the nature of the things. The sounds imitate the quality of the object that the names constructed out of them signify (SVF II, 146). The Stoic attempted to support this claim
with often forced etymologies.

219. Whereas linguistic signs are material sounds, what
is signified by them is immaterial. The Stoics called it "lecton," or the "said," which corresponds approximately to our
word 'meaning'. The distinction between lexis and lecton
results from that between hearing and understanding. One
can hear a person speak without understanding him. When
we understand him, we recognize the state of affairs intended
by his words. It is different not only from the linguistic signs
but also from the perceivable things signified by them. But
states of affairs do not exist as independent Platonic entities
either. The Stoics advanced a conceptualist position: the lecta
exist exclusively in human understanding (SVF II, 166; DL
VII, 63). The highest division of lecta is oriented toward
whether the linguistic expression is complete or incomplete.
An example of an incomplete expression is '. . . writes'. It
designates a "categorema" (katēgorēma): a thing (in contrast
to a linguistic expression) that is unsaturated, or requires
supplementation, and can be attributed to either one or several objects (DL VII, 64). It corresponds approximately to
what we understand today by the meaning of a predicate expression or a propositional function (see GK 10, par. 162).
Complete lecta are represented linguistically by sentences,
for example, 'Socrates writes'. Under the respect of the speech
act performed by them one is to distinguish within complete
lecta between assertions, questions, commands, desires, and
so on. A sign of an assertion is that it has a truth value.
"Whoever says 'It is daytime' claims that it is day. If it is daytime, the asserted claim is true; if not, it is false" (DL VII,
65). On the contrary, for example, questions claim nothing;

instead an answer is requested. The question itself is neither true nor false.

220. Assertions are divided into simple ones, into whose kinds we cannot delve, and nonsimple ones. Nonsimple assertions are those in which various assertions (or the same one repeatedly) are combined by one or more conjunctions. DL VII, 69 mentions implicative assertions ("if p, then q"), subimplicative assertions ("because p, q"), conjunctive assertions "p and q"), and disjunctive assertions ("p or q"). Syllogisms also belong to the complete lecta. The Stoic syllogistic stood in Aristotle's shadow for a long time. It is especially to J. Lukasiewicz's credit (1935) to have pointed out its importance. The Stoics can be seen as precursors to modern propositional logic. In Aristotelian syllogistic, the truth value of the conclusion is conditioned by the domain of the terms involved. The variables stand for terms. In the Stoic syllogistic the truth value of the conclusion is conditioned by the meaning of the conjunctions and the truth values of the assertions combined by them. The variables stand for the truth values of assertions. The Stoics assumed five elementary syllogisms that did not require a proof. They viewed all and only those inferences as valid that can be derived from the elementary syllogisms. These elementary syllogisms are (DL VII, 79):

(1) if p, then q; p is given, therefore q
(2) if p, then q; not q is given, therefore not p
(3) not both p and q; p is given, therefore not q
(4) p or q; p is given, therefore not q
(5) p or q; not q is given, therefore p.

2. THE PHYSICS

221. Aristotle uses 'physis' (nature) for the personified cause that determines the entirety of cosmic events as well as for the principle of change in every individual organism (Bonitz, *Index* 836a18). As a defined philosophical term, the

word has the second meaning (*Phys.* II, 1; *Met.* V, 4). A corresponding distinction can be found in the Stoics' linguistic use. Physis holds the entire cosmos together, and it is the self-moving principle that is contained in the sperm and causes its development into a fully mature organism of the corresponding species (DL VII, 148). The two concepts are related in such a manner that the Stoics viewed the entire cosmos as a single organism. Before we follow up on this, we need to ask how the concept of physis is related to that of logos (reason). According to DL VII, 134 the Stoics presumed two principles for the cosmos: the active and the passive. They identified the passive with propertyless matter, the active with the logos active in matter. Physis and logos coincide in that they are both an active principle in opposition to matter. Physis is "artificial fire that proceeds along its path to creation; this is firelike and artificial breath" (DL VII, 156). The difference lies in the mode of observation. The physis develops the organism according to a plan within the sperm (spermatikos logos). "Physis" thus emphasizes the origin of motion, whereas "logos" underlines the information that controls the process.

222. The difference becomes clearer when we turn to the conception of the cosmos as an organism. The correspondence consists in one sense in the development. Like individual living beings the cosmos is subject as a whole to coming to be and passing away. The beginning and end point of the development is (artificial) fire. From DL VII, 136; 142 (See SVF I, 497) the following picture results. In the beginning reason or nature exists as fire per se. Then it turns into water via air. This water is the sperm that contains the origin of movement and the plan for the cosmos. How the cosmos arises out of it in particular is described differently in both passages. Similarly, we find no clear picture as to how the cosmos passes away. According to various other testimony the Stoics taught that the cosmos would become fire again (SVF II, 585; 596ff.). That the cosmos is an organism also explains why, despite the universality of logos, not all

beings are rational. Nature or logos penetrates the matter as fire (as the Early Stoics claimed) or pneuma (breath; since Chrysippus), but in varying degrees, just as the various organs in the human body are more or less "ensouled" (DL VII, 138). Various designations of the active principle correspond to the varying degrees of its presence. In rocks and in wood it is only present as breath which holds together the components of the mixture and is called "hexis." It is called "physis" (in the narrow sense) as the life principle of plants. It reveals itself as the soul in sensitive beings and as reason in the central organ of human beings, the heart (DL VII, 139; 159; SVF II, 368; 710; 714).

223. According to the Stoics' teaching the active principle is "artificial fire" or "artlike breath" (DL VII, 156). These expressions suggest the position often maintained that the Stoics are materialists. In favor of this interpretation speaks the fact that the Stoics viewed activity and passivity as the criteria of reality; only bodies are capable of these criteria (SVF I, 90; II, 525; 359). On the other hand, one must not overlook that the Stoics decisively rejected the mechanistic worldview of the Epicureans and argued for the existence of reason that has the best as its goal (Cicero, *De nat. deorum* II, 81–87). Thus the following interpretation is more accurate: every reality must prove itself through its effects in the material world. No faculty can be active without a body; it exists only as long as the body to which it is attached does. In the phrase 'artificial fire' not only the element of fire but also the faculty of art that is active according to its own laws is at issue. In contemporary terminology one could perhaps call the element fire the carrier of information.

224. Whereas Aristotle assumed ten categories (*Cat.* 4), the Stoics believed that four suffice. Their categories are ontological concepts as well. It is difficult to tell what method is used to determine them. Plotinus (VI, 1), who via Simplicius (SVF II, 369) is our most important source, criticized the division as inconsistent. What appears certain is that the

teaching of the categories must be seen as the development and differentiation of the teaching of the two ontological principles: the passive, propertyless matter and the active logos, bound to fire or pneuma (DL VII, 134). The first category is the substrate (hypokeimenon); it is to be equated with matter. The remaining three categories depend upon the activation of the active principle. The matter becomes initially an individual thing due to an "individuating quality" (idia poiotēs); we refer to this quality with proper names, for example, 'Socrates'. Within the second category the "common quality" (koinē poiotēs) is distinguished from the individuating one. It is called by an "address" (sortal term) (par. 218), for example, "human being," "horse" (DL VII, 58). What ontological status do these common qualities (universals) have? The fact that the species (eidos) and the genus (genos) are treated, not under the lecta, but rather under the linguistic signs (DL VII, 60f.) suggests that the Stoics held a nominalist position. At any rate the individuating quality is ontologically prior. If the first two categories are principles that constitute the individual, the third category summarizes the changing determinations that can be attributed to the individual. Under the category of accidental constitution (pōs echon) the Stoics summarized various (and contradictory) things (as their ancient critics claimed), for example, quantity, time, place, and quality (SVF II, 399f.). The relations of one individual to another, for example, "is the father of," "lies to the right of," fall under the fourth category of "relative accidental constitution" (pros ti pōs echon) (SVF II, 402–404).

225. The logos that creates the cosmos from matter is god according to the Stoics' conception. "God is one, is reason and fate, and Zeus; but he is named by many other names" (DL VII, 135f.). Theology is thus part of physics. The most extensive reports are by Cicero, *De natura deorum* (On the Essence of the Gods) II, and Sextus Empiricus, *Adversus mathematicos* IX. Whereas Sextus takes the arguments out of their context, Cicero's reports are "controlled by an

overview"; it is "perhaps the most complete, but at any rate the most systematic presentation of this school's theology" (Boyancé, 1962 [1971], p. 450; 447). Cicero's report deserves interest in an epistemological respect as well. It inquires into the origin of the thought of god and the function of proofs for god's existence. In the beginning there is neither traditional teaching nor a philosophical or theological theory. The conviction that god exists is innate in human beings. It develops naturally and alone, that is, without any human interference (see SVF II, 83). This first, naturally given intuition can find expression in various pictures of god. The variety and historical change of religions is, not an argument against, but rather a certain indication of God's existence. "For the day destroys the made-up opinions; it solidifies the judgments of nature" (*De nat. d.* II, 5). Cleanthes named four causes through which the thought of god was imprinted upon human beings: 1. the premonition of coming events; 2. the experience of advantages that secure the earth's climate and fertility for human beings; 3. the fear that overcomes human beings in the face of natural catastrophes; 4. (the most important cause) the experience of the beauty of the ordered motion of the stars. These four causes make clear the character of natural intuition. Feeling and knowledge are unseparated in it; it has the same degree of certainty that the assumptions of everyday life have, for example, that the sun will rise tomorrow.

The content of natural preconception is not only the existence of god but also an initial characterization: God has a soul and is the most perfect of all beings. Natural intuition can be developed in trains of thought with varying argumentative garb. A simple consideration works with the analogy between the cosmos and an orderly household. Order is common to both. If a house is controlled by a rational being, the same is to be expected of the universe. On a more reflective level the same consideration can be carried out with the comparison between nature and art. "When what is by nature is better than the completed works of art, and when

art brings forth nothing without reason, then reason cannot be denied of nature" (*De nat. d.* II, 87). According to
the natural preconception god is the most perfect being. Zeno
constructs the following argument: "What possesses the capacity to think is better than what does not possess this capacity; there is nothing better than the universe; therefore
the universe possesses that capacity" (*De nat. d.* II, 21). The
proofs can also be supported by natural science. In this manner, from the fact that all processes of life are bound to
warmth it can be shown that there must be a rational nature
(the artificial fire) that conserves the cosmos. A series of observations is claimed to demonstrate that the teleology of the
world is caused by divine reason and inexplicable by chance.

226. The Stoics were concerned to and attempted to integrate the people's religion into their philosophical system.
The teaching of the "threefold division of theology" helped
in this endeavor (SVF II, 1009). Mythical theology is that
of the poets, political theology that of the public culture,
and physical (natural) theology that of the philosophers. The
distinction shows that the people's religion is indispensable
for the resoluteness of the state and morality according to
the Stoics' conception. It attributes the highest status and
the task of criticism to natural theology. The etymological
explanations of the gods' names and the allegorical interpretation of myths served to mediate the people's religion
with philosophical theology (*De nat. d.* II, 60–71; DL VII,
147).

227. The Stoic conception of god is indivisibly connected
with concepts of "providence" (pronoia) and "fate" (eimar-
menē). As the four major points of Stoic theology that Cicero
mentions in *De nat. d.* II, 3 we count in addition to the existence and properties of the gods the claims that the world
is guided by them and that they are concerned about human
beings. The final claim is true not merely for the species of
human beings but also for each particular individual (ibid.
II, 164). Providence is nothing other than the "artificial fire,"
or the divine reason, insofar as it steers everything for the

best of human beings (ibid. II, 57f.). Similarly, the Stoics identify God with fate (DL VII, 135): the eternal, complete, exceptionless, and unavoidable causal connection of events with each other (SVF II, 1000; DL VII, 149). This concept of fate corresponds to the rationalist strand in the Stoics' philosophy, for only exceptionless causal determination allows a complete explanation (logos) of all occurrences. Apparently there was a discussion among the Stoics as to how the two concepts are to be combined. According to Chrysippus they have the same extension: what happens due to fate is desired by providence and vice versa. Conversely, according to Cleanthes the concept of fate is broader than that of providence: not all events of fate are desired by providence (SVF II, 933). Without a doubt Chrysippus' claim is more consistent with the Stoic system. If Cleanthes were correct, there would be events that are caused by divine reason without being steered by it toward the best. The teachings of fate and providence have difficult consequences. Determinism leaves no room for ethics whose demands rely on the freedom of the human being. And "Why, if providence steers the world, do human beings experience so much unhappiness?" Seneca asks at the beginning of his work on providence that is devoted to the problem of theodicy. If Cleanthes limited the omnipotence of providence, this attempt at a solution was insufficient. For Chrysippus physical pain is the unavoidable consequence of the good. In this manner, for example, the human head can only function when it is built of small and thin bones. But that necessarily brings with it the disadvantage of fragility (SVF II, 1170). According to Marcus Aurelius (V, 8) the individual cannot look only at himself but must also consider the whole. Misfortune is to be compared with a medicinal prescription that serves the health of the cosmos.

3. ETHICS

228. Physics, as Cicero writes at the end of his summary of Stoic ethics in *De finibus bonorum et malorum* (Of the

Highest Good and the Worst Evil), is itself a moral virtue, for no one could judge about good and evil without knowing nature's plan (III, 72f.). With this he is repeating Chrysippus' teaching: "For one cannot attain knowledge of the good and bad or of virtue and happiness any other way or more adequately than by proceeding from the universe and the endowment of the world" (SVF III, 68). Today we are critical of a justification of morality that relies so heavily on nature because we suspect a "naturalist fallacy" of inferring from is to ought (see GK, §§52–60). Thus it is important to note that both of our passages speak of the universe. It reveals itself in the preservation of plants, in the desire of sensitive beings, and in human beings' reason. For human beings to live naturally is to live according to reason (DL VII, 86). This nonnaturalist definition is underlined by the definition of the good as what is "perfect according to the nature of the rational as rational" (DL VII, 94). If we want to interpret the Stoic ethics as a nonnaturalistic rational ethics, it is all important not to limit the concept of reason to that of human reason. In order to act properly, a human being must be oriented toward how the universal reason is manifested in the parts of nature that are not endowed with reason. Such a human being must be convinced that it controls everything for the best for him, when either through no fault of his own he does not achieve the goals he followed in accord with reason or others inflict injury upon him with their irrational actions (see Cleanthes' Zeus-hymn, SVF I, 537). One can characterize the Stoic ethics as a theological rational ethics. The theological premise allows a teleological view of nonrational nature; in this manner its goals become morally relevant. Through it misfortunes that cannot be interpreted positively for natural goals and with the finite reason of human beings can also be interpreted rationally.

229. As an introduction to ethics, Cicero (*De fin.* III, 16–22) and Diogenes Laertius (VII, 85f.) both sketch (which is in agreement in its basic features) how human consciousness develops. This sketch also serves to distinguish human beings from other natural beings. Every being has a self-

relationship from the first moment of life, even before it can experience feelings of pain or pleasure. It is related to what belongs to it prior to anything else, and that is its own existence. It is every living being's "first possession" (prōton oikeion; this point of the Stoic ethics is thus called the "teaching of oikeiosis"). Living beings love their existence and fear destruction. This is revealed by their striving toward what is agreeable and avoiding what is harmful. At this level there is no difference between animals and plants. Plants also have this sense for and love of their own existence, and many of the processes essential for the preservation of animals are achieved at this vegetative level. The Stoics' argumentation is directed against the view that living beings ultimately strive for pleasure. According to their teaching, pleasure is only a subsequent phenomenon; it arises when a (sensitive) being has received what is agreeable to its existence. In their further development animals obtain an additional possibility to relate to what is required for their preservation: the perceived drive (hormē). Reason as a third level of development distinguishes human beings. Human beings can deliberately strive for their preservation through reason; it can steer desires and correct them if necessary.

230. The level of morality has not been reached with the self-relationship described above. Morality proceeds from self-love in order to transcend it. Human beings are not determined by necessity in their actions; they must choose whether they should follow their desires, and they must choose between mutually exclusive desires. In order to be morally good the choice must be made with a certain kind of motive. Reason has the capacity of knowing the teleological structure of the self-relationship described above. Chrysippus argues that this is the only rational possibility: if nature creates living beings, then it is only consistent to equip them with self-love; if living beings were foreign to themselves, they could not preserve themselves and the act of creation would have been foolish (DL VI, 85). Whoever has the teleological order of the universe as such as a motive acts morally. The satis-

faction of natural desires becomes a morally good action when the agent recognizes that she is thereby obeying the universe. Correspondence (homologia; convenientia) with the universe becomes the only good to be desired for its own sake.

231. In connection with the teaching of oikeiosis Cicero introduces two important distinctions within the Stoic ethics. The first (par. 232) is related to goods, the second (par. 233) to actions.

232. Everything that is natural in the sense that it is the goal of a natural desire has value (axia; *De fin.* III, 20; DL VII, 104f.). It is preferred under otherwise equal conditions. For this reason the Stoics distinguished between "preferred things" (proēgmena) and "rejected things" (apoproēgmena) (*De fin.* III, 52; DL VII, 105). Examples of preferred things, that is, things that are valuable, are mental and physical health, vocational ability, life, beauty, wealth, and fame. Valueless things (apaxia) are, for example, death, sickness, poverty, and being of low descent (DL VII, 106). The value of preferred things lies in their contribution to a life in accordance with the universe (DL VII, 105), for they fulfill the desire created by it. For this reason they are not only preferred de facto, but they also deserve being preferred. Cicero (*De fin.* III, 50) attacks Zeno's student Ariston, who denied any nonmoral value. This removes the foundation of, and outlet for the moral decision of, choosing between nonmoral goods. Again and again opponents of the Stoics objected that the Stoics contradicted themselves by claiming that there is a nonmoral value and at the same time designating the nonmoral "goods" as "indifferent things" (adiaphora; DL VII, 104; SVF I, 190).

Several points of Stoic ethics are expressed in the concept of adiaphora. First, even if one understood only the useful under the good, the preferred things are only good in a limited sense. Wealth and health, for example, can also be harmful; they can be used well and badly (DL VII, 103). Second, the claim of adiaphora results from the Stoic concept of happiness. Happiness is independent of the fulfillment of natu-

ral desires. The Stoic concept of happiness is distinguished
from the Aristotelian concept (par. 188) in this respect. The
Stoics equated happiness with the moral end; its ideal is independent of all external conditions (*De fin.* III, 26). "Only
what is moral (honestum) is good (bonum), and to live in
happiness means to live morally, and that means to live vir-
tuously" (ibid. 29). Third, the concept of adiaphora underlines the essential difference between the moral good (kalon;
honestum) and other goods. Cicero (*De fin.* III, 54) illustrates this with a comparison to a game in which it is important to roll the series of numbers 1, 3, 4, 6 with four dice.
One can only hit or miss this series. How close one comes
is of no importance whatsoever. The same is true of the preferred things and the morally good. The nonmoral goods
have a relation to the moral goal; yet one can still achieve
the former without the latter and vice versa.

233. Corresponding to the goods the Stoics distinguish
between the morally good (or bad) and "middle" (mesa;
media) actions which they designate as "suitable" (kathē-
konta). This concept was introduced by Zeno. DL VII, 107f.
uses it in a broader sense for plants and animals. Whatever
corresponds to its natural capacities is "suitable" for a being; we can speak of the natural achievement of a task. Cicero
chooses the word 'officium', for which the English translation of 'duty' has become traditional. The normative character results for him from the theory of oikeiosis (*De fin.* III,
20; 22). Natural desire shows us things that have value. From
this arises the necessity of actions through which we realize
these goals. The "first duty" consists in "retaining one's own
natural state." Diogenes Laertius defines the narrower concept, which is applicable to human beings only, as an "action that can be justified with good reasons." That a behavior corresponds to a desire does not turn it into a suitable
action; rather a choice guided by reason is required. He provides as examples: to honor one's parents, relatives, and fa-
therland; to care for one's friends; to care for one's health.
Whoever performs actions in accord with nature does not

yet act morally (*De fin.* III, 22). Cicero thus distinguishes between "common duty" (commune officium; kathēkon) and "perfect duty" (perfectum officium) (*De officiis* I, 8). The Greek word for "perfect duty" (katorthōma) means "right action"; Cicero translates it with 'recte factum' (*De fin.* III, 24).

Why is this distinction required? Isn't someone who fulfills common duty acting correctly? Cicero raises the following example (*De fin.* III, 59): whoever returns an entrusted good fulfills a common duty; whoever does it for the sake of justice, acts perfectly. An example is taken from Plato's *Republic* 331c which shows that one and the same action can be just or unjust according to the circumstances. One is acting unjustly, for example, if one returns a borrowed weapon to a friend who has become mentally ill since the weapon was lent out. Thus an action is only perfect not only if the agent does what is appropriate in most cases but when the agent can judge whether this course of action is right in the circumstances given here and now. For this reason Cicero (*De fin.* III, 46) mentions in addition to correspondence with nature the correct time (opportunitas; eukairia) as a further criterion for right action. He emphasizes that one can return a borrowed item for various reasons. If one does it due to natural self-love, one is fulfilling a common duty; the perfect action occurs for the sake of the morally good. Finally, it must be done with the right internal attitude: free from reprehensible emotions and in characteristically unmistakable firmness (*De fin.* III, 20; 32).

234. Perfect duty is an ideal moral demand which only the wise are capable of satisfying (*De fin.* III, 32). A human being can fulfill all her common duties without exception: as long, however, as she lacks a perfect attitude of character and perfect practical judgment, she will not be acting morally and will not be happy (SVF III, 510). There is no continuous transition between the middle and the right actions. "For like someone drowning who is just under the surface of the water can breathe as little as one very far below the

surface . . . , similarly, one who has proceeded a ways toward moral behavior is in as miserable a state as one who
has taken not a single step on the path toward virtue" (*De
fin.* III, 48).

235. The first step in justifying a social ethics (*De fin.*
III, 62–71) is mere reference to the fact that nature has
equipped human beings with the capacity for reproduction.
Nature would contradict itself if it did not also implant love
for their descendents that widens into consciousness of the
togetherness of all human beings. The insight that human
beings rely upon each other supports this natural feeling;
it is the origin of political and other communities. The world
is the common state of the gods and human beings. Because
every individual human being is a part of this whole and
relies upon it, the common utility of the whole is to be preferred to that of the individual. In this manner the Stoics
justify duties to future generations. They discussed another
question of contemporary environmentalist ethics: Do animals have rights? Chrysippus denied this with an anthropomorphic justification. The rest of nature is for the sake of
the gods and human beings. Human beings are for each
other's sake. For this reason human beings are justified in
using animals for their own purposes. The legal order is not
limited to the particular political community. Due to their
nature every human being is a legal subject. That the world
belongs to all human beings does not exclude property rights.
Cicero brings up the comparison with a theater that is intended for the public and where each person can rightfully
claim that the seat she is sitting in belongs to her.

236. The moral concepts of value presuppose that it is
up to the agent whether the agent acts well or badly. Virtue
and vices are attributed to human beings. Praise and blame,
commands and prohibitions, penalties and rewards assume
that the agent could have done otherwise (SVF II, 984). Yet
the Stoics maintain the exceptionless causal connection of
all events. "If there could be a mortal who had come to know
the connection of all causes, nothing could deceive him. For

whoever knows the causes of all future events necessarily knows everything that will be the case" (Cicero, *De divinatione* I, 127 = SVF II, 944). How are the two to be rendered consistent? Does not the teaching of providence (par. 227) renounce the possibility of moral action? Chrysippus attempted to solve the problem by distinguishing two kinds of causes (Cicero, *De fato* 39–43). He explains them with the example of a cylinder. If the cylinder receives a push from without, its process of motion is determined by its construction. The external impulse stands for the immediate, triggering cause (causae adiuvantes et proximae); the construction or nature stands for the perfect, first cause (causae perfectae et principales). Only the immediate, triggering causes stand in the necessary causal connection. Applied to action, the distinction means: the impressions received from without are the immediate causes. They affect us, but they do not necessitate us. Whether we give our assent depends on the perfect cause, and that is our moral character.

Initially, this distinction only explains that we ascribe actions to a person; one of the causal factors is the character of the agent. But can we hold the person responsible for the actions? For this we would have to show that the person is responsible for his or her character. For this purpose Chrysippus removes the character from the necessary causal nexus. But does the Stoic ontology admit this dualism? And if so, the question still remains open whether a two-world theory is possible as a consistent solution to the problem of freedom.

II. Epicurus
Life and Works

237. Epicurus was born in 341 B.C. on the island of Samos as the son of an Athenian immigrant. He is reported to have heard his first philosophical lectures from a Platonist by the name of Pamphilus, about whom little else is known (DL X, 14). His studies with the Democritean Nausiphanes in the Ionian city of Teos on the mainland of Asia Minor were decisive for his own philosophy. When eighteen years old Epicurus went to Athens in order to serve two years of mandatory military service. During this time his parents had to leave Samos; Epicurus followed them to Colophon in Asia Minor (DL X, 1). When thirty-two years old he began to teach philosophy first in Mitylene at Lesbos and later in Lampsacus (DL X, 15). He made friendships there that were to become important for the later development of the school. Hermarchus, his successor as the leader of the school, stemmed from Mitylene (DL X, 15), and his lifelong colleague Metrodorus came from Lampsacus. Around 307/306 Epicurus returned to Athens and bought a garden that gave the school its name. The emphasis was probably less on teaching and research than in the Academy and among the Peripatetics, and more on common life; Epicurus counted friendship as one of ethic's highest goods. Women and slaves were admitted as well. Metrodorus' brother Timocrates left the school and wrote a diatribe against Epicurus in which he accused the latter of gluttony, philosophical incompe-

tence, naivete, and of leading a sexually promiscuous life (DL X, 6f.) To the contrary, Diogenes Laertius' biographies praise Epicurus' immense radiance of personality, goodness, social consciousness, and extremely modest life-style (DL X, 9–11).

238. Epicurus is thought to have written more than all other philosophers before him (DL X, 26). In Diogenes Laertius' biographies three pedagogic letters are preserved. The letter to Herodotus provides a summary of the atomic theory; the letter to Pythocles concerns astronomy and meteorology; the letter to Menoeceus is a protreptic work containing his most important ethical teachings. The *Main Teachings* (Kuriai doxai; abbrev.: KD) were also preserved by Diogenes, containing a summary of Epicurus' philosophy in 40 theses which his students learned by heart. A similar collection, the *Gnomologium Vaticanum,* was discovered in the previous century in a Vatican manuscript. At the eighteenth-century excavations in Herculaneum papyri were found with fragments from Epicurus' main work, the 37 books of *On Nature,* and from the Epicurean Philodemus of Gadara (first century B.C.). A reliable and extensive source of Epicurus' natural philosophy is Lucretius' poem *De rerum natura* (first century B.C.). Around 200 A.D. an Epicurean of the name Diogenes had Epicurus' teachings chiselled into a monumental wall in Oenoanda in Lucian (southwest Asia Minor); parts of this inscription have been preserved. Of the indirect, partially polemic sources, in addition to Lucretius, especially Cicero, Diogenes Laertius, Seneca, Plutarch, and Sextus Empiricus are to be mentioned.

1. THE CANONIC

Diogenes Laertius divided Epicurus' philosophy into the canonic, physics, and ethics (X, 29f.; see par. 128). The term 'canonic' is derived from the title of one of Epicurus' works *On the Criterion,* or *Canon* (DL X, 27). 'Kanōn' means literally "straight stick." 'Canon' and 'criterion' (means of judgment) signify the standard of the means of determining an assertion's truth value. Epicurus recognizes three criteria of truth: 1. perception (aisthēseis); 2. concepts (prolēpseis); 3. feelings (pathē) (DL X, 31). Feelings are criteria of value judgments; for this reason they are treated in the section on ethics. According to Epicurus the foundation of knowledge is perception. It carries certainty in itself; it requires for its confirmation neither reflection nor memory. It can be falsified by no example: neither by a perception of the same kind, for both have the same epistemic value; nor by a perception of another sense organ, for they refer to different objects; nor by reason either, since it relies upon perception. Epicurus presumes that perception is a movement caused by the perceived object and that it hits the sense organs as it is caused by the object without anything being added or taken away from the movement. He compares perceptions of sight and hearing with pain; I can be deceived about them as much as I can about sensations of pain; as little as pain can perceptions be true or false (DL X, 31f.; see KD XXIII).

239. The word 'concept' (prolēpsis; literally: anticipation) signifies the meaning of a universal term. It consists in a universal representation that is formed from the memory of an often-repeated perception of the same object. With the help of concepts we create an "opinion" or "assumption," that is, an assertion that has a truth value. Concepts thus enable us to speak about our perceptions. They contain the criteria with which we decide the truth of an assertion. For this purpose they must be clear. They serve to "anticipate" perceptions and to pose questions of a perception that is still unclear, for example, "Is what is standing over there a horse or a cow?" We can only decide on the truth or falsity of a statement when we are in a situation that allows a reliable perception (DL X, 33f.). Error arises when we assent to a proposition without waiting for confirmation or falsification by a clear perception (*To Her.* 50f.; see KD XXIV).

240. That perception is the foundation of knowledge does not of course mean that knowledge is exhausted in perception. The described activities of concept and proposition formation show this; knowledge requires other operations in addition to perception. Epicurus also admits this openly. Concepts do not arise only through repeated perceptions; they can also be formed by particular operations of the understanding. Epicurus mentions (DL X, 32) the composition of a concept from those actions that derive directly from repeated perceptions: *analogy,* through which, for example, concepts or propositions are taken from the realm of the perceivable and applied to imperceivable atoms (*To Her.* 58); *similarity,* that is, we form a higher concept that summarizes the common characteristics of subordinate concepts; *coherence,* that is, we form the concept of an imperceivable reality that serves to explain perceivable things.

241. The rules that determine when a proposition is true or false are also not derivable from perception. Sextus Empiricus (*Adv. math.* VII, 212–216 = Quest. 247; see DL X, 34; *To Her.* 51) attributes four such rules to Epicurus:

(1) An assertion about a perceivable object is true if it is *confirmed* by perception.

(2) An assertion about imperceivables is true if it coheres with perceivable states of affairs. Such an assertion is, for example, that a void exists. It coheres with the phenomenon of motion. In contrast to (1) it is not confirmed but rather only *not falsified.*

(3) An assertion about imperceivables is false if it contradicts perceivable states of affairs, for example, the assertion that a void does not exist. Such an assertion is to be *rejected.*

(4) An assertion about perceivables is false if it is *not confirmed* by perceptions.

Rule (2) deserves special interest. Epicurus assumes that many phenomena admit several explanations. The moon's phases, for example, can be explained by the rotation of the moon or by changes in the atmosphere or by heavenly bodies that move in between. Each of these explanations coheres with the observable facts. According to rule (2) all of these explanations are to be viewed with equal validity (*To Pyth.* 87; 92–96).

2. PHYSICS

242. The letter to Herodotus initiates the portrayal of physics (38–45) with three ontological principles. They clearly reveal their origin from Parmenides, but Epicurus attempts to justify them with his canonic.

(1) *Nothing comes to be from not-being.* The negation of this assertion would contradict experience. This shows us that every being arises from a cause that corresponds to it, its sperm or seed.

(2) *Nothing perishes into not-being.* Epicurus relies on experience for this as well. If everything that perishes in the perceivable world perished into not-being, nothing more would exist, for we can constantly perceive the (phenomenal) process of perishing.

(3) *The universe was always the way it is now and will always remain so.* This principle is a consequence of (1) and (2). Epicurus then shows that the universe consists of bodies and void. The existence of bodies is testified to by perception. Void must be assumed because without it the phenomenon of movement cannot be explained. There can be no beings per se in addition to bodies and void but rather only necessary or accidental properties of bodies. This excluding assertion is justified by the fact that any other being per se is inconceivable. We can form no concept of it, for there is no concept formation independent of perception, and what we perceive are bodies, their properties, and their changes. Epicurus' ontology is thus to be understood as a consequence of his epistemological approach.

243. Bodies are partially composites, partially elements of which the composites are composed. These elements are indivisible and unchanging. Their indivisibility results from

their being full, that is, they contain no empty space within, which is a necessary condition for divisibility. That such elements must be presupposed results for Epicurus from his second ontological principle. The universe is infinite. If it were finite, it would have a limit that separated it from something else. But that is not possible, since the universe encompasses everything and does not admit anything distinct from it. Thus not only the void is infinite but also the set of atoms. Otherwise the atoms would disperse in the infinite space; they would neither collide nor combine with other atoms. The set of different shapes is not infinite but inconceivable (for us); only in this manner can the great variety of the perceivable world be explained. It follows from the infinite number of atoms that nothing stands in the way of the assumption that there are infinitely many worlds.

244. Not least due to Aristotle's objections to the older Atomists, Epicurus furthers Democritus' atomic theory in two points.

For Democritus the relation between physical and mathematical divisibility remained unclear (par. 52). Epicurus clearly takes a stand by rejecting the mathematical concept of the potentially infinitely divisible. The *atom* is *physically* indivisible but mathematically divisible. The latter results from it having a certain shape in which we can distinguish various parts. The *parts of the atom,* however, are *mathematically* indivisible; we must assume smallest sizes (minima). Lucretius I, 599–634 (see *To Her.* 56–59) argues most clearly: if the atoms were composed of infinitely many parts, they would be infinitely large, for even in an infinite division every part is extended, and an infinite number of extended parts results in an infinitely large thing. The mathematically indivisible minima cannot, however, be the principles of the perceivable world, since not having any parts, they cannot have (different) shapes and thus cannot cause the variety of appearances.

Epicurus (*To Her.* 56) also provides an ontological argument for the minima: if division into infinity were possible, the ultimate components could also be dissolved into nothing, which would contradict the second ontological principle.

This train of thought is not convincing, since regardless of how far we continue the process of division, the divided thing will always be extended, and in this sense it does not dissolve into nothing. A plausible argument can be provided for the physical indivisibility of the atoms (if we abstract from the argument in par. 243) but not for the mathematical indivisibility of the minima. Lucretius' consideration is this: only the physical indestructibility of atoms that have differing shapes can explain the variety in the empirical world.

245. Second, Epicurus has, when compared with Democritus, a worked-out theory of atomic motion. The infinite empty space has no absolute up or down; we can only state these directions relative to our bodies. Relative to a viewpoint, the atoms move downward due to their weight. Despite the different weights they all fall with the same velocity (*To Her.* 60f.). This falling motion does not suffice, however, to explain the origin of compositions. If this were the only motion, atoms would fall like raindrops in a straight line into the infinite without colliding with each other. Epicurus thus recurs to the assumption that the atoms swerve a little from their vertical line of fall at an indeterminate time and place without a cause (Lucretius II, 216–224). This deviation also explains free will (ibid. 251–293). This deviation leads to the atoms colliding with one another, and because they are hard, they bounce off each other, which results in another change of direction. Collision and repulsion cause the atoms to be in a constantly oscillating motion. They remain intact even in compositions; the varying density of perceivable bodies is explained by the varying sizes of the amplitudes of the oscillations. In addition to this theory Epicurus retained the position, taken over from Democritus, that the atoms latch onto one another. How both are to be maintained is difficult to discern (*To Her.* 43f.; Lucretius II, 80–141; 445f.).

3. ETHICS AND PHILOSOPHY OF RELIGION

246. Like all other judgments, value judgments must be justifiable ultimately by immediate sensation. The criterion for what is to be strived for and what is to be avoided is pleasure and pain. Epicurus appeals to the perceivable behavior of all living beings and to immediate sensation. That pleasure is to be strived for and pain to be avoided is perceivable as directly as fire being warm or honey being sweet (DL X, 34; Cicero, De fin. I, 30). In the Philebus Plato defined pain as the sensation of dissolution of the natural state and pleasure as the sensation of its restoration (31e–32b). He distinguished from these two the state in which neither of these processes is occurring; in that state a living being is perceiving neither pleasure nor pain (32e; 43de). Epicurus picks up on this distinction, but he alters the concept of pleasure. Not only the sensation that accompanies the process of restoring the natural state is viewed as ("kinetic") pleasure (Lucretius III, 963–966), but also the mere absence of pain, which Epicurus calls "catastematic," that is, pleasure connected with a state in accord with nature (katastēma) (DL X, 136). Thus he disputes that there is a neutral state on the scale of sensation between pain and pleasure. The reason for this terminological ruling was, according to Cicero, De fin. I, 37, that we can spontaneously evaluate the condition of being free of pain due to the background of painful experiences. Catastematic pleasure is the highest form of pleasure and the goal of life. "The limit of the degree of pleasure is the removal of all painful things" (KD III). "For it is the goal of all of our actions that we be free of pain and fear" (To Men. 128). Epicurus distinguishes himself in this respect from the Cyrenaics, who view the highest good in kinetic pleasure (DL X, 136). Mental pain is worse than physical pain. But here, too, Epicurus remains faithful to his canonic. Every mental pain is referred to bodily pain; it is the expectation or memory of a bodily pain (DL X, 137; Cicero, De fin. I, 41). If it can be shown that the expectation

of bodily pain is unjustified, the mental pain dissolves. Epicurus argues in this manner against the fear of death: "Every good or evil consists in sensation; but death is the loss of sensation" (*To Men.* 124). In the same way reason can prevent us from letting our desires unnecessarily disappoint us. Epicurus distinguishes between natural and imagined desires. The natural desires divide up into the necessary and the merely natural desires. Only the necessary desires that would otherwise cause pain must be satisfied; all others can be abrogated (*To Men.* 127; *KD* XXVI; XXIX). Epicurus replies to the objection that we do not think of every pleasure as good in the same way as modern utilitarianism does with its calculus of pleasure. We avoid a pleasure if disproportional pain results from it; we choose a pain if the corresponding pleasure outweighs it (*To Men.* 129).

247. The value of virtue lies in it being the necessary and sufficient condition for a life full of pleasure (*To Men.* 132). DL X, 138 and Cicero, *De fin.* I, 42 compare it with a doctor's practice which has no value in itself but rather serves health. Moral insight is the practice of life. "One would not strive for it if it were without effects. But it is strived for because it is like an artist in finding and creating pleasure" (Cicero, ibid.). Passions and vices are sicknesses of the soul. "Where inclination is pitted against inclination and plans against plans, the soul can find no peace, no tranquility" (*De fin.* I, 58). In *KD* XXXI–XXXV Epicurus develops this approach with the example of justice (see *De fin.* I, 50–53). His arguments are reminiscent of the Sophist's theory that Plato summarizes in *Rep.* II. For Aristotle human beings are naturally determined with respect to the community of the polis, because in contrast to animals they are endowed with language. Animals also have sensations of pleasurable and painful things; only beings endowed with language, however, can be concerned with justice (*Pol.* I, 2 1253a12). This path is closed to Epicurus due to his canonic; language does not reveal any genuinely new realm of reality beyond perception (DL X, 31). Epicurus expressly disputes against Aristotle that

there is a natural community of rational beings (Frg. 523). The legal order is the contract of not harming each other that human beings consent to for the sake of their individual utility. No legal relation exists between peoples that are unable to form such a contract. This contract is binding, not due to the moral norm that contracts are to be adhered to, but exclusively due to its consequences. Illegality in itself is not an evil. Because norms are internalized, it makes the transgressor uneasy when she breaks the contract. She can never exclude the possibility of being discovered and must therefore fear the sanctions of society.

248. Whether friendship, which influenced Epicurus' life and personality so much, could be justified egoistically, as justice was, was disputed among the Epicureans. Cicero, *De fin.* I, 66–70 reports three conceptions: 1. Our own utility receives priority over that of the friend; friendship can be justified purely egoistically. 2. Friendship arises from one's own utility; the enduring time spent together leads to the friend being loved for his own sake. According to *Gn. Vat.* 23 (see 39) Epicurus maintained this position: "Every friendship is desirable for its own sake; it begins, however, from utility." 3. The wise sign a contract to love their friends no less than they love themselves. Here it is unclear whether this contract is motivated egoistically or altruistically.

249. According to the portrayal so far Epicurus' ethic is essentially an egoistic hedonism, and it is subject to all the objections that are raised against such a theory today. This criticism is justified. It should not, however, obscure the difference between our and the ancient understanding of ethics. For Hellenism ethics is primarily the teaching of happiness and of the correct attitude toward life. That leads to a central concern of Epicurus, theology. Lucretius I, 62ff. celebrates Epicurus as the liberator from inhumane repression of religion. Epicurus' battle against Plato's and Aristotle's teleological philosophy of nature is directed against the fears caused by religion. They can only be overcome if it can be shown that the divinity cannot interfere in the course

of the world's events (*KD* XI–XIII). The letter to Menoeceus and the *Main Teachings* start with the idea of god. "First,
understand god as an immutable and happy being, as the
general understanding of god is for human beings, and do
not attribute anything to him that is inappropriate for his
immutability or his happiness. Rather believe of him everything that allows you to maintain his immutability and happiness. For there are gods; knowledge of them is of obvious
clarity. They are not, however, as the many think" (*To Men.*
124). Like the Stoics (par. 225) the Epicureans were of the
opinion that the universal consent of all human beings allowed an inference to a naturally given idea of god, and this
to the existence of god (Cicero, *De nat. d.* I, 44).

250. Does theology have a positive function for Epicurus?
Is he concerned exclusively with a criticism of religion or
with a catharsis of the picture of god? Is only the destruction of false ideas of god sufficient for happiness or is positive belief in the existence of the holy god required? The texts
favor the second alternative. Epicurus' idea of god has a certain similarity with Aristotle's. According to both, god does
not interfere with the events of the world. He is a happy being to whom all human emotions are foreign. Like Aristotle's, Epicurus' god is a moral ideal. The immutability of
god is unattainable for human beings, but they can partake
of it in their own way if they live in the present (*To Men.*
124; *KD* XIXf.). If you follow my teachings, the letter to
Menoeceus concludes, "you will live as a god among men.
For a human being who lives among immortal goods is similar to an immortal being." Epicurus, so it reads in Cicero's
report (*De fin.* I, 71), listened to the voice of nature and understood it. In this lies liberation from societal coercion and
false needs. "You must serve philosophy so that you receive
true freedom" (Frg. 199). Especially Lucretius' poem shows
clearly that despite atomism the ancient piety toward the
cosmos is a basic feature of Epicurean philosophy: a theological relationship with nature whose limits are determined,
as are those of the moral ideal, by the sensualistic canonic.

III. Skepticism

1. PYRRHONIAN SKEPTICISM

251. There is little of any reliability about the founder of the school, *Pyrrho of Elis* (ca. 365–ca. 275 B.C.) (DL IX, 61–70). His attitude is thought to have been one of emphatic indifference and a deep conviction of the frailty, transience, and vanity of human life. He mistrusted all caution, gave way to no wagon or dog, and always had in mind the *Iliad*'s verse "The family of mankind is like the leaves" (Book VI). Perhaps he was motivated toward this attitude by the Indian ascetics whom he is thought to have met on Alexander the Great's military expeditions. He received philosophical inspiration from Democritus' skepticism (DK 68B6–10) and the Megarics' eristic. Pyrrho wrote nothing. We owe the earliest reports of his teachings to the fragments of poems and works in prose by his student *Timon of Phlius* (ca. 325–ca. 235 B.C.). He was the student of a Megarean. Timon had no successor. The Pyrrhonian school was founded anew by Ptolemy of Cyrene. We know only the names of the succession following him, with two exceptions. *Aenesidemus of Knossos* taught between 80 B.C. and 130 A.D. in Alexandria. An excerpt from his *Pyrrhonian Investigations* is preserved in Photius. He probably collected the ten tropes of epoché.

The most important source for Pyrrhonian skepticism is the doctor *Sextus Empiricus* who lived in Alexandria during the second half of the second century A.D. His earliest and most fundamental work is the *Outline of Pyrrhonian Skepticism* (*Pyrrhoneae hypotyposes*). Book I explains the character of skeptical philosophy; Books II and III, ordered according to the disciplines epistemology, physics, and ethics, is directed against the dogmatists, that is, philosophers that advance a teaching (dogma). A second work is preserved under the title *Adversus mathematicos*. But two different works are involved here. The earlier one encompasses Books VII–IX; it is a worked out version of *PH* II and III; it is also quoted as *Adversus dogmaticos*. The later one (M I–VI) is directed against grammarians, rhetoricians, geometers, arithmeticians, astrologers, and musicians.

252. Sextus portrays the basic experience of the skeptic with an anecdote: Apelles wanted to paint the foam of a horse's mouth. Because he was unsuccessful at painting it, he threw the cloth with which he cleaned the paint from the brush against the picture. As the cloth hit, the portrayal of the foam was successful (PH 27f.). Like the Stoics and the Epicureans, the Skeptics followed a practical goal, inner peace and independence (ataraxia). The Skeptics assume that they can only reach this goal if they are capable of making a justified judgment about reality. Whoever wants to be happy, as Timon teaches, must keep three questions in mind: "First, how the things are in reality; second, what attitude we ought to have toward them; third, what results from this attitude" (Aristocles of Eusebius, *Praep. ev.* XIV 18, 2). For this reason the Skeptics attempt to judge their representations in order to determine which of them are true and which false. But this epistemological undertaking fails.

The practical question cannot be answered along this path toward knowledge of reality. For it can be shown that every assertion can be countered by an opposing assertion that is supported by equally good reasons. If, for example, the Stoics prove the existence of providence from the ordered movement of the stars, the Skeptic claims that the opposite follows from the fact that good human beings are often miserable and bad ones happy. Because the Skeptic does not claim to be in a position that could decide between the two opinions, judgment is suspended. The Skeptic has the same experience as the painter Apelles: the practical goal is achieved via an unexpected path. Abandoning judgment graces him with inner freedom. In retrospect it is clear that it can only be found in this manner. The knowledge that something is in reality a good or evil leads necessarily to inner discontent. If a human being does not possess certain goods, she believes that she must acquire them; if she does possess them, she must fear their loss. Only renouncing all value judgments can bestow inner peace (PH I, 26–28).

253. Sextus defines skepticism as "the art of opposing all appearing and conceived things in all possible ways, from which we move first from the opposed things and arguments to renunciation (epochē) and then to peace in the soul (ataraxia) due to indifference (isostheneia)" (PH I, 8). In order to induce epoche, the Pyrrhonians introduced various "ways" (tropoi) of opposition. Three lists have been preserved. The oldest with ten tropes probably stems from Aenesidemus. The first trope refers to the variety of living beings; it shows that the same things can appear different to the different kinds of beings. The second refers to the differences between human beings; the third to the different construction of the sense organs; the fourth to the difference in states like health and sickness, sleep and waking; the fifth to the various distances and positions which causes the tower to appear round from afar and square close up; the tenth to the difference in mores, laws, and myths (PH I, 36–163; DL IX, 79–88). Agrippa added five further tropes: that of the conflict between views; of infinite regress; of relativity; of unprovable assumptions; of circles (PH I, 164–177; DL IX, 88f.). A third list encompasses two tropes: everything comes to be either from itself or from another, and neither of these is possible (PH I, 178f.). In order to verbalize his attitude and sensations in the application of the tropes the Skeptic uses certain slogans, for example, "Not this [before that]," "Perhaps"

and "Perhaps not," "It is possible" and "It is not possible," "I abstain" (PH I, 187–205).

254. The Pyrrhonians attacked philosophical systems that endeavored to demonstrate the existence of realities beyond experience with scientific means (PH I, 16). For this reason Sextus distinguishes a special section that is concerned with the dogmata of the philosophical schools (PH I, 5f.) from the general section in whose center stand the explanations of the goal of skepticism, the tropes and the slogans. But the Pyrrhonians also rejected all worldly assertions that attribute properties to things. We may say that the honey appears sweet to us; yet it is questionable whether the claim that it is sweet is justified (PH I, 19f.; 22). This should not be understood as if the Pyrrhonians maintained a theory like phenomenalism or an epistemology that claims or demonstrates the impossibility of knowledge. The problem of self-contradiction does not apply. Pyrrhonian skepticism is the art of abstaining from any judgment. The Skeptic should not express anything about the demonstrative force of the tropes (PH I, 35). The use of slogans does not at all imply any claim to truth. They express a sensation that abrogates itself with this expression (PH I, 206). The isosthene is not *claimed*. Insofar as claims are important for argumentation Skeptics do not argue. The view inconsistent with the opponents' claim is opposed to that claim under the sign of a skeptical slogan.

255. It is often objected against the Pyrrhonians that complete abstention of judgment is not livable. Mustn't we agree with certain states of affairs in order to live, like that this bread is not wood or that it has such and such consequences when a car drives into a wall at a high speed? Sextus, PH I, 24 is of the opinion that there can be a world without existential claims that suffices as an orientation for our actions. The Pyrrhonian holds to the feelings of displeasure that are forced upon him without judging that they are evil (PH I, 30). He orients his life according to the traditional mores and laws without judging them and uses the practi-

cal, technical experience without inquiring into a theoretical foundation.

256. One of the puzzles that the Pyrrhonians place in front of us is their motivation. If one proceeds from Sextus' Apellus story and Eusebius' Diocles report, the Skeptic wants to know reality because the practical question can only be answered in this manner. The skeptical attitude is only the result of the search for truth failing (see PH I, 12). On the other hand, according to Sextus' definition PH I, 8 it looks as if resignation is present even in the beginning: the Skeptic does not want to know and therefore looks for strategies that vilify any claim. Is the soul's peace a consequence of the failed search for truth or is it to be found in the Pyrrhonian programmatically and systematically avoiding the question of truth? The Stoic can think of things indifferently because the only concern is following the logos. What positive content for life does the Pyrrhonian find in the epoche?

2. ACADEMIC SKEPTICISM

257. Around 268 B.C. *Arcesilaus of Pitane* in Musia (Asia Minor) took up the leadership of the Academy (see par. 127). He is the founder of the Middle (PH I, 220; DL IV, 28) or the New (Cicero, *Acad.* I, 46) Academy. He is believed to have heard Theophrastus initially and then joined with the Academician Crantor (DL IV, 29). DL IV, 32f. emphasizes Plato's, Pyrrho's and the Megarean dialectician Diodorus Cronus' influences. Like Pyrrho, Arcesilaus wrote nothing. He too taught the epoché that results from exclusive assertions, both of which can be justified (DL IV, 28). Arcesilaus subjected the Stoic epistemology to sharp criticism. He objected to the cataleptic representation: 1. The object of our assent is not a representation but a proposition. 2. There is no nondeceitful representation. Through many and differing examples it can be shown that every representation can be false. Thus the wise person only has the option of ab-

staining from judgment. For practical life, however, we need a criterion to distinguish between correct and incorrect actions. Here Arcesilaus appears to follow the Stoic doctrine of suitable actions (par. 233): an action is correct if it can be justified with good reasons (M VII, 150–158). Normative statements are not true either, but apparently there is a difference in the weight of the reasons for them.

258. Socrates claimed to know that he knows nothing. Arcesilaus expresses that we cannot even know that. Thus he too was obviously not a dogmatic skeptic. According to Cicero's testimony his skepticism was motivated by the search for truth. The wise person must abstain from assenting in order not to err (*Acad.* I, 45; II, 60; 76). Sextus PH I, 234 tells a rumor according to which Arcesilaus was a Pyrrhonian in appearance but a Platonic dogmatist in truth. "From the front Plato, from the back Pyrrho, in the middle Diodorus." He is thought to have initially tested his students in aporetics in order to then teach the talented ones Platonic dogmata. The true core of this story is probably that Arcesilaus' skepticism was inspired by the aporetic of the Platonic Socrates.

259. The second important proponent of academic skepticism is *Carneades of Cyrene,* the founder of the New Academy (PH I, 220). Along with the Stoic Diogenes of Babylon and the Peripatetic Critolaus he was an Athenian messenger in Rome, where on two successive days he held a speech for and against justice (Cicero, *De republica* III, 6). He is primarily a sharp critic of the Stoics. "If Chrysippus hadn't been, I would not have been either." His passion for work was so great that he let his hair and fingernails grow long (DL IV, 62f.). He wrote nothing himself. The doxographic reports on him derive mainly from the comprehensive production of his student and successor *Cleitomachus of Carthage* (DL IV, 67). Carneades, who is believed to have been especially competent in ethics (DL IV, 62), is reported to have been concerned with the Stoic teaching of the goal of action (see Long 1967). Cicero reports in *De nat. d.* III

of his criticism of the Stoic theology and in *De fato* on his controversy with Chrysippus regarding causality, determinism, and freedom.

260. Carneades developed a remarkable epistemology (M VII, 166–189). Like the Stoics (par. 219) he proceeds from the concept of representation (phantasia). First, every representation stands in a relation to the object it represents. In this respect it can be true or false. It is true if it corresponds with the represented object; otherwise false. Second, the representation stands in a relation to the human being entertaining the representation. It can appear to her as true or false. In this respect one can distinguish between probable (pithanos) and not-probable representations. (Literally 'pithanos' means "plausible"; Cicero *Acad.* II, 99 translates it with 'probabilis'.) Carneades' epistemology is skeptical or empirical insofar as he assumes that we do not have access to the relation between the representation and the represented object. We cannot pass over from the representation to the thing-in-itself. Assent can only be oriented toward the relation between the representation and the representer. The not-probable representations are eliminated as a criterion. Among the probable representations one is to distinguish between the indistinct ones, for example, those that stem from a small or distant object or are perceived by a weakened faculty of sight, and those that offer themselves as very probable due to the quality of perception. The latter is the first criterion that still requires, however, two further criteria. A probable representation is not an infallible criterion. It can be false. But because it is true in most cases, it is reasonable to use it as a criterion of assent. A representation never arises in isolation but rather always in conjunction with other representations. The second criterion is thus, whether the whole system of representations in which the representation in question is found has the requisite qualifications. If that is the case, Carneades speaks of a "probable and also unimpeded representation." That this man is Socrates is probable if we can observe his usual size, bodily posture, clothing, and so

on. Finally, as the third criterion we have the possibility of "going through" the whole system of representations. We can check the perceiving subject, whether her faculty of sight is sufficiently sharp and in what mental attitude the faculty can be found; the perceived object, whether it has the required size; the medium through which we perceive the object; the distance; and so on. Whether we use only the probable representation or also the unimpeded and the "going through" as a criterion depends on the importance of the thing in question and the circumstances.

F. Neoplatonism

261. Neoplatonism is the dominating philosophy of the late ancient period. From the last decades of the third century A.D. Plato and Aristotle are handed down and commented on by Neoplatonists. Until the beginning of the nineteenth century Plato was interpreted for the most part Neoplatonically. Beginning with apologetics in the second century up to the recovery of Aristotle since the middle of the twelfth century Christian philosophy and theology are influenced by Middle and Neoplatonism. Neoplatonism is connected with Stoicism by its religious interest. Especially the Stoic concept of logos is integrated into the Platonic system. Plotinus' philosophy, especially the teaching of the three hypostases — namely, the One, the Intelligence, and the Soul — had the way prepared for it by Middle Platonism beginning in the first century B.C., which ties in with the later Plato's and the early Academy's theory of principles as well as with the *Timaeus'* creation myth. Neoplatonism, and along with it ancient philosophy, ends in the West with the closing of the Academy in Athens by Emperor Justinian I in the year 529 and in the East with the Arabian conquest of Alexandria in the year 642.

I. Middle Platonism

262. Under Arcesilaus the Academy had turned toward skepticism (par. 257). *Antiochus of Ascalon* (ca. 130–ca. 68 B.C.) led it back to dogmatism. He is strongly influenced by Stoic philosophy, especially physics. Perhaps the theory that the Forms are God's thoughts stemmed from him. Antiochus cannot, however, be seen as the founder of Middle Platonism because the later Plato's and the early Academy's theory of principles is not to be found in his philosophy. *Eudorus of Alexandria* (dec. ca. 25 B.C.) does, however, tie in with this theory. He prepares the way for Plotinus' monism and theory of hypostases: the One is the cause of everything, even matter. He distinguishes between the first and the second One. Eudorus comments on the *Timaeus*. The Hellenistic Jew *Philo* (ca. 25 B.C.–ca. 50 A.D.) also taught in Alexandria. He connects Jewish monotheism with Platonic theology by means of his allegorical interpretation of the Bible, especially of Genesis. God is the transcendent One and the cause of all being. Matter is created. God orders it by giving it his son, the logos, who penetrates, forms, and holds it together as a mediator of creation in the manner of the Stoic pneuma. The divine logos is the pattern for human reason. The Forms are God's thoughts; logos is the Form of Forms. Like Philo, *Plutarch of Chaeronea* (ca. 45–ca. 125 A.D.), well known due to his biographies and moral works, is not a systematic thinker. Again, like the former, he emphasizes the transcendence of God. The causes of the world which came to be

in time are, tying in with the *Timaeus,* the demiurge, the Forms, and matter. Plutarch recognizes a good and an evil World-Soul. Matter is neutral. His religious interest is revealed in an extensive demonology and teaching of reincarnation.

263. *Albinus* (second century A.D.) and *Apuleius of Madura* (born ca. 123 A.D.) are attributed, according to several scholars, to a common school founded by Gaius, the teacher of Albinus. Albinus' *Didaskalikos* (Outline of Platonic Philosophy) combines Platonic with Aristotelian and Stoic teachings. He recognizes two triads: matter, Forms, and the first God that corresponds to the *Timaeus'* demiurge; and the first God, whose ineffability he emphasizes, the Intelligence, and the World-Soul. Albinus distinguishes a twofold concept of Forms. The immaterial (Platonic) Forms are God's thoughts; their copies are (Aristotelian) forms bound to matter. Clearer than in Albinus, Plotinus' theory of hypostases is anticipated by Apuleius' triad (*De dogmate Platonis*) "first God, Intelligence and Forms, Soul." Here as in Plotinus the original Forms are clearly assigned to the second principle.

Whereas Albinus assumes a fundamental correspondence between Plato and Aristotle, *Atticus* (around 176 A.D.) is an orthodox Platonist who sharply criticizes Aristotle and all attempts of harmonizing him with Plato. Aristotle denied the immateriality and the immortality of the soul, probably with his teaching of entelechy (par. 168). Aristotle's theology of the unmoved mover does not admit providence and is thus a form of atheism. In his *Timaeus* interpretation Atticus assumes an uncreated matter that is held in chaotic motion by the evil World-Soul. The demiurge gives the Forms to matter and intelligence to the evil World-Soul.

264. Authors and pseudoepigraphs that stem from the Pythagorean tradition reveal similarities with Middle Platonism. *Moderatus of Gnades* (first century A.D.) claims that Plato, Aristotle, and the early Academy stole all of their most important teachings from Pythagoras. According to him there is a first, a second, and a third One. The first One is beyond

ousia, or being; the second is to be equated with the Forms; the third, the Soul, participates in the first and second. *Nicomachus of Gerasa* (second century A.D.) equates numbers and deities in his *Arithmetic Theology. Numenius'* (second century A.D.) proximity to Plotinus is testified to by Plotinus being accused of plagiarizing his works (Porphyrios, *Vita Plot.,* par. 82). Theology, Numenius claims in his work *On the Good,* must originate back beyond Plato to Pythagoras and integrate the teachings of the Brahman, the Jews, magicians, and Egyptians (Fr. 1a). Plato is nothing other than an "attic speaking Moses" (Fr. 8). Numenius' first god is only related to itself. The second and third gods are only two different functions of the next hypostasis. It contemplates the Forms in the first god, and it combines with matter in order to give the Forms to it, and in doing so loses its unity (Fr. 11).

II. Plotinus
Life and Works

265. We possess a valuable biography of Plotinus by his student Porphyry. Plotinus was born in 205 A.D.; place of birth and nation are unknown. When twenty-eight years old he turned to philosophy and found a teacher in Ammonius Saccas, who impressed him so much that he stayed with him eleven years. We know about Ammonius only that he maintained the immateriality of the soul and the fundamental correspondence between Plato and Aristotle. In 243 Plotinus joined Emperor Gordian III's Persian expedition in order to become acquainted with Persian and Indian philosophies. This information has caused a discussion about whether oriental influences can be found in Plotinus' philosophy. This is to be denied; Plotinus stands in the Greek tradition. In the beginning of 244 Gordian was murdered in Mesopotamia. Plotinus then went to Rome, and there he began to give lectures at the age of forty. Only after lecturing for ten years did he begin to write. Many men and women from the most distinguished circles for whom death was near took their children to Plotinus and entrusted them to him as a guardian along with their whole estate. Plotinus took the children into his house. In many disputes he took on the office of arbitrator. Porphyry reports Plotinus' religiousness: "Here [in a quoted oracle] it is said that he . . . was awake without falling asleep, that his soul was pure, and that he always aspires to the divine which he longs for with his entire soul.

. . . To precisely this demonic man, when he rose to the first transcendent God on the path that Plato described in the *Symposium*, appeared the God who has no shape or form and is enthroned above the Intelligence and the whole intelligible world [. . .] it was namely his goal and target to be close to and one with the God that is above all; during the time that I was with him he attained this goal four times due to his ineffable power" (chap. 23). Plotinus died in 270 A.D. at the estate of a friend in Minturnae at Campagna.

266. The biographies introduce the edition of Plotinus' works obtained by Porphyry. It contains 54 works in the temporal series of their origin. Porphyry did not, however, want to leave the works in their chronological order. Thus, he ordered the works according to subject matter and summarized them into six enneads.

1. THE INTERPRETER OF PLATO

267. Plotinus understands himself to be an interpreter of Plato's philosophy. "These teachings are not new, not just now, but were said long ago, even if not clearly and expressly, and our present teachings are only presented as interpretations of the old teachings, and the fact that these teachings are old is corroborated by the testimony of Plato's own writings" (V 1, 8). This passage makes clear that Plotinus is aware of standing in a tradition. The age of the teaching is the guarantor of its objective authority. Plato is the distinguished witness of this tradition. Plotinus abbreviated Plato, however, especially with respect to his political dimension. Porphyry's characterization of his personality reveals that he is first a philosopher of religion. Cosmology, psychology, and philosophy of mind are done with an interest in philosophy of religion in the forefront. Ethics is the teaching of internal catharsis. Plotinus develops a metaphysics of "longing for the completely other," whose fundamental concept is not that of being but rather that of Beauty and Goodness.

From the biographies the twofold origin of his philosophy becomes clear: the Platonic tradition and his own mystic experience. Plotinus unified the elements of Middle Platonic philosophy into an organic unity due to his own personal experience. He utilizes the language of the Platonic-Aristotelian metaphysics in order to portray his own mystical experience with these means. It follows from the combination of metaphysics and mysticism that Plotinus' philosophy combines two perspectives with each other. On the one hand he stands in the tradition of Greek cosmology. Like the pre-Socratics and Aristotle, he inquires into the first causes in the universe. The path to God for him is an ascent in the series of causes. The other perspective consists in this ascent simultaneously being the path to oneself, into the heart of one's soul. The three hypostases—Soul, Intelligence, and the One—are found not only in the cosmos but also in individual human beings. One can certainly find intimations for this perspective in Plato and Aristotle, but it is only expressly developed by Plotinus for the first time, who thus prepares the way for idealism. For Plotinus cosmology and metaphysical psychology are only two different ways of looking at one and the same reality.

2. METAPHYSICS OF BEAUTY

268. We will attempt to gain access to Plotinus' thought through the work I, 6 *The Beautiful*. It is a metaphysics of aesthetic experience and is concerned to attain a representation of the One. The presupposition for that is that one rises above the visible world into the realm of the intelligible. Aesthetic experience is supposed to be the starting point for that. I, 6 is Plotinus' earliest work; it ties in closely with Diotima's *Symposium* speech (par. 99). Like Plato, Plotinus starts at the level of bodily beauty. In this manner the whole investigation is undeniably placed on a phenomenal foundation.

In it the erotic and the aesthetic experience are not distinguished. Plato and Plotinus retain this unity for the higher
levels as well. The beautiful is not only admired but also
loved and desired. This aesthetic experience is one of harmony, correspondence, relatedness, agreement, and accord.
It is explained with the help of an ontological language; the
central concept is that of eidos. Aesthetic knowledge is recollection. Plotinus proceeds from the ontology of Book Zeta
(par. 159). The soul is "what something is": it is what a human being is, its human beingness, its form. As such it is
primary being in a first sense when compared with matter
and the composite substance. At the same time the form of
visible substances that the soul perceives is the cause of beauty.
Something is ugly if it has no form or is not completely controlled by the form. A whole is beautiful in which the matter is completely determined by the form, in which the form
comes to its complete expression and its complete development and for this reason can be perceived. When the soul
perceives the form that is completely developed in the beautiful object, it is aware of itself and its own ontological status. These thoughts are to be explained in some more detail.

269. The eidos as being proper is the cause of beauty.
This consideration is universalized in the work V, 8. Plotinus expounds, as one could say in scholastic terminology,
the claim of the transcendentality of the beautiful. "For where
would beauty be if it were robbed of being? And where would
being be if it lacked beauty? For by lacking beauty it would
also be lacking in being [. . .] Who should investigate which
is the cause of the other if they are one and the same being?"
A perceivable substance *is* due to the form, and that means
it is only insofar "as it has received a part of the beauty of
the eidos, and the more it partakes of this, the more perfect
it is. For it is more than being (ousia) if it is beautiful" (§
62f.). Reality is not disclosed entirely through concepts. The
function of eidos is not exhausted in its causality; it is not
merely a theoretical, ontological concept. Aesthetic experi-

ence reveals an original mode of access to being. Being is always also an object of desire. That is shown prior to the aesthetic experience in the phenomenon of preservation. Plotinus' aesthetics and the later teaching of transcendentals are directed on the one hand against a rationalistic abridgment of the concept of being. That a being is beautiful according to the rank of its being is a synthetic proposition. The independence of the phenomenon is protected. They are directed on the other hand against irrationalism. The assertion that the beautiful has being to the extent that it is beautiful places the beautiful in the whole framework of reality. The world of aesthetics is not a separate world. The object of aesthetic experience can also be described in ontological language. Aesthetic experiences can be justified by ontological propositions.

270. Aesthetic knowledge is recollection. A look at the beautiful reminds the soul "of itself and of what it carries in itself" (I, 6, §10). Like Plato and Aristotle Plotinus distinguishes different faculties of the soul. Knowledge of the beautiful or of the form is an achievement of the soul's highest faculty. Yet it is not an exclusively rational process but is also an emotional one; the other faculties of the soul are active along with it. Knowledge presupposes a twofold mode of being for the eidos. First it appears in the variety of parts in the perceived object. Plotinus distinguishes between form and shape. Shape is the appearance of the indivisible form in the variety of the parts. At the same time the eidos is in the soul as a higher undivided mode of being. Knowledge creates a relation between the eidos' two modes of being. The eidos in the soul is the norm according to which the eidos of the perceived object is judged. Perception summarizes the eidos which is spread out over the variety of the parts into its indivisible unity. It brings the unity into the inner part of the soul where correspondence with the eidos which was always already present in the soul can be ascertained.

3. THE INTELLIGENCE

271. The starting point of the work I, 6 is passive aesthetic experience. The later work V, 8 attempts, conversely, to gain access to metaphysics from the active aesthetic process, the artist's creative activity. The work concerns, as does the entire fifth Ennead, primarily the second hypostasis, the Intelligence (*Vita*, §145). We encountered it briefly in I, 6 since the undivided forms in the soul were the subject matter. The cause of an artwork's beauty is its eidos. Before the artist imprints the form on the matter, it is present in her insofar as she partakes in art. The comparison of the Intelligence with art is developed under three points of view.

272. a) Creativity. An artist produces something new. Originality is characteristic for art. Plotinus attacks the false understanding that art imitates nature. For him nature and art are original to the same extent. Creativity is the artist's ability. His art is the unity from which the variety of ideas and forms that he creates arises. The Intelligence is not form but is rather the producer of all forms. Plotinus compares the soul with the matter and the Intelligence with the artist. The soul possesses, as we saw, the undivided forms. It can only know because it is capable of grasping the individual, distinct forms. The Intelligence is the original unity in which the forms are not yet distinct from each other. Differentiation only begins when it imprints them on the soul, as the artist does to matter. The Intelligence as cause of the forms is beautiful in a more proper sense than the forms. The relation of the visible world to the Intelligence is interpreted with the concept of "picture." Plotinus emphasizes that not an artificial but rather a natural picture is involved here. An artificial picture is a painting or a statue; a natural picture is a reflection or a shadow (see Plato, *Rep.* 510a). This concept of picture has an epistemological function; the beauty of the original can be discerned from the beauty of the copies. This concept is also supposed to show the kind of causality

the Intelligence has. The Intelligence does not create the cosmos in the same manner as an artist or craftsman does a product. The latter deliberate and decide to produce something. The Intelligence, however, creates the cosmos as necessarily as the sun does light or an object produces its reflection or shadow. From this it follows that the cosmos is eternal like the Intelligence.

b) Intuition. The artist does not construct. The whole is prior to the details. She knows, not discursively, but rather intuitively. Intuition is the unity that forms the artwork into its final details. It is in this that Plotinus sees the difference between art and science. Science works with premises and conclusions. An artist's intuitive knowledge is prior to scientific thought, which is always only the development of an original intuition. Plotinus illustrates the difference between the understanding's discursive thought and the Intelligence's intuitive knowledge with the difference between alphabetic script and hieroglyphics. Whoever reads alphabetic script takes up one sign after the other. Reading and speaking are a process of passage in the dimension of succession. Correspondingly, discursive thought works with definitions that analyze a concept and with axioms that combine concepts with each other. Hieroglyphics' symbols stand for the forms in the Intelligence. Every picture is the whole wisdom, every form the whole Intelligence.

c) Wholeness. Every work of art reflects the entirety of reality. It only communicates its message to who grasps it intuitively as a whole. Plotinus illustrates the wholeness of the Intelligence with a comparison to homogeneous matter—for example, gold—with light. In contrast to an organism or a house, gold does not consist in different kinds of parts. Even the smallest part is gold in the full sense of the word. In this sense every part is the whole. Light is completely transparent, and it permeates itself. In a certain sense the various forms are parts of the Intelligence. Each of these forms is, however, the entirety of the forms, and the entirety of the forms is the Intelligence, so that each form is the entire Intelligence. Knowledge is described with the help of the metaphor of light as a reciprocal permeation. Every form is known exhaustively and through it the entire reality with which it is identical. The individual form is the whole Intelligence and thus a knowing principle. When the Intelligence knows a form, it knows all of reality and thus itself. The work V, 9 (§32) compares the Intelligence with science. Science is the entirety of its sentences. But every particular sentence is in a sense the whole science. Only whoever understands the whole science can understand a particular sentence. It receives its meaning only through the system of the entire science.

4. THE ONE

273. Not only being beautiful but also being the One is a transcendental predicate of being according to Plotinus. "All being," work VI, 9 *The Good (The One)* begins, which we shall follow initially, "is a being through the One." A plant and an animal are one; they lose their essence along with their unity. The perfection of a being corresponds to its degree of unity. The soul as the cause of the unity of the body is one in a higher degree than its body. But the soul too is a plurality; it has different faculties, for example, thinking, desiring, perceiving. The step decisive for the following considerations is that Plotinus reveals a difference between the Soul and the One and more generally between the eidos and the One. If we assume that the eidos is being in the proper sense, this consideration leads to a difference between being and the One. The soul gives the body unity but, as itself a plurality, relies upon a principle of unity. Every eidos is a principle of unity, but, according to Plotinus, it too is a plurality. So the Intelligence cannot be the ultimate principle of reality. If every being is by being the One, and the Intelligence cannot be the ultimate cause of unity, it cannot be the ultimate principle of reality either. The concept of In-

telligence contains a difference between the thinker and the thought. The Intelligence reflects on itself in its thought. Plotinus gives this self-relation a specific accent: by inquiring into itself the Intelligence inquires into its origin. It experiences its plurality in its reflection, and it inquires into the unity in which it is grounded. In this manner it becomes aware that it is not the Ultimate. Thus the Intelligence can only be at home with itself such that it is with its origin, the One. By thinking the One it thinks itself, and by thinking itself it thinks the entirety of reality. The Intelligence is being in the proper sense; it is the entirety of being. Being is conceived of from the perspective of predication. It can be said what being is, and this assertion reveals a plurality in any case. Therefore the One cannot be a being. It is eidosless and is in this sense nothingness. "To the extent that the soul forges into the shapeless, which it is completely incapable of grasping because the soul is not determined by it, not even stamped with rich variety, it slides and is afraid of grasping nothingness" (VI, 9, §16). The One is neither a something nor a being. It does not fall under the categories of quantity or quality. It is neither moving nor at rest, neither in space nor in time. When we say that it is the cause of everything, we are not saying what it is in itself; we are merely uttering an assertion about our relation to the One. If we say that it is the One, we are thus only negating plurality and divisibility without being able to think the unity positively.

274. But how do we have access to it nonetheless? It is the last point of retreat to which all life acts return and in which they come together such that "everything depends on it, looking up to which everything lives and thinks; for it is the cause of life, thought, and being" (I, 6, §33). "For all things aspire to it, they drive toward it, forced by their natures, as if they intuited that they could not be without it. The beautiful is deeply stirred and is gazed at by those who already know and are awakened, and this waking oc-

curs through the Eros; the Good, however, which has always accompanied us as the object of our natural desire, even as long as we are still slumbering, this Good does not amaze us if we see it one day because it is always with us and we never need to remind ourselves of it, only we do not see it, because it is present to us even in our sleep" (V, 5, §76f.). Plotinus uses the metaphor of a circle for this unconscious presence of the One or the Good (V, 1, §60; VI, 9, §56). It is the midpoint of the soul, and the soul performs its own essential motion if it does not flee into the extremities, but rather circles around its midpoint. This metaphor requires more precise clarification, however. The One is not the midpoint of the soul but rather the midpoint of all being. But the soul has the possibility of touching this absolute midpoint with its own midpoint. The One is always in us, but we are not always with it. It does not desire us, but we desire it because we only truly live if we have made it our middle. As the absolute midpoint it is the primitive ground of being, source of the Intelligence, cause of the Good, and root of the soul (VI, 9, §60). The metaphor of the source is not to be understood such that the One loses something of its perfection by bringing forth the Intelligence and the Soul. It suffers neither a lessening nor a change. The rising forth of the Intelligence from the One corresponds to that of light from the sun. Like the sun's light, the Intelligence is the expression of the perfection of the One. Light is necessarily there as long as the sun exists. Thus the Intelligence and the Soul are eternal and necessary like the One. But just as the light cannot be without the sun, the Intelligence and the Soul cannot be without the One. The Intelligence has the faculty of love in addition to that of thinking. Thinking can only grasp what is in the Intelligence. Only love is capable of touching the Good that lies beyond the Intelligence (VI, 7, §273). This encounter cannot be achieved due to one's own power alone; human beings can only prepare themselves and wait until it appears (V, 5,

§53). Then the Soul becomes one with the One "by having the midpoints touch." The union is no viewing "but rather another mode of sight: moving out of oneself, making oneself simple and sacrificing" (VI, 9, §§71–76).

III. Neoplatonism after Plotinus

275. Like Plotinus the later Neoplatonists are primarily philosophers of religion. Plato and Aristotle are viewed as complementary proponents of *one* philosophy who are distinguished only verbally from each other. In Athens, Alexandria, and Constantinople there were teaching chairs that were financed by public means. That is one of the reasons for the scholastic character of Neoplatonism. Plato and Aristotle are authorities; the greatest part of their preserved works are commentaries, especially on Aristotle. The religious interest allowed not only myths and cults but also a theurgy, a magic that was based on religious revelation and served religious aims, to appear philosophically important. Characteristic of their metaphysics is the plurality of hypostases that are divided into Plotinus' triad; it is to help humans ascend to the first principle, conceived in exaggerated transcendence. The standard work on the divisions of the movements and schools was and still is today that of Karl Praechter (1910; 1926), whose systematization I shall adopt in the following.

1. THE METAPHYSICAL-SPECULATIVE MOVEMENT

a) Plotinus' School

276. Plotinus' school is represented especially by *Porphyry* (ca. 234–301/305), who was Plotinus' student in Rome from

ca. 262 to ca. 267. He takes over the basic thoughts of his teacher, whose works he publishes (par. 266) and explains and whose philosophy he makes accessible to the general public. One difference with Plotinus is the stronger emphasis on the religious-practical setting of goals. Philosophy serves the soul's welfare. Porphyry's interest in theurgy is testified to by his work *Chaldaic Oracle,* which originated between 160 and 180 A.D. and was repeatedly used by later Neoplatonists. He is the first Neoplatonic commentator of Aristotle. His *Eisagogé,* an introduction to Aristotle's work on categories, was very influential in the medieval period. In it Porphyry explains the five concepts ("quinque voces") — genus, differentia, species, proprium, and accident — and formulates the problem of the mode of being of universal concepts (the problem of universals). In his knowledgeable and comprehensive work he fights against Christianity.

b) The Syrian School

277. Its founder is *Iamblichus* (ca. 250–ca. 330), a student of Porphyry. He underlines the transcendence of the Absolute and multiplies the number of hypostases in order to make the ascent to it easier. "The completely ineffable Origin" stands above Plotinus' One. He divides Plotinus' second hypostasis into the intelligible world of Forms and the intellectual world of thinking beings that are both in turn divided into three more groups. A second nous mediates between them and the threefold soul. Knowledge of the gods is immediately given along with the soul's essential desire for the Good. Nonetheless, it requires a metaphysical justification. The Greek and oriental gods are integrated into the system of hypostases. Belief in miracles and theurgy play an important role for Iamblichus. He justifies the Neoplatonic exegesis of Plato with his systematic interpretation of the dialogs that is oriented toward the threefold division of metaphysics, mathematics, and physics.

c) The Athenian School

278. The most important figure of Neoplatonism after Plotinus is *Proclus* (ca. 411–485). He is the great scholastic to whom we owe the most closed portrayal of the system. His works encompass, among other things, commentaries on Plato, systematic works—for example, the *The Elements of Theology* and *On Plato's Theology*—and mathematical investigations. He is a worshipper of the gods, an unmarried ascetic, visionary and theurgean. As for Plotinus, the basic problem for Proclus is the relation between the One and the Many. Plotinus had already distinguished between a higher and a lower hypostasis: the lower flows from the higher (emanation) and returns to it. Proclus analyzes this process into three moments: 1. The caused is similar to the cause; to this extent it "remains" in it (monē). 2. It it distinct from the cause; to this extent it "leaves" it (proodos). 3. To the extent the cause is efficacious in the effect it is everywhere in the effect; insofar as it is distinct from it it is nowhere. For this reason the effect "returns" to the cause (epistrophē). The entirety of reality is determined by the law of this triadic circular motion. Proclus agrees with Plotinus in the teaching of the One. An important addition is that the One initially brings forth unities (henaden). They are absolutely simple, but insofar as they are distinct from each other they form a unity. In the realm of the Intelligence Proclus furthers Iamblichus' twofold division into a threefold one by distinguishing between being (the intelligible), thought (the intellectual), and life (the intelligible-intellectual). Proclus equates natural religion's gods with metaphysical entities.

Hegel's admiration for Proclus is opposed by Zeller's sober judgment, for whom Proclus' immense systematizing achievement is only gained at the price of a "boring and monotonous formalism" (III, 2, p. 846). The great influence Proclus had on the late patristic period, the medievals, renaissance philosophy, and German Idealism with his transmission of

Pseudo-Dionysius the Areopagite and the *Liber de causis* is undisputed.

279. The last scholarch of Plato's Academy is *Damascus* (born ca. 458). He works out the aporias in Proclus' system and arrives at the result that the bringing forth of the Many from the One and their reciprocal relation is not rationally conceivable; all representations of this are only makeshifts due to human weakness. This agnosticism is combined with subtle distinctions and an uncritical mysticism. Along with Damascus, his student *Simplicius* emigrated to Persia after the closing of the Academy and returns with him to the Roman Empire two years later. Simplicius' scholarly commentaries on Aristotle are a valuable treasure chest of fragments and doxographic reports ranging from the pre-Socratics to lost Aristotle commentaries. He maintains a complete agreement between Aristotle and Plato in all essential points.

2. THE RELIGIOUS-THEURGICAL MOVEMENT

280. The founder of the school of Pergamon is *Aedesius,* a student of Iamblichus. The school is best known due to Emperor *Julian* (331–363). Stemming from the family of Constantine the Great and raised as a Christian, in 351 he professed himself a member of a Neoplatonically interpreted sun cult. The attempted pagan restoration during his rule (361–363) earned him the nickname "Apostata" (the Apostate). *Sallustius'* small work *On the Gods and the World* is an outline of Neoplatonic dogmatism, which might have been written for Julian's religious politics.

3. THE SCHOLARLY MOVEMENT

a) The Alexandrian School

281. Whereas the schools mentioned so far were all decidedly opponents of Christianity due to their emphatic con-

nection with Greek and oriental religions, an encounter between Neoplatonism and Christianity takes place in the Alexandrian school. Metaphysical-religious speculation recedes
behind the special sciences and an exegesis of Plato and Aristotle that is oriented less toward a system and more toward
the texts. *Hypatia,* celebrated female philosopher with a
teaching chair in Platonic philosophy, mathematician, and
astronomer, is also known for her tragic death; she was murdered in 415 by Christians. Synesius of Cyrene, bishop of
Ptolemy after 411, combines in his hymns the Christian doctrine of the Trinity with Iamblichus' metaphysics. *Hierocles
of Alexandria* (fifth century) is more of a Middle Platonist.
He recognizes only the Demiurge as a transcendent divinity; the Neoplatonic theory of hypostases is not found in his
works. We owe a series of preserved commentaries on Aristotle to *Ammonius,* the son of Hermias (Ammonius Hermeiu), and his school, to which Simplicius also belongs (par.
279). The Christian *Ioannes Philoponus* (ca. 490–ca. 570),
student of Ammonius, defended the Christian teaching of
creation ex nihilo against Aristotelian natural philosophy.
Especially in his work *On the Eternity of the World* he argues against Proclus that not only the world, as several Middle Platonists taught, but also matter has a beginning in time.

b) The Neoplatonists of the Latin West

282. Their importance stems mainly from the fact that
they provided Platonic and Aristotelian thought to the Latin
medievals with their translations and commentaries. The partial Latin translation and commentary on the *Timaeus* (31c–
53c) by *Chalcidius* (fourth/fifth century), who used the
Peripatetics Adrastus and Porphyry, is one of the most important sources of Platonic cosmology and theology for the
medieval period. The rhetorician *Marius Victorinus* (around
350), who became a Christian late in life and whose example impressed Augustine (*Conf.* 8, 2–5), translated parts of
the Organon and probably Plotinus and Porphyry. He inter-

preted the Trinity with Neoplatonic concepts. *Macrobius'* influential commentary on Cicero's *Somnium Scipionis,* who used Porphyry's *Timaeus* commentary, renders discernible a Plotinian-Porphyrian Neoplatonism. More than all of these, however, *Boethius* (ca. 480–524) is to be mentioned, who was accused of treason and executed by Theodoric the Great. His plan to translate and comment on Plato's and Aristotle's entire corpus, whose agreement he presumed, could only partially be fulfilled (for most of the works in the Organon). His theological works contain influential definitions, for example, of 'eternity' (aeternitas) and for the terms 'person' and 'nature' which are so important for the doctrine of the Trinity and Christology. The famous *Consolation of Philosophy* which he wrote in prison combines Cynic, Stoic, and Middle Platonic thoughts.

Works

Anaxagoras, *The Fragments of Anaxagoras,* ed., intr., comm. by D. Sider, Meisenheim 1981
Antisthenis fragmenta, coll. F. D. Caizzi, Milano 1966
Aristippi et Cyrenaicorum fragmenta, ed. E. Mannebach, Leiden 1961

Aristotle

The Works of Aristotle, translated into English under the editorship of W. D. Ross, 12 vols., Oxford 1908ff.

Commentaries

———, *Categories and De Interpretatione,* trsl. with notes by J. L. Ackrill, Oxford 1974
———, *Prior and Posterior Analytics,* ed. with intr. and comm. by W. D. Ross, Oxford 1949; reprt. 1965
———, *Posterior Analytics,* trsl. with notes by J. Barnes, Oxford 1975
———, *Physics,* ed. with intr. and comm. by W. D. Ross, Oxford 1936; reprt. 1966
———, *Physikvorlesung,* übers. von H. Wagner, 4th ed. Berlin 1983
———, *Physics I, II,* trsl., intr., notes by W. Charlton, Oxford 1970
———, *Physics III, IV,* trsl. with notes by E. Hussey, Oxford 1983
———, *On Coming-to-Be and Passing-Away* (De generatione et corruptione), ed. with intr. and comm. by H. H. Joachim, Oxford 1922; reprt. Hildesheim 1970
———, *De generatione et corruptione,* trsl. with notes by C. J. F. Williams, Oxford 1982
———, *De anima,* ed. with trsl., intr., notes by R. D. Hicks, Cambridge 1907; reprt. Amsterdam 1965
———, *De anima,* ed. with intr. and comm. by W. D. Ross, Oxford 1961
———, *De anima II, III,* trsl., intr., notes by W. D. Hamlyn, Oxford 1968

——, *Metaphysics,* ed. with intr. and comm. by W. D. Ross, 2 vols., Oxford 1924; reprt. 1966
——, *Metaphysics IV, V, VIII,* trsl. with notes by Chr. Kirwan, Oxford 1971
——, *Metaphysics XIII, XIV,* trsl., intr., notes by J. Annas, Oxford 1976
——, *The Nicomachean Ethics: A Commentary* by H. H. Joachim, ed. by D. A. Rees, Oxford 1962
——, *Eudemian Ethics I, II, VIII,* trsl. with a comm. by M. Woods, Oxford 1982
——, *The Politics of Aristotle,* ed. with intr., two pref. essays, notes by W. L. Newman, 4 vols., Oxford 1887–1902; reprt. New York 1973
——, *The Politics of Aristotle,* trsl., intr., notes, appendices by E. Barker, Oxford 1946; reprt. London 1976

Cicero in twenty-eight volumes, lat./engl., London (The Loeb Classical Library)
——, *De natura deorum,* ed. with comm. by A. S. Pease, 2 vols., Cambridge, Mass. 1955–1958
Democritus, *Griechische Atomisten,* ed. by F. Jürss, R. Müller, E. G. Schmidt, Leipzig 1977; reprt. Berlin 1984
Diogenis Laertii vitae philosophorum, ed. H. S. Long, 2 vols., Oxford 1964
——, *Leben und Meinungen berühmter Philosophen,* übers. u. erl. von O. Apelt, 2nd ed. Hamburg 1967
Epicurus, *Opere,* ed. G. Arrighetti, Turin 1960, 2nd ed. 1973
——, *The Extant Remains,* ed. with trsl. and notes by C. Bailey, Oxford 1926; reprt. Hildesheim 1975
——, *Epistulae tres et ratae sententiae,* ed. P. von der Muehll, Stuttgart 1922; reprt. 1966

Heraclitus, *Greek Text with a Short Commentary* by M. Marcovich, Merida, Venezuela 1967; ital. Ausgabe Florenz 1978
——, *The Art and Thought of Heraclitus: An Edition of the Fragments with Translation and Commentary* by Ch. H. Kahn, Cambridge 1979
——, *The Cosmic Fragments,* ed. with comm. by G. S. Kirk, Cambridge 1954; reprt. 1978
Hesiod, *Works and Days,* ed. with proleg. and comm. by M. L. West, Oxford 1978; reprt. 1980
——, *Theogony and Works and Days,* trsl. with an intro. and notes by M. L. West, Oxford, New York 1988
——, *Theogonie,* hg., übers. u. erl. von K. Albert, 2nd ed. St. Augustin 1983

Parmenides, ed. with trsl., comm., critical essays by L. Tarán, Princeton
1965
———, *Vom Wesen des Seienden: Die Fragmente,* griech./dt., hg., übers.
u. erl. von U. Hölscher, Frankfurt 1969

Plato

Platonis opera, ed. I. Burnet, 5 vols., Oxford 1900–1907

Commentaries

———, *Protagoras,* trsl. with notes by C. C. W. Taylor, Oxford 1976
———, *Gorgias,* trsl. with notes by T. Irwin, Oxford 1982
———, *A Commentary on Plato's Meno,* by J. Klein, Chapel Hill 1965
———, *Meno,* ed. with intr. and comm. by R. S. Bluck, Cambridge 1964
———, *Phaedo,* trsl. with notes by D. Gallop, Oxford 1975
———, *The Republic,* ed. with comm. and appendices by J. Adam, 2
vols., Cambridge 1902, 2nd ed. 1963
———, *Plato's Republic: A Philosophical Commentary* by R. C. Cross,
A. D. Woozley, New York 1964
———, *Theaetetus,* trsl. with notes by J. McDowell, Oxford 1973
———, *Plato's Theory of Knowledge: The Theaetetus and the Sophist,*
trsl. with a running comm. by F. M. Cornford, London 1935
———, *Plato and Parmenides: Parmenides' Way of Truth and Plato's Par-
menides,* trsl. with an intr. and a running comm. by F. M. Cornford,
London 1939
———, *Sophist: A Commentary* by R. S. Bluck, ed. by G. C. Neal, Man-
chester 1975
———, *Philebus,* trsl. with notes by J. C. B. Gosling, Oxford 1975
———, *A Commentary on Plato's Timaeus* by A. E. Taylor, Oxford 1928;
reprt. 1962
———, *Plato's Cosmology: The Timaeus of Plato,* trsl. with a running
comm. by F. M. Cornford, London 1937

Plotini opera, ed. P. Henry, H.-R. Schwyzer, 3 vols., Paris 1951–1973;
editio minor, 3 vols., Oxford 1964–1982
Posidonius, I: The Fragments, ed. by L. Edelstein, I. G. Kidd, Cambridge
1972
*The Presocratic Philosophers: A Critical History with a Selection of
Texts* by G. S. Kirk, J. E. Raven, M. Schofield, Cambridge 2nd ed.
1983.
Sextus Empiricus, with an English translation by R. G. Bury (Greek/
Engl.), 4 vols., London (The Loeb Classical Library) 1933–1949

Stoicorum verterum fragmenta, ed. H. von Arnim, 4 vols., Leipzig 1903–1924; reprt. Stuttgart 1968

Xenophanes, *Die Fragmente* hg., übers. u. erl. von E. Heitsch, München 1983

Zeno, *Testimonianze e frammenti,* ed. M. Untersteiner, Florenz 1963

Bibliography

Ackrill, J. L., *Aristotle the Philosopher,* Oxford 1981

Allan, D. J., *The Philosophy of Aristotle,* Oxford 1952, 2nd ed. London 1970

Allen, R. E. (Ed.), *Studies in Plato's Metaphysics,* London 1965

——, *Plato's 'Euthyphro' and the Earlier Theory of Forms,* London 1970

Annas, J., *An Introduction to Plato's Republic,* Oxford 1981

Annas, J., Barnes, J., *The Modes of Scepticism: Ancient Texts and Modern Interpretations,* Cambridge 1985

Armstrong, A. H., *The Architecture of the Intelligible Universe in the Philosophy of Plotinus: An Analytical and Historical Study,* Cambridge 1940; reprt. Amsterdam 1967

—— (Ed.), *The Cambridge History of Later Greek and Early Medieval Philosophy,* Cambridge 1967

Arnim, H. v., "Karneades," in *RE* X 2 (1919) 1964–1985

Bailey, C., *The Greek Atomists and Epicurus,* Oxford 1928; reprt. New York 1964

Barker, E., *Greek Political Theory: Plato and His Predecessors,* London 1918; reprt. 1970

Barnes, J., Schofield, M., Sorabji, R. (Eds.), *Aristotle: A Selective Bibliography,* Oxford 1977

Barnes, J., *The Presocratic Philosophers,* 2 vols., London 1979, 2nd ed. 1982

Barnes, J., Brunschwig, J., Burnyeat, M., Schofield M. (Eds.), *Science and Speculation: Studies in Hellenistic Theory and Practice,* Cambridge 1982

Berti, E. (Ed.), *Aristotle on Science: The "Posterior Analytics,"* Padua 1981

Bonitz, H., *Index Aristotelicus,* Berlin 1870; reprt. Graz 1955

Boyancé, P., "Les preuves stoïciennes de l'existence des dieux d'après Cicéron," in *Hermes* 90 (1962) 45–71; Germ. in Büchner, K. (Ed.), *Das neue Cicerobild,* Darmstadt 1971, S. 446–488.

Brandwood, L., *A Word Index to Plato*, Leeds 1976

Brentano, F., *Von der mannigfachen Bedeutung des Seienden nach Aristoteles*, Freiburg 1862; reprt. Darmstadt 1960 (Eng. trsl.: *On the Several Senses of Being in Aristotle*, ed. and trsl. by Rolf George, Berkeley 1975)

Burkert, W., *Weisheit und Wissenschaft: Studien zu Pythagoras, Philolaos und Platon*, Nürnberg 1962 (Eng. trsl.: *Lore and Science in Ancient Pythagoreanism*, trsl. by Edwin L. Minar, Jr., Cambridge, Mass. 1972)

Burnet, J., *Early Greek Philosophy*, 4th ed. London 1930

Burnyeat, M. (Ed.), *The Sceptical Tradition*, Berkeley 1983

Cassin, B., *Si Parménide, Le traité anonyme "De Melisso Zenophane Gorgia": Edition critique et commentaire*, Lille 1980

Chadwick, H., "Philo and the Beginnings of Christian Thought," in Armstrong, A. H. (Ed.) 1967, pp. 137–192

Charles, D., *Aristotle's Theory of Action*, London 1984

Cherniss, H., *Aristotle's Criticism of Presocratic Philosophy*, Baltimore 1935, 2nd ed. New York 1964

————, *Aristotle's Criticism of Plato and the Academy*, vol. 1, Baltimore 1944, 2nd ed. New York 1964

Christensen, J., *An Essay on the Unity of Stoic Philosophy*, Copenhagen 1962

Colish, M. L., *The Stoic Tradition from Antiquity to the Early Middle Ages*, 2 vols., Leiden 1985

Cornford, F. M., "Was the Ionian Philosophy Scientific?" in *Journal of Hellenic Studies* 62 (1942) 1–7; reprt. in Furley, Allen (Ed.) 1970, pp. 29–41

————, *Principium Sapientiae: The Origins of Greek Philosophical Thought*, Cambridge 1952; reprt. Gloucester, Mass. 1971

Crombie, J. M., *An Examination of Plato's Doctrines*, London vol. 1 1962, vol. 2 1963

Diller, H., "Hesiod und die Anfänge der griechischen Philosophie," in *Antike und Abendland* 2 (1946) 140–151; reprt. in Heitsch, E. (Ed.) 1966, pp. 688–707

Dillon, J., *The Middle Platonists*, Ithaca, N.Y. 1977

Dirlmeier, F., "Aristotles," in *Jahrbuch für das Bistum Mainz* 5 (1950) 161–171; reprt. in Moraux, P. (Ed.) 1968, pp. 144–157

Düring, I., *Aristotle in the Ancient Biographical Tradition*, Göteborg 1957

————, *Aristoteles*, Heidelberg 1966

————, "Aristoteles," in *RE Supplementband* 11 (1968) 159–336

Edelstein, L., *The Meaning of Stoicism*, Cambridge, Mass. 1966

Engberg-Pedersen, T., *Aristotle's Theory of Moral Insight*, Oxford 1983

Epp, R. H. (Ed.), *Recovering the Stoics,* Memphis, Tenn. 1985 (*Southern Journal of Philosophy* 23 [1985] Suppl.)

Field, G. C., *The Philosophy of Plato,* 2nd ed. Oxford 1962
Findlay, J. N., *Plato: The Written and Unwritten Doctrines,* London 1974
Flashar, H. (Ed.), *Ältere Akademie, Aristoteles, Peripatos,* Basel 1983
Fortenbaugh, W. W., Huby, P. M., Long, A. A. (Eds.), *Theophrastus of Eresus: On His Life and Work,* New Brunswick, N.J. 1985
Fränkel, H., *Wege und Formen frühgriechischen Denkens: Literarische und philosophiegeschichtliche Studien,* 2nd ed. München 1960
Frank, E., *Plato und die sogenannten Pythagoreer,* Halle 1923; reprt. Darmstadt 1962
Frede, M., *Essays in Ancient Philosophy,* Oxford 1987
Friedländer, P., *Platon,* 3rd ed. Berlin vol. 1 1964, vol. 2 1964, vol. 3 1975
Fritz, K. v., "Xenophanes," in *RE* 2. Reihe vol. 9, 2 (1967) 1541–1562
Furley, D. J., *Two Studies in the Greek Atomists,* Princeton, N.J. 1967
Furley, D. J., Allen, R. E. (Eds.), *Studies in Presocratic Philosophy,* London vol. 1 1970, vol. 2 1975

Gaiser, K., *Platons Ungeschriebene Lehre,* Stuttgart 1963 (mit Anhang, Testimonia Platonica: Quellentexte zur Schule und mündlichen Lehre Platons); reprt. (mit Nachwort) 1968
Glucker, J., *Antiochus and the Late Academy,* Göttingen 1978
Gosling, J. C. B., Taylor, C. C. W., *The Greeks on Pleasure,* Oxford 1982
Gotthelf, A. (Ed.), *Aristotle on Nature and Living Things.* Festschrift D. M. Balme, Pittsburgh, Penn. 1985
Grünbaum, A., *Modern Science and Zeno's Paradoxes,* Middletown 1967
Guthrie, W. K. C., *A History of Greek Philosophy,* 5 vols., Cambridge 1962–1978

Hägler, R.-P., *Platons "Parmenides,"* Berlin 1983
Hardie, W. F. R., *Aristotle's Ethical Theory,* Oxford 1968
Hartman, E., *Substance, Body, and Soul: Aristotelian Investigations,* Princeton, N.J. 1977
Heinaman, R., "Self-Predication in the "Sophist," in *Phronesis* 26 (1981) 55–66
Hintikka, J., "The Varieties of Being in Aristotle," in Knuuttila, S., Hintikka, J. (Eds.) 1986, pp. 81–114
Hölscher, U., *Anfängliches Fragen: Studien zur Frühen griechischen Philosophie,* Göttingen 1968

Inwood, B., *Ethics and Human Action in Early Stoicism,* Oxford 1985; reprt. 1987

Irwin, T., *Plato's Moral Theory: The Early and Middle Dialogues*, Oxford 1977

Jaeger, W., *Aristoteles: Grundlegung einer Geschichte seiner Entwicklung*, Berlin 1923, 2nd ed. 1955; reprt. 1967 (Eng. trsl.: *Aristotle: Fundamentals of the History of His Development*, 2nd ed. Oxford 1948)
——, *Die Theologie der frühen griechischen Denker*, Stuttgart 1953; reprt. 1964 (Eng. trsl.: *The Theology of the Early Greek Philosophers*, trsl. by Edward S. Robinson, Oxford 1964)
Jantzen, J., *Parmenides zum Verhältnis von Sprache und Wirklichkeit*, München 1976

Kahn, Ch. H., "Religion and Natural Philosophy in Empedocles' Doctrine of the Soul," in *Archiv für Geschichte der Philosophie* 42 (1960) 3–35; reprt. in Mourelatos, A. P. D. (Ed.) 1974, pp. 426–456
——, *Anaximander and the Origins of Greek Cosmology*, 2nd ed. New York 1964
——, "The Thesis of Parmenides," in *The Review of Metaphysics* 22 (1968/69) 700–724
——, "Pythagorean Philosophy Before Plato," in Mourelatos, A. P. D. (Ed.) 1974, pp. 161–185
——, "Some Philosophical Uses of to be in Plato," in *Phronesis* 26 (1981) 105–134
——, "On the Intended Interpretation of Aristotle's 'Metaphysics,'" in Wiesner, J. (Ed.) 1985, pp. 311–338
——, "Retrospect on the Verb 'To Be' and the Concept of Being," in Knuuttila, S., Hintikka, J. (Eds.) 1986, pp. 1–28
Kenny, A., *The Aristotelian Ethics*, Oxford 1978
——, *Aristotle's Theory of the Will*, London 1979
Kerferd, G. B., "Anaxagoras and the Concept of Matter before Aristotle," in *Bulletin of the John Rylands Library* 52 (1969) 129–143, reprt. in Mourelatos, A. P. D. (Ed.) 1974, pp. 489–503
——, *The Sophistic Movement*, Cambridge 1981
——, (Ed.), *The Sophists and Their Legacy*, Wiesbaden 1981 (1981a)
Kerschensteiner, J., *Kosmos: Quellenkritische Untersuchengen zu den Vorsokratikern*, München 1962
Knuuttila, S., Hintikka, J. (Eds.), *The Logic of Being: Historical Studies*, Dordrecht 1986
Krämer, H. J., *Arete bei Platon und Aristoteles: Zum Wesen und zur Geschichte der platonischen Ontologie*, Heidelberg 1959, reprt. Amsterdam 1967
——, "Die platonische Akademie und das Problem einer systematischen Interpretation Platons," in *Kant-Studien* 55 (1964) 69–101, reprt. in Gaiser, K. (Ed.) 1969, pp. 198–230

―――, *Der Ursprung der Geistmetaphysik: Untersuchungen zur Geschichte des Platonismus zwischen Platon und Plotin,* Amsterdam 1964 (1964a)

Lee, H. D. P., *Zeno of Elea,* Amsterdam 1935, 2nd ed. 1967
Leisegang, H., "Platon," in *RE* 20,2 (1950) 2342–2537
Leszl, W., *Aristotle's Conception of Ontology,* Padua 1975
Lloyd, A. C., "The Later Neoplatonists," in Armstrong, A. H. (Ed.) 1967, pp. 272–325
Lloyd, G. E. R., *Polarity and Analogy,* Cambridge 1966
―――, *Magic, Reason and Experience,* Cambridge 1979
Long, A. A., "Thinking and Sense-Perception in Empedocles," in *Classical Quarterly* 16 (1966) 256–276
―――, "The Principles of Parmenides' Cosmogony," in *Phronesis* 8 (1963) 90–107; reprt. in Furley, D. J., Allen, R. E. (Ed.) 1975, pp. 82–101
―――, "Carneades and the Stoic Telos," in *Phronesis* 12
―――, (Ed.), *Problems in Stoicism,* London 1971
―――, "Freedom and Determinism in the Stoic Theory of Human Action," in Long, A. A. (Ed.) 1971, pp. 173–199 (1971a)
―――, *Empedocles' Cosmic Cycle in the Sixties,* in Mourelatos, A. P. D. (Ed.) 1974, pp. 397–425
―――, *Hellenistic Philosophy,* London 1974 (1974a)
Long, A. A., Sedley, D. S., *The Hellenistic Philosophers,* vol. 1, *Translations of the Principal Sources: With Philosophical Commentary,* Cambridge 1987
Lukasiewicz, J., "Zur Geschichte der Aussagenlogik," in *Erkenntnis* 5 (1935) 111–131

McKirahan, R. D. Jr., *Plato and Socrates: A Comprehensive Bibliography 1958–73,* New York 1978
Mansfield, J., "Aristotle and Others on Thales, or the Beginnings of Natural Philosophy," in *Mnemosyne* 38 (1985) 109–129
Merlan, Ph., "Greek Philosophy from Plato to Plotinus," in Armstrong, A. H. (Ed.) 1967, pp. 14–132 (1967a)
Mohr, R. D., *The Platonic Cosmology,* Leiden 1985
Moraux, P. (Ed.), *Aristoteles in der neueren Forschung,* Darmstadt 1968
Morrow, G. R., *Plato's Cretan City: A Historical Interpretation of the "Laws,"* Princeton, N.J. 1960
Mourelatos, A. P. D. (Ed.), *The Pre-socratics: A Collection of Critical Essays,* Garden City, N.Y. 1974
―――, "Some Alternatives in Interpreting Parmenides," in *The Monist* 62 (1979) 3–14

O'Brien, D., *Empedocles' Cosmic Cycle*, Cambridge 1969
O'Meara, D. J. (Ed.), *Studies in Aristotle*, Washington, D.C. 1981
Owen, G. E. L., "Eleatic Questions," in *Classical Quarterly* 10 (1960) 84–102; reprt. in Furley, D. J., Allen, R. E. (Eds.) 1975, pp. 48–81; Owen G. E. L. 1986, pp. 3–26
————, *Logic, Science and Dialectic: Collected Papers in Greek Philosophy*, Ithaca, N.Y. 1986
Owens, J., *The Doctrine of Being in the Aristotelian "Metaphysics,"* Toronto 1951, 3rd ed. 1978

Patzig, G., *Die Aristotelische Syllogistik*, Göttingen 1959, 3rd ed. 1969 (Eng. trsl.: *Aristotle's Theory of the Syllogism: A Logicophilological Study of Book A of the Prior Analytics*, trsl. by Jonathan Barnes, Dordrecht 1969)
Popper, K. R., *Die offene Gesellschaft und ihre Feinde I: Der Zauber Platons*, Bern 1957, 4th ed. München 1975 (Eng. trsl.: *The Open Society and Its Enemies*, 2 vols., London 1945
————, "Back to the Presocratics," in *Proceedings of the Aristotelian Society* N.S. 59 (1958, 59); reprt. in Furley, D. J., Allen, R. E. (Eds.) 1970, pp. 130–153
Praechter, K., "Richtungen und Schulen im Neuplatonismus," in *Genethliakon für Carl Robert* (1910) 105–156; reprt. in ders., *Kleine Schriften*, Hildesheim 1973, pp. 165–216

Rankin, H. D., *Sophists, Socratics and Cynics*, Beckenham 1983
Reale, G., *The Concept of First Philosophy and the Unity of Metaphysics of Aristotle*, New York 1980
Reiner, H., "Die Entstehung und ursprüngliche Bedeutung des Namens Metaphysik," in *Zeitschrift für philosophische Forschung* 8 (1954) 210–237, reprt. in Hager, F.-P. (Ed.) 1969), pp. 139–174
Reinhardt, K., *Parmenides*, Bonn 1916; 3rd ed. Frankfurt 1977
Rist, J. M., *Plotinus*, Cambridge 1967
————, *Stoic Philosophy*, Cambridge 1969
————, *Epicurus: An Introduction*, Cambridge 1972
———— (Ed.), *The Stoics*, Berkeley, 1978
Robin, L., *La théorie platonicienne des idées et des nombres*, Paris 1908; reprt. Hildesheim 1963
Robinson, R., *Plato's Earlier Dialectic*, 2nd ed. Oxford 1953; reprt. 1985
Rorty, A. O. (Ed.), *Essays on Aristotle's Ethics*, Berkeley 1980
Ross, W. D., *Aristotle*, London 1923, 5th ed. 1949
————, *Plato's Theory of Ideas*, Oxford 1951
Rowe, C. J., *Plato*, Brighton, Sussex 1984

Sandbach, F. H., *The Stoics,* London 1975

Schleiermacher, F., "Einleitung," in ders., *Platons Werke,* Erster Teil, vol. 1, Berlin 1804, 3rd ed. 1855, pp. 5–36; reprt. (3rd ed. 1855) in Gaiser, K. (Ed.) 1969, pp. 1–32

Schofield, M., *An Essay on Anaxagoras,* Cambridge 1980 (1980a)

Schofield, M., Striker, G. (Eds.), *The Norms of Nature: Studies in Hellenistic Ethics,* Cambridge 1986

Solmsen, F., *Plato's Theology,* Ithaca, N.Y. 1941; reprt. 1967

Sorabji, R., *Philoponus and the Rejection of Aristotelian Science,* London 1987

Stenzel, J., *Zahl und Gestalt bei Platon und Aristoteles,* Leipzig 1924, 3rd ed. Darmstadt 1959

Stough, Ch. L., *Greek Scepticism,* Berkeley 1969

———, "Sextus Empiricus on Non-Assertion," *Phronesis* 29 (1984), 137–164

Striker, G. "The Role of Oikeiosis in Stoic Ethics," in *Oxford Studies in Ancient Philosophy* 1 (1983) 145–167

Taylor, A. E., *Plato: The Man and His Work,* London 1926; reprt. 1960

Tugendhat, E., TI ΚΑΤΑ ΤΙΝΟΣ, Freiburg 1958, 3rd ed. 1982

———, "Das Sein und das Nichts," in Klostermann, V. (Ed.), *Durchblicke: Martin Heidegger zum 80. Geburtstag,* Frankfurt 1970, pp. 132–161

———, "Über den Sinn der vierfachen Unterscheidung des Seins bei Aristoteles (Metaphysik Δ7)," in Bolz, W., Hübener, W. (Eds.), *Spiegel und Gleichnis: Festschrift für Jacob Taubes,* Würzburg 1983, pp. 49–54

Vlastos, G., "Ethics and Physics in Democritus," in *The Philosophical Review* 54 (1945) 578–592; 55 (1946) 53–64; reprt. in Furley, D. J., Allen, R. E. (Eds.) 1975, pp. 381–408

———, "The Physical Theory of Anaxagoras," in *The Philosophical Review* 59 (1950) 31–57; reprt. in Mourelatos, A. P. D. (Ed.) 1974, pp. 459–488

———, "The Third Man Argument in the Parmenides," in *Philosophical Review* 63 (1954) 319–349

———, "Zeno of Elea," in Edwards, P. (Ed.), *The Encyclopedia of Philosophy* vol. 8 (1967) 369–379

——— (Ed.), *The Philosophy of Socrates: A Collection of Critical Essays,* Notre Dame 1980

——— (Ed.), *Plato: A Collection of Critical Essays,* 2 vols., Notre Dame 1978

———, *Platonic Studies,* Princeton, N.J., 2nd ed. 1981

———, *Plato's Universe,* Seattle, Wash. 1975

Waterlow, S., *Nature, Change, and Agency in Aristotle's "Physics,"* Oxford 1982
――――, *Passage and Possibility: A Study of Aristotle's Modal Concepts*, Oxford 1982 (1982a)
Wedberg, A., *Plato's Philosophy of Mathematics*, Stockholm 1955; reprt. Westport, Connecticut 1977
Wehrli, F., "Der Peripatos bis zum Beginn der römischen Kaiserzeit," in Flashar, H. (Ed.) 1983, pp. 459–599
West, M. L., *Early Greek Philosophy and the Orient*, Oxford 1971
Wieland, W., *Die aristotelische Physik*, Göttingen 1962, 2nd ed. 1970
――――, *Platon und die Formen des Wissens*, Göttingen 1982
Wiesner, J., Ps.-*Aristoteles, MXG, Der historische Wert des Xenophanesreferats: Beiträge zur Geschichte des Eleatismus*, Amsterdam 1974
Wolf, U., *Möglichkeit und Notwendigkeit bei Aristoteles und heute*, München 1979

Zeller, E., *Die Philosophie der Griechen in ihrer geschichtlichen Entwicklung*, 6 vols., 6th ed. Leipzig 1919; reprt. Hildesheim 1963 (Eng. trsl.: *Aristotle and the Earlier Peripatetics*, London, New York 1897)

Index